FACTS, RESEARCH AND
IN GERIATRICS

WOMEN, AGING AND HEALTH

NUTRITIONAL INTERVENTION AND WOMEN
AFTER MENOPAUSE

Preface A. Kabache, Chief, Ageing and Health
World Health Organization

Foreword M.C. Bertière, Director,
Center for Research and Information on Nutrition

Serdi Publisher
Springer Publishing Company
Paris - New York

Serdi Publisher, 320, Rue Saint-Honoré, F75001 Paris, France
Springer Publisher Company, 536 Broadway N-Y 10012-3955, USA

ISBN 2-909342-53-0 (France)
ISBN 0-8261-8174-0 (USA)

Serie : Facts, Research and Intervention in Geriatrics 1998

We wish to express our sincere thanks to CERIN for their support of this publication

Facts, Research and Intervention in Geriatrics Contents are listed in : Experta Medica, ISI/IST P&B online database, Current Book Contents - Current Contents / Life Sciences and Clinical Medicine Philadelphia, CNRS / Pascal, Paris, Current Literature on Aging, Washington, C.P.A: New Literature on Old Age and Age Info, London; CAB International, Biosis.

The material contained in this volume was submitted as previously unpublished material, except in the instances in which credit has been given to the source from which some of illustrative material was derived.
Great care has been taken to maintain the accuracy of the information contained in this volume. However, Serdi cannot be held responsible for errors or for any consequences arising from the use of the information contained herein.

FACTS, RESEARCH AND INTERVENTION IN GERIATRICS 1998

Invited Editors

F.E. KAISER M.D. (Saint-Louis - USA)
F. NOURHASHEMI M.D. (Toulouse - France)
M. C. BERTIERE M.D. (Paris - France)
Y. OUCHI M. D. (Tokyo - Japon)

Editors

B. VELLAS, J.L. ALBAREDE, P.J. GARRY
(Toulouse - France ; Albuquerque - USA)

Serdi

320, Rue Saint-Honoré, F-75001 Paris
Fax: (33) 5 61 75 11 28 • E-mail: 100775.1315@CompuServe.com

Springer Publishing Company

536 Broadway, N-Y 10012-3955, USA
Tel : 212 431 4370 - Fax : 212 941 7842

RECOMMENDATIONS TO AUTHORS

Manuscripts proposed to "Facts, Research and Intervention in Geriatrics" must be submitted in accordance with the standards established by the International Committee of Editors of Medical Journals, Annals of Internal Medicine, 1982, 96, part 1 : 766-771, summarized below:

* The text should be submitted in the following format : title page, abstract and key words, text, acknowledgements, references, tables, illustrations and captions. It should be typed with single spacing, on one side only on paper measuring 21 x 29,7 cm, leaving a left hand margin of 4 cm.
* The title page includes : 1) the title of the article ; 2) the authors' fornames and surnames ; 3) the names of departments and institutions to which the authors belong ; 4) the main author's name and complete address ; 5) the funding sources (donation award, grant etc...).
* The second page should include the abstract and the key words.
* The third page includes a very short title (less than 40 characters) as a header for each edited page.
* The text will be eventually divided into : introduction, material and methods, results, discussion and conclusion.
* References in the text should be cited by numbers, placed in line with the text and numbered in order of appearance. They should be listed in numerical order at the end of the paper in the form prescribed in the Uniform Requirements.
** Table : All tables must be written in the same version than the text **with maximum dimensions of : large = 115 mm and high = 183 mm**. Each table should be inserted in the text. It should have a title and, if desired, an explanation. Each table should be cited in the text and should be numbered according to the order of appearance.*
* Illustration for diagrams, original artwork : Black ink on white paper and glossy prints will usually be acceptable. All illustrations should bear author's name and the number of the illustration on the reverse side, also an indication in soft pencil if only part of the illustration is required.
*Captions should be typed on separate sheets. **All illustrations or figures must be cited and inserted in the text and in the disk**, and the space must be shown in the text. It is the responsibility of the author(s) to ensure that any requirements of copyright and courtesy are fulfilled in reproducing illustrations and appropriate acknowledgements included with the captions.*
* Copyright : Authors of accepted manuscripts must transfer copyright to "Facts, Research and Intervention in Geriatrics", which holds the copyright to all articles, comments, reviews and notes published in "Facts, Research and Intervention in Geriatrics".
* Submission of manuscripts : Contributions and correspondence should be sent to :
- Professor Bruno VELLAS, Centre de Gériatrie, C.H.U. Purpan-Casselardit - 31300 Toulouse (France) or Clinical Nutrition Program, UNM, Rm. 215 Surge Building, 2701 Frontier Place N.E., Albuquerque, NM 87131, USA.
* Two copies must be submitted. Submission of an article is taken to imply that its content has not previously been published and is not being considered for publication elsewhere.
* Manuscripts are sent to reviewers for recommendation and comment. Reviewers' comments are provided to authors.

The submission of electronic manuscripts is requested. Electronic manuscripts have the advantage that there is no need for rekeying of text, thereby avoiding the possibility of introducing errors and resulting in reliable and fast delivery of proofs. The desired storage medium is a 3 1/2 inch disk in Macintosh format, and the preferred Microsoft is "Word Version 4., 5. or 6.". Although the Microsoft "Word Perfect 5.1" is welcome in IBM PC Format. After final acceptance, your disk plus one final, printed and exactly matching version (as a printout) should be submitted together to the accepting editor. It is important that the file on disk and the printout are identical. Both will then forwarded by the editor. Please label the disk with your name, Microsoft used, and the name of the file to be processed.

CONTENTS

CONTENTS

PREFACE

A. KALACHE

MD, PhD, Chief, Ageing and Health, World Health Organization, Geneva

A gender perspective is indispensable for a full understanding of ageing and health. Both from a physiological and from a psycho-social point of view, the determinants of health as we age are intrinsically related to gender. Yet until recently the gender perspective was rather neglected by researchers and policy makers alike. It is only over the last few years that it has been recognized that research and programmes (clinical and in public health) which do not acknowledge these differences are not effective. That is in spite of the fact that we have long known that while men die earlier, women experience greater burdens of morbidity and disability. In the great majority of countries, life expectancy at birth for women is substantially higher than that for men. While the difference is around six to seven years in most western, fully-industrialized countries, in Eastern Europe it has now reached 13 years (in Russia, for instance). Furthermore, women worldwide constitute the majority of care givers. The rapidity of population ageing, combined with the clear "feminization" of ageing, contribute to the need for a sharp focus on gender issues if meaningful policies are to be developed.

For these reasons, the newly established WHO programme on ageing and health has embraced gender as one of its key perspectives, the others being life course (older people not compartmentalized as a population sub-group but part of the life cycle as is any other age group); health promotion (with a focus on healthy ageing and ageing well); cultural (the settings in which individuals age will determine their health status at older ages); inter-generational (emphasis on strategies to maintain cohesion between generations); and ethical (multiple considerations such as equity issues, undue hastening or delaying of death, long-term care, and abuse of elders emerge and/or are magnified as populations age). To a large extent all these perspective are inter-connected and overlap, and gender issues permeate them all.

Not only has the WHO Ageing and Health Programme adopted gender as a key perspective to its programme components, it is also developing a strategy through which other WHO programmes and divisions might be stimulated and develop their own activities on gender, ageing and health. Programmes such as reproductive health, child health, women health and development, non-communicable diseases, nutrition and many others share common interests and responsibilities that relate to how gender issues should be highlighted in the context of a life course perspective on ageing. Furthermore, the Programme is also actively seeking to stimulate a broader, intersectoral movement towards "healthy ageing" with a strong gender dimension. Without such strong partnership - to which the academic sector can uniquely contribute - the message, however powerful, that gender is at the centre of the ageing and health debate, will be heard by only a few.

For all these reasons, we enthusiastically welcome the initiative of Professor Vellas in dedicating this special issue of Facts, Research and Intervention in Geriatrics to the theme of **Women, Aging and Health,** Nutritional Intervention and Women after Menopausis. The issue contains precious information that has been contributed by a wide range of distinguished experts from around the world and serves as an important vehicle for disseminating knowledge and ideas that will help us to reach our common goal - healthy ageing for all.

FOREWORD

M.C. BERTIERE

Director, Center for Research and Information on Nutrition (CERIN), Paris, France

Although life expectancy is increasing in women, longevity is also associated with increased morbidity. We may live longer, but not necessarily better lives. Accumulating evidence suggests that good nutritional practices over a lifetime can improve health and reduce disease incidence.

There are a number of health issues which affect women specifically. A woman's dietary and nutritional status may have profound effects on her reproductive capacity and efficiency, and on her own health and well-being throughout life, as well as that of her off-spring.

With menopause, hormonal and behavioral modifications have major health consequences, both as a result of acute or short-term symptoms and of more chronic effects such as increased risks of cardiovascular disease, cancer and osteoporosis.

Scores of previous or running studies strongly suggest that both cancer and heart disease could be partly preventable by simple dietary modifications. Osteoporosis and related bone fractures is the key example of the relationship between poor nutrition and pathology. There is now sound scientific evidence that adequate calcium and vitamin D intake -even in late menopause- can help prevent the onset or reduce the severity of osteoporosis which affects nearly one third of all post-menopausal women.

Prevention will be all the more efficient as health professionals and Public Health Organizations will feel truly involved through better access to information and better training. This has been for more than a decade the main objective of CERIN in partnership with academics, scientists and health organizations.

WOMEN, AGING AND HEALTH
ACHIEVING HEALTH ACROSS THE LIFE SPAN

WORLD HEALTH ORGANIZATION (a)

I - INTRODUCTION: SETTING THE AGENDA

1.1. Building on past initiatives

While the social position and health status of women have advanced in many areas since the United Nations Decade for Women was launched at the First International Conference of Women in Mexico in 1975, the report of the Conference made only a brief mention of older women. Since then, women's issues have been placed on the agenda of the international community and the special needs of aging populations have been raised at a number of major international meetings, but none have provided an adequate basis or conceptual framework for addressing issues of aging women in a lifespan perspective. A time line of these key events is set out in Box 1.

```
BOX 1: Key events, 1975-1999

1975   United Nations Decade of Women launched, Mexico
1982   International Plan of Action on Aging, Vienna
1983   World Programme of Action Concerning Disabled Persons
1985   The Forward-looking Strategies adopted, Nairobi
1986   United Nations Commission on the Status of Women
1991   United Nations Principles for Older Persons
1993   World Conference on Human Rights, Vienna Assembly
1994   United Nations International Conference on Population and Development, Cairo
1995   United Nations Social Development Conference, Copenhagen
1995   Fourth World Conference on Women, Beijing
1997   Fourth International Conference on Health Promotion, Delhi
1999   United Nations International Year of Older Persons
```

(a) Originally prepared by Dr Ruth Bonita for the Global Commission on Women's Health, under the guidance of the WHO Ageing and Health Programme and issued by the World Health Organization (document WHO/HPR/AHE/HPD/96.1) Copies available on request from WHO, Distribution and Sales, CH-1211 Geneva 27, Switzerland.

The earlier plans and agreements gave some general guides for policy and long term planning, but these were not widely taken up at national level. The Vienna International Plan of Action on Aging agreed at Vienna Assembly identified particular areas of concern for aging women and provided a starting point for approaching the subject in a systematic manner by recognising the multiple dimensions of aging [1]. In the Forward-looking Strategies adopted in 1985 at the culmination of the United Nations Decade for Women, aging as a process was mentioned for the first time in an international statement on women, but only one paragraph was devoted to elderly women.

The Fourth World Conference on Women, held in Beijing in September 1995, was a major opportunity to raise awareness of the status of aging women and their health. It provided the opportunity for the Global Commission on Women's Health to advocate on behalf of aging women. Looking to the future, two events offer further opportunities. First, at the fourth International Conference on Health Promotion to be held in 1997 in New Delhi, aging and women's health are both key areas for discussion. Second, the UN International Year of the Older Person in 1999 will provide an important subsequent opportunity to monitor progress and to ensure that continuing attention is given to the health of aging women.

1.2. The Global Commission on Women's Health

The Global Commission on Women's Health was established to promote the adoption and implementation of effective actions related to women, to ensure that women's health is firmly established on national and international agendas, and to advocate on behalf of women's health concerns at an international level.

Health issues of aging women were raised in the initial Issues Paper "Women's Health : Towards a Better World" presented at the first meeting of the Global Commission on Women's Health in April, 1994. The paper noted:

As life expectancy increases in most countries, it is estimated that the number of women over the age of 65 will increase from 330 million in 1990 to 600 million in 2015. Many of these elderly women will have experienced poor nutrition, reproductive ill-health, dangerous working conditions, violence and life style related diseases, all of which exacerbate the post-menopausal phenomena of increased likelihood of breast and cervical cancers and osteoporosis. Poverty, loneliness and alienation are common. Little data exists on the health conditions of the elderly female population except in industrialized countries from which extrapolation is made [2].

In subsequent discussions, the Global Commission determined that a background paper on aging and health should be prepared, covering:

* major health issues facing aging and postmenopausal women;
* social, cultural, political and economic determinants of the health of aging and postmenopausal women;
* specific needs of aging women for health care; and
* future action plans.

This report is one of a number of documents being prepared for the members of the Commission and, as such, is not a stand alone document. These discussion documents all adopt a lifespan approach to women's health and take up six key themes identified at the Commission's first meeting as having major impacts on women's health. These themes are:

* nutrition,
* reproductive health,
* health consequences of violence;
* lifestyle related conditions; and
* the work environment.

1.3. The WHO Aging and Health Programme

The preparation of this report coincided with the re-activation of the WHO Aging and Health Programme, which followed on from the previous Health of the Elderly Programme as summarised in Box 2.

BOX 2: History of the WHO Aging and Health Programme	
1974	Publication of Report of Expert Committee on Health of the Elderly
1979	World llealth Assembly adoption of Resolution on health care of the elderly, leading to the establishment of the Global Programme for Health of the Elderly (HEE)
1982	Incorporation of International Plan of Action on Aging into HEE activities
1987	Research agenda established under HEE to investigate determinants of healthy aging, osteoporosis, age-related dementias, and age-related changes in immune fiunction
1989	WHO Expert Committee Meeting
1992-94	WHO Divisions, Geneva, and Regional Office collaboration on HEE - inter-regional meetings in Alexandria and New Delhi
1995	Reorientation of the prograrnrne adopting the new title 'Aging and Health'

Earlier work on aging at WHO has provided a number of key sources for the present report. These include: the 1984 report on The Uses of Epidemiology in the Study of the Elderly [3]; the report of the 1989 Expert Committee, Health of the Elderly; Improving the Health of Older People: A World View, published in 1990 [4]; and Family Support for the Elderly: The International Experience, published in 1992 [5].

A background document on Aging and Health released in January 1995 details the reorientation of the WHO programme. Significantly, it includes specific mention of a gender perspective and points out that research and programmes in aging which do not recognise gender differences will not be effective. The higher morbidity and disability rates experienced by older women are pointed out, as is their major role as carers. The key components of the Aging and Health Programme provide the framework in which strategies for advancing the health of aging women have been proposed in this report.

1.4. Defining health and aging

The definition of health adopted in this report follows the broad WHO definition of health as a state of complete physical, mental, and social well-being. In applying this definition to aging women, a first requirement is to recognise that aging is a continuing process. Since the health of a woman in earlier periods of her life forms the basis of her health in later stages of her life, it is essential to consider the health of aging women within a life course perspective; the strategic implication for promoting the health of aging women is that both primary and secondary prevention initiatives must be taken during the later life span.

Another requirement is that older women throughout the world be given opportunities to advocate on the health issues of concern to them and to participate in developing programmes to address the problems they identify. It is only through such approaches to defining health that the value placed on different aspects of health by aging women will be given due recognition.

There are major differences in the life course of aging women in countries at different levels of development, and transitions across the life course vary accordingly. In societies where life expectancy is short, "older" may be defined at an age which other societies would define as "young". Some societies regard menopause as the start of "old age" for women; in others, women achieve old age with the birth of their first grandchild. Retirement from the work force based on chronological age is also used to denote entry to the later stage of life, although this definition is of limited applicability to older women. Although participation of aging women in the paid work force is relatively low even in the developed countries, the majority of women keep working, unpaid, until they die.

When defining "old" for the general population, demographers and others have made distinctions between "mid-life", "young old" and "old old". Paradoxically, the age set for defining old age for women has commonly been five years or so younger than for men, notwithstanding women's greater life expectancy. The use of an arbitrary cut-offpoint of 55 or 60 years to denote the older segment ofthe female population, and 60 or 65 for men, masks tremendous diversity in the two to three decades which follow. Such chronological definitions have little biological, social or cultural meaning.

One event that carries a unique meaning in women's life course compared to men's is the menopause. The menopause is a universal event, or more correctly a universal process, that occurs at around 50 years in both developed and developing countries. While development brings major changes in life course events that occur before menopause - notably the narrowing of the span of child bearing years and major extension of the life cycle stages following menopause - the age of menopause itself remains relatively constant. The age of menopause thus provides a useful defining point for this paper, but at the same time it is recognised that menopause carries a wide variety of cultural and social meanings.

In developed countries the majority of women are in good health at this age. Yet it is in these countries that menopause itself is increasingly being depicted as an illness, or oestrogen deficiency "disease", to justify increasing medical intervention. In many developing countries, by the time a woman reaches menopause, her health may already have been undermined, not by her hormonal state, but by the aftermath of health problems in reproductive years and the social and environmental conditions under which she lives.

This report will cover the life course from age 50, covering stages labelled as "mid-life", the "young old" and the "old old". An extended later life is as yet the experience of a minority of women in developing countries, but it is becoming a more common experience. More women will reach old age in future in these countries and this stage of their life span will also be increased.

For the majority of women in the developed regions of the world, the experience of aging lasts for many decades. With the expectation that the life course will run to an extended period of aging and old age now a reality for women world wide, the life course perspective offers the potential for addressing the promoting of health in preparation for and throughout the later lifespan.

1.5. Scope and aims of the report

There is enormous diversity among older women. Some live extended lives and others have their lives shortened. Some live in abject poverty, others with vast wealth. Some expand their roles with increasing age, others face reduced status. Some are in excellent health even at advanced ages, and others have to rely on formal assistance for their everyday personal care. Whatever their situation, aging women deserve much more attention if their health is to be advanced and lasting improvements in the quality of their lives are to be achieved.

While health issues of aging has been identified as a policy concern in many developed countries, greater attention needs to be given to cohort differences of factors affecting the health of aging women.

The health of women who are aging now is in many ways different to that of those who are already older. Aging has not yet been defined as an issue in many developing countries, but already two thirds of the net annual increase in the number of older women in the world is occurring in less developed countries.

Three considerations impel the greater recognition of health of aging women as a major concern:

* the numbers of aging women are increasing worldwide;
* women's life course beyond 50 now extends for a significant period and is increasing; and
* there is very significant scope for improving the health of aging women.

Taking action to improve the health of aging women is imperative if these women are to achieve an acceptable quality of life in the extended period of old age that will be their experience and if all societies are to avoid the consequences that will otherwise ensue. With a view to the future returns from investing in health, the scope of this report encompasses the coming generation of older women (those now in their 50s and 60s) as well those already in older age groups.

This report aims to propose a framework for action on héalth for aging women within the Health for All context, a goal which encompasses WHO's aspirations for the elderly people of the world. It is not possible to present a comprehensive framework that addresses the health needs of all aging women, in all countries. Rather, in recognition of the diversity of older women and their health, the framework aims to set directions and give some examples of actions that can be taken.

The report begins with a brief account of the particular features of demographic aging of relevance to the life course of aging women. The social, cultural and economic determinants of health of aging women are reviewed next. Attention then turns to priority health issues for aging women and several common strategies are identified for addressing a number of major preventable conditions, chronic disabling conditions and mental health problems. The framework proposed in the final section draws together these and other strategies identified in each section of the report. In line with the key components of the WHO Aging and Health Programme, strategies for action are grouped in four areas: policy development; advocacy; community-based programmes (including the support of carers) ; and training and research.

II - LIFE COURSE AND DEMOGRAPHIC TRANSITIONS

"An aging society is evolving, which, for the most part, is female. " [6]

The health outcomes of demographic aging in terms of improved survival and changing patterns of morbidity are the product of changes in underlying economic, social and cultural determinants of health. Demographic aging not only brings about major changes in the duration of life course stages, but also in the social experience of these stages. Of all these changes, the increase in women's life course after age 50 is the most obvious; it is also the change that presents most challenges in achieving quality of life for aging women over these years.

This section begins with an account of later life course stages as now experienced in developing and developed countries and then presents a brief analysis of the demographic processes underlying population aging, focusing on the differential aging of the female population in developing and developed regions of the world.

2.1. Population aging and lifespan transitions

As seen in Table 2.1, the later lifespan of women in developed and developing countries appears markedly different when life expectancies at birth are compared. Female life expectancy at birth ranges from just over 50 years in the least developed countries through the 60s and 70s in those undergoing rapid development. In developed countries, female life expectancy at birth of 80 years and more is now becoming the norm. These differences are accounted for not only by high infant mortality but also high maternal mortality.

Life expectancies at birth however disguise the duration of later life in developing countries. For women in developing countries who survive the early lifespan stages to reach middle age, life expectancy approaches that of women in developed countries. Life expectancies at age 65 show much greater similarity between developing and developed countries, at around 15 and 19 years respectively. At age 65, women in developing countries now have about three quarters of the remaining life expectancy of their counterparts in developed countries, and the gap will narrow in future as mortality declines not only at younger ages but also at later ages.

It is the likelihood of reaching older age rather than the total duration of life in old age that differs most markedly between countries at different levels of development. The smaller proportion of the population reaching old age makes it a less individual and social experience in developing countries than in developed countries. At the same time, the already considerable duration of this life stage for those who do reach it explains why there are some very old individuals in countries with low average life expectancies.

The life course transitions indicated by these demographic data bring major restructuring of family relationships and social roles of aging women. In developed countries, these roles are well established but are undergoing change. Even more so in developing countries, traditional roles of older women are being overtaken and new norms have yet to emerge. The economic, social, cultural and political factors which will affect the health of aging women as these social transformations proceed and which will have a major impact on the quality of life of women as they age, are taken up in Section 4. As these impacts will be felt increasingly in the future, particular attention needs to be paid to the next cohorts of aging women - that is, those now aged from 50 to 60 years.

2.2. The gender transition

The theory of demographic transition has been widely used in analysing population aging. Within it, a gender transition emerges. Three phases of population aging can usefully be identified on the basis of changing patterns of survival of women relative to men and the associated gender balance of the older population. Data on selected countries presented in Table 2.1 illustrate these three stages.

In the early stages of the transition, life expectancy at birth for men and women is similarly low, as seen in Mozambique, Nigeria and India. Female life expectancy is still limited by high maternal mortality and is close to that of males.

"The neglect of women's health and nutrition is so serious in some countries, particularly in Asia, that it even outweighs women 's ... tendency to live longer than men. " [7]

In some developing countries, particularly in South Asia, women's life expectancy at birth is lower than or only equal to that of men, and has improved only marginally more than has men's life expectancy over the last 20 years. Further, it has been estimated that early deaths and the alleged infanticide of girl babies in these countries have caused up to 100 million women to be "missing" from the statistics [8].

The second stage of the gender transition reflects two trends in mortality which are well established in more developed countries and are becoming evident in many developing countries. By far the major factor is reduced maternal mortality which ensures the survival of a larger proportion of women to middle age. This decline is due to reduced exposure to childbirth and improved standards of living; the decline in birth rates that also occurs in this phase contributes to the aging of the population as the growth of younger cohorts decreases. Second, improvements in mid- and later life mortality lead to the survival of higher proportions of middle age cohorts into old age and to advanced old age. Life expectancy at birth and at age 65 both increase, and it is the combined effects of improved female survival to middle age, followed by improved survival at older ages, that leads to the marked shift in the gender balance in the older population.

The contrast between the rapidly developing Asian and Latin American countries and Eastern European countries illustrates these differential trends. The Eastern European countries are exceptional in the lack of improvement in life expectancy over the last 20 years; improvements in infant and maternal mortality that achieved increases in life expectancy at birth in the first two post-war decades have not been followed by improvements in life expectancies in later years. It is this failure to increase life expectancy at age 65 that has kept overall life expectancies in Eastern Europe below those of established market economies.

Populations in the second stage of the gender transition are characterised by increasing proportions of older females. A high proportion of these women live alone; many are widows while others may never have married. This process, which has been described as the "feminisation of aging", is the current experience of many developed countries and also of many rapidly industrialising countries such as Thailand and the Republic of Korea. In some developed countries (for example, Sweden), there are two elderly women for every elderly man; the ratio widens considerably with increasing age [9]. The pronounced gender imbalance of the Eastern European countries resulting from the Second World War will reduce as those cohorts pass. In the developing countries where female life expectancy at 65 already exceeds that of men, the increasing proportion of women reaching this age and then surviving longer is set to make aging at least, if not more, feminised than it has been in the developed countries.

The main social effect of the extension of later life for women at this stage of the gender transition is an extended period of widowhood. Widowhood occurs at a later age in developed countries (close to 70 years) but the greater differential life expectancy of women compared to men at age 65 in these countries means that it extends for a longer period. To the extent that trends in life expectancy at older ages in developing countries follow the pattern of women's life expectancy improving ahead of that of men, similarly protracted periods of widowhood can be expected. The markedly lower status of women at earlier stages of the life span in many of these societies stands to be compounded.

A third stage of the gender transition is now emerging in advanced industrial societies. At this stage, very high life expectancies for women mean that there is limited scope for further improvement, while recent improvements in male life expectancy at older ages are starting to narrow the gap between males and females. If these trends strengthen, the gender balance of the older population will shift, but only slowly, towards a more even balance. Of those who are still married on reaching old age, more will experience a longer period of old age with their partner.

Table 2.1
Life expectancy of women and men, 1991, and improvements 1970-91
[9, 10, 11]

Country	Life expectancy at birth, 1991		Increase in life expectancy 1970-91		Life expectancy at age 65, 1991	
	Female	Male	Female	Male	Female	Male
Sub-Saharan Africa						
Mozambique	48	45	6	6	n.a.	n.a.
Nigeria	53	50	10	10	n.a.	n.a.
South Africa	66	59	10	9	n.a.	n.a.
India	60	60	11	10	n.a.	n.a.
China	71	67	8	6	16	14
Other Asia and Islands						
Bangladesh	52	53	8	7	n.a.	n.a.
Philippines	67	63	8	7	14	12
Malaysia	73	68	10	8	15	3
Korea	73	67	11	9	15	13
Middle Eastern Crescent						
Egypt	62	60	10	10	13	12
Turkey	70	64	11	9	n.a.	n.a.
Tunisia	68	67	13	13	14	13
Latin America						
Brazil	69	63	8	6	n.a.	n.a.
Mexico	73	67	9	7	17	15
Argentina	75	68	5	4	17	14
Former Socialist Economies of Europe						
Romania	73	67	2	0	15	13
Poland	75	67	1	0	16	12
Hungary	74	66	1	-1	16	12
Established Market Economies						
United States	79	72	4	5	19	15
Spain	80	74	5	4	18	15
Australia	80	73	5	5	19	15
France	81	73	5	5	20	15
Japan	82	76	7	7	20	16

n.a.: not available

As well as the positive improvements in male mortality contributing to these trends, there are some emerging negative trends in female mortality at mature ages. A large part of the gap between life expectancy of men and women is due to differences in alcohol and tobacco consumption as well as accidents, suicide and chronic diseases. However, the impact of increased smoking rates among women is now becoming more evident. Death rates from smoking-related diseases have plateaued in men whereas they are increasing in women at older years. The example of Denmark, presented in Figure 2.1, shows the increase in smoking-related deaths among the large cohorts of women who took up smoking at young ages and who are now reaching old age [10]. Cigarette smoking by women has not yet become widespread in developing countries, and there is still time to take global action to protect the health of older women by halting the spread of these toxic substances in these countries.

Figure 2.1
Percentage of total deaths in women attributed to smoking, Denmark (1955-1995)

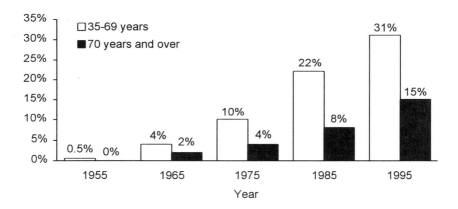

2.3. Diversity within global aging

2.3.1. Where are the world's aging women?

Most of the world's aging women are living in developing regions of the world. Already, more than half of the world's women aged 60 years and over live in developing regions; 148 million compared to 121 million in developed regions. It is only at age 70 years and over that the number of women in the developed regions exceeds the number in the developing regions, but even at this age, the margin is small (60 million compared to 58 million).

The future growth in the numbers and proportion of aging women in developing countries is foreshadowed in the distribution of those now aged 45 to 59 years. Two thirds of the women in this age group (213 million) live in developing countries and one third (98 million) live in developed countries. The distribution of the world's aging women for the eight World Bank regions [11] is shown in Figure 2.2. The imminent large increase of older women in the developing world contrasts with the age structures of the established market economies and former socialist economies of Europe, where the cohorts aged 45 to 59 are smaller than those now aged 60 years and over.

2.3.2. Differences in life expectancy

Population aging is accompanied by a greater life expectancy at birth and at older ages for women than for men, although the gap is closing at older ages. In developed countries, women live on average about six years longer than men [12].

Differences in life expectancy between women in countries at different levels of development have received less attention.

Figure 2.2

Geographical distribution of the world's aging women

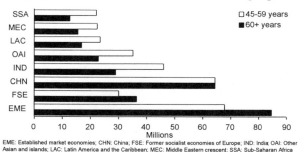

EME: Established market economies; CHN: China; FSE: Former socialist economies of Europe; IND: India; OAI: Other Asian and islands; LAC: Latin America and the Caribbean; MEC: Middle Eastern crescent; SSA: Sub-Saharan Africa

Life expectancy at birth for women in developed countries exceeds that of women in middle income developing countries by 15 years and by as much as 30 years for women in the poorest countries [7]. The disparity in life expectancy at birth of women in rich and poor countries has improved only a little over the past 20 years, and these differences in women's life expectancies represent major inequities that must be addressed.

While less pronounced, differences in life expectancy at age 65 between rich and poor countries are nonetheless evident. That later life expectancies in many developing countries are already approaching those of developed countries can be taken as an indicator of what can be achieved with improved health over the lifespan. Further narrowing of this gap will be an indicator of improved life expectancy at birth and at older ages in developing countries. The extended lifespan already experienced by older women in both developing and developed countries calls attention to issues of quality of life in these years.

There are also major differences in life expectancy and the quality of life of aging women within countries, largely associated with class differences. Strategies to address these differences mean that health interventions must take into account quality of life as well as quantity of life.

2.3.3. Differences over the age range

There are not only differences in the proportions of older men and women in national populations, but also shifts in the age structure of the population. Notwithstanding their dominance on a global scale, aging women in developing countries remain a smaller proportion of the population than in developed countries. Whereas women aged 60 years and older account for around 20% of the female population in the developed regions, they account for only some 7% of women in developing countries. The equivalent proportions for men 60 years and over are nearly 15% in developed regions and 6% in developing regions.

The main trend in aging in developed countries is the increase in the "oldest old", that is, those 85 years or older. The great majority in this age group are women, and this trend will continue in the foreseeable future. It is largely this group which will require access to a range of health and long term care services. It is, however, important that the small absolute size of these very old cohorts be recognised so that the demographic aspects of the rapid increases projected for the oldest old in developed countries do not overwhelm other considerations. The oldest old constitute only a small fraction of the total population in the developed countries; Sweden has the highest proportion of "oldest old", 4.4%. In the least developed countries, less than 1% of the population is in the "oldest old" cohort; in countries such as Bangladesh and Indonesia, the proportion is as low as 0.2%, although the absolute numbers are substantial.

2.3.4. Cohort differences

Future cohorts of older women will be very different to those of the current generation. A cohort approach which follows each particular generation or age group over time is essential for developing social and health policies for women as they age. Encouraging each cohort to consider its own future health is an important means of stimulating policies for health promotion that will address the different problems and potentials of each group.

An example is Latin America where it is projected that 60% of women who were aged 45-49 years in 1990 will survive to age 75-79. The health that these survivors can expect in their old age will depend on the social and physical environments in which they live over the next 30 years. Monitoring such environments and their influence on the health of these aging women through cohort studies would be instrumental for policy makers.

Cohort shifts can take place rapidly. For example, in Japan and Spain, shifts to separate living arrangements for older people have been occurring very quickly, as the desire to continue living an independent life becomes a preferred, and increasingly feasible, option. To sustain this trend, more options for housing for independent elderly women and care arrangements for those who become dependent will be required. Providing independent living options within a larger supportive environment will be an important means of ensuring appropriate social contact.

In both developed and developing countries, older women are the main carers for their partners, and many of the women who are carers of frail elderly parents are themselves aging. In developing countries, changes in living arrangements associated with urbanisation suggest that even more of the care of older women will fall to other older women in the future.

2.4. Monitoring demographic trends and changes in health status and wellbeing

The marked difference in the health experiences of successive cohorts of aging women and the differences between countries at different levels of development mean that aggregate data on total aged populations is inadequate for monitoring trends in health status. A simple but significant contribution could be made by the presentation of all relevant data by more detailed age and sex and economic status categories. A second important basic development is the use of age and sex specific life expectancies rather than only life expectancies at birth as indicators of changes in later life.

Improvements in demographic data are of direct importance in monitoring trends in the health status of aging women. Further indicators, such as the WHO recommended [12] indices of healthy life expectancy, need to be developed. This poses a number of technical problems, and must also take into account the differences in social and cultural meanings of disability and handicap. Methodological issues of this kind have begun to be addressed in the work of the REVES group and others [13]. Gender factors need continued attention and recognition.

As women live longer than men, the quality of their longer life becomes of central importance. Quality of life, measured in terms of older women's capacity to maintain physical, social and mental well-being notwithstanding varying levels of illness and disability, is of as much relevance as increased life expectancy and years of life free of disability. Measures of quality of life must reflect older women's experience and their expectations about acceptable levels of functioning in their daily lives.

Emerging measures such as Disability Adjusted Life Years (DALYs) or Quality Adjusted Life Years (QALYs) have yet to consider to these issues [14, 15]. Indeed, there is a risk that such measures of the burden of illness will give an overly negative account of the health of aging women, in turn affecting the way in which these issues are recognised in policy. To avoid these consequences, indicators which more adequately reflect the health of aging women need to be developed.

2.5. Longer lives - healthier lives

The changes in the life course of aging women outlined in this section, and the diversity of experience of later life, have significant implications for the health of aging women. Above all, the greater life expectancy for women in developed countries sets the basic goal for strategies for the health of aging women globally, namely to reduce the inequities in life expectancy of women in developed and developing countries. These inequities are not measured simply in the number of years of life, but reflect underlying inequities in the determinants of health and the quality of life that must be addressed if life expectancies are to be improved.

The benefits of improvements in life expectancy free of disability as individuals age are obvious; not only would it reduce the cost of disability (to themselves, their families and society) but it would expand their roles and, in the process, improve the public image of older persons as active citizens. As yet there is no clear evidence that women's greater life expectancy has any significant advantage in terms of remaining years lived free of disability. If longer lives for women are to be years of quality, policies must then be directed to ensuring the best possible health for women as they age.

An important adjunct to these policies, and an area in which WHO has a key role, is the establishment of data sets for monitoring demographic trends and health outcomes. Strategies are needed to expand the range of indicators, in order to take into account functional status and well-being in terms relevant to the experience of aging women.

Strategies proposed to these ends are:

* that Member States review national health goals and targets to ensure that the health of aging women is fully addressed;
* that intersectoral policy initiatives be developed by Member States to reduce the differences between developing and developed countries in life expectancy of aging women, and between groups of aging women within countries at different levels of development;
* that age- and sex-specific life expectancies be used in conjunction with life expectancies at birth as basic indicators for monitoring changes in the later life course; and
* that appropriate and relevant indicators of the health of aging women be developed, involving the critical analysis of current global measures of health status from the perspective of aging women, taking into account the way in which aging women perceive their quality of life and value their health.

III - HEALTH PRIORITIES FOR AGING WOMEN

3.1. Defining health priorities for aging women

Before discussing any health issue as a priority for aging women, the basis on which priorities have been defined must be made explicit. The approach to defining priorities adopted here involved applying the WHO definition of health to the situation of aging women, and the development of criteria by which various health problems could be assessed as priorities. The criteria adopted for defining a health issue as a priority for aging women cover three dimensions:

(a) The scale of the problem means it is

*   of major significance in both developed and developing countries;
*   of high prevalence in women over age 50 compared with younger women; and
*   of greater impact in aging women than men.

(b) The nature of the problem is such that it

*   has a progressive impact on women as they age, if not addressed;
*   has a major impact on functioning and independence as well as mortality;
*   is preventable, through primary prevention during the whole life course and secondary prevention at older ages; and
*   can be substantially addressed by primary health care measures, including selfcare management.

(c) The presentation of the problem is

*   overstated in some cases, under-rated in others, or generally under-researched;
*   often at risk of over-medicalisation or inappropriate interventions; and
*   already recognised in national health goals and targets in some countries, but requires a greater focus on aging women.

When these criteria are applied to a wider range of health problems, a number of conditions are identified that can be grouped into three major areas:

*   Major preventable causes of morbidity and mortality: heart disease and stroke ; cancer; and communicable diseases, especially in developing countries;
*   Major chronic disabling conditions: musculoskeletal; osteoporosis; and incontinence;
*   Mental health : depression and dementia.

3.2. Major preventable causes of morbidity and mortality

It is because the major preventable causes of morbidity and mortality all take effect over extended time periods that a life course perspective on the health of aging women is most appropriate. Primary prevention strategies will be most effective when initiated as early as possible. These strategies are also applicable to older women, and where problems are already apparent at older ages, secondary prevention and self care strategies are also relevant. Heart disease, stroke and lung cancer are the conditions which primary prevention needs to address, while secondary prevention strategies are applicable to the other cancers.

3.2.1 Heart disease and stroke

Heart disease and stroke are the major causes of death and disability in aging women. The common view of heart disease and stroke as men's health problems has tended to overshadow the recognition of their significance for aging women's health and there is a need to bring their importance into sharper focus.

In a typical developed country, heart disease and stroke are the major causes of death among older women, accounting for close to 60% of all adult female deaths. Cardiovascular diseases are also the major cause of death among women aged 50 years and over in developing countries, despite the incomplete control of communicable diseases. Half of all deaths of women over 50 in developing countries are due to these conditions; although communicable diseases are not fully controlled in these countries, they are no longer important causes of sickness and death in old age. As death from cardiovascular diseases is frequently preceded by a period of morbidity and disability, they also account for a high proportion of disability.

Trends in heart disease and stroke over the last two decades show the extent of improvement that can be achieved (Table 3.1). The control of stroke in Japan has resulted in a decline of 43% from 1970 to 1990, from a rate as high as that which now prevails in many developing countries, to a level commensurate with current rates in the United Kingdom, Germany and Australia. In the majority of developed countries for which trend data are available, declines in death rates have been greater for women than men, but cardiovascular disease will continue to be the major health issue for older women, even if favourable trends in mortality rates are sustained. The exceptions are the Eastern European countries, where the lack of improvement in life expectancy shown in Table 2.1 is largely due to the lack of progress in controlling these conditions.

Table 3.1 shows that trends in developing countries are less positive. An analysis of the global burden of stroke [16] has shown that age-specific mortality rates for stroke are higher at younger ages in developing countries and that improvements in mortality for women from 1970 to 1990 have been far less in many developing countries than in developed countries.

The patterns of morbidity and disability that accompany these mortality patterns indicate that developing countries carry a substantial part of the global burden of stroke. As increasing age is the main risk factor for stroke and cardiovascular disease more generally, this burden will increase as greater proportions of the population in developing countries reach older ages. There is a possibility that any decrease in the high rates (due to low standards of living in these countries) may be offset by an increasing adoption of western lifestyles without the benefits of economic development.

Further, since in developing countries the chances of surviving a stroke are currently less than in developed countries, improvements in survival rates could add to the burden of disability and see increased years of life being years with handicap.

Studies of both heart disease and stroke show that some aspects of health behaviour among younger and older women are similar. However, age can bring specific health management problems bearing in mind that signs and symptoms are assessed differently in men and women. Women also modify their perception of themselves and their abilities to cope with effects of illness in different ways to men. Information to empower older women to adopt self-care approaches to prevention of heart disease, stroke and other chronic diseases can also include assisting older women to cope with any caring needs that may arise as a result of these conditions.

Despite the importance of cardiovascular disease in aging populations, few studies have specifically examined women in this age group. Most longitudinal studies have begun with a cohort of middle-aged men and, as the cohorts have aged, conclusions have been drawn about the significance of risk factors for cardiovascular disease in older age groups. However, even these data are limited and cardiovascular disease policy decisions - especially those relating to older women - have long been hampered by inadequate data [17]. The dearth of data is even greater for developing countries, yet the levels of morbidity and mortality indicated by what data are available show an even more pressing need for information.

Table 3.1

Stroke mortality for women in developing and developed countries [19]

	Age specific stroke mortality rate, 1990 (per 100,000)			% of deaths > 55 caused by stroke	
	55-64	65-74	75+	1990	Change 1970- 1990
China	197.9	664.9	2408.2	n.a.	n.a.
Argentina	104.8	254.1	1118.8	12.6	- 13 %
Romania	177.4	572.0	2286.2	20.6	+ 2 %
Japan	- - -	262	- - -	17.4	- 43%
USA	42.2	126.9	778.5	9.1	-41 %

Since heart disease and stroke are due to the prevalence of risk factors in the population - primarily cigarette smoking, raised blood pressure and raised cholesterol - there is great scope for primary prevention through reduction of smoking, promotion of exercise and improved diet [18].

The two approaches to primary prevention for the whole population (including aging women) are the high risk strategy and the population strategy [19]. The high risk strategy involves finding and treating individuals who are deemed at high risk of developing cardiovascular disease. This strategy is costly and limited, and does not offer a realistic solution, especially in developing countries.

In contrast, reducing the average risk of the population at all ages is likely to have the greatest impact and can be justified by the fact that most new cases of cardiovascular disease will occur in people who may be at only mildly raised levels of risk. For example, a comprehensive nutrition policy in Norway has been successful in reducing the consumption of fat [20]. A reduction in the consumption of tobacco has also been achieved in many countries through a population strategy. A further major advantage of population-based approaches is that substantial benefits accrue for addressing other health disorders with the same contributing factors. Thus, the same population-based strategies for heart disease and stroke are applicable to the other priority areas taken up below.

BOX 3: Primordial prevention: lessons for developing countries

Primordial prevention is the avoidance of the emergence and establishment of the social, economic and cultural patterns of living that are known to contribute to an elevated risk of disease. In some developing countries coronary heart disease is becoming increasingly common, particularly in urban populations, which have already acquired high risk behaviours. Cigarette smoking is increasing rapidly in developing countries while the overall consumption of cigarettes in many developed countries is dropping. It has been estimated that by the year 2010 there will be over two million deaths each year in China from smoking-related disease unless a major effort is made now to reduce smoking. The indirect impact on women will take the form of increased numbers of widows [21].

The scope for primordial prevention in developing countries is considerable (Box 3). Coronary heart disease occurs on a large scale only if the basic underlying cause is present, that is, a diet high in saturated fat. Where this cause is largely absent, as in China and Japan, coronary heart disease is less common than stroke. Any increase in the frequency of cigarette smoking will, however, result in an increase in cardiovascular disease; changes in traditional dietary habits will compound this increase.

Dissemination of information about the extent of cardiovascular disease in the older female population is essential to ensure that women do not become complacent about this condition which is too often seen as a male problem.

3.2.2 Cancer

It is the long latent period for most cancers that dictates the importance of early detection. Age is thus an important factor in preventative strategies, but the known benefits of these strategies vary. It is among women in mid-life rather than those who are younger that available interventions are likely to be most effective, yet applications at younger ages have been more common to date. There is a need to review the available evidence and develop guidelines to ensure the most clinically appropriate and cost-effective use of these interventions.

The major cancer in women in developing countries is cervical cancer, followed by breast cancer. By contrast, in developed countries, breast cancer ranks first, followed by lung cancer. Because lung cancer is most amenable to primary prevention, it is discussed first.

Lung cancer

Lung cancer is the most preventable of all cancers; over 90% is attributable to cigarette smoking. The levels of morbidity and mortality among older women due to lung cancer are now similar in developed and developing countries [14] and likely to grow worldwide, given that increasing numbers of women smoke.

There is no cure for lung cancer. Prevention is not only the only option, but it is the most effective one. Strategies to promote giving up smoking will also yield major benefits in relation to other health problems.

Although lung cancer is not yet widespread in most of the developing world, the lessons from developed countries where women have now been regular smokers for some decades, are very clear. Lung cancer in women has increased fourfold over the past 30 years in many developed countries. As shown in Figure 3. I, it has overtaken breast cancer as the leading cause of cancer death in women in the United States who were the first women to take up cigarette smoking in large numbers. This pattern is being repeated elsewhere in developed countries where women have started smoking.

If current smoking patterns persist, or get worse, even higher costs associated with ill health and disability will occur. For example, in Spain few deaths in older women are attributed to smoking at present because only a very small proportion of 60 year old Spanish women have ever smoked. However, the situation has changed recently; 50% of young women now smoke cigarettes. If most of them continue to smoke, it can be anticipated that there will be an epidemic of smoking-related deaths when these women reach middle and old age [13].

Figure 3.1
Trends in mortality for cervix, breast and lung cancer in US women, age adjusted to the US 1970 population

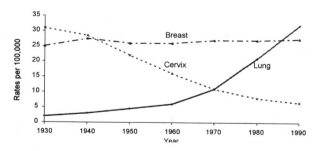

In most developed countries and Eastern European countries, between one quarter and one-third of women smoke; anti-smoking policies and health education strategies are aimed at containing these levels and especially at countering cigarette advertising targeted at young women. Even higher levels are to be found in many Latin American countries, where up to two-thirds of young women smoke. In most African and Asian countries levels are considerably lower (less than 10%). There are also a number of traditional societies where smoking has long been common practice among women. Everywhere, strategies are needed to counter the aggressive marketing policies in developing countries by the tobacco industry.

Cervical cancer

About 500,000 new cases of cervical cancer are diagnosed each year, mostly in developing countries [22]. For instance, mortality is three to six times higher in Latin American countries such as Brazil, Argentina, and Bolivia, than in Canada or the United States [23].

Cervical cancer is one of the few cancers with a readily detectable and treatable precursor stage. Pap smear screening is relatively simple and effective, but there are logistical and cost considerations in establishing effective screening and treatment programmes, particularly in developing countries. Screening is rarely accessible to women in rural areas, or aging women who are at greatest risk; even in developed countries, screening rates are usually higher in younger than in older women. Screening once every five years can result in an 85% reduction in mortality from cervical cancer; screening every 10 yeras could result in a 64% reduction [24]. Screening older women even once in their lifetime will prevent more cases of cervical cancer than screening a small proportion of younger women every few years. For these reasons, a stepwise approach to the frequency of screening has been recommended where resources are limited; screening should not be encouraged to a level beyond which it cannot be matched by the diagnostic and therapeutic facilities [25]. In other words, for screening to be effective, the associated cytology and treatment facilities must be available and of a high standard. Prerequisites for establishing complete population programmes and political commitment to action are the recognition that cervical cancer is a preventable major cause of death.

Where cytology-based screening programmes are not feasible, alternative approaches are being investigated such as using nurses or trained non-medical health workers to examine visually cervices treated with an acetic acid solution that highlights abnormal tissue.

Breast cancer

In developing countries, breast cancer is similar to cervical cancer in terms of its impact on women. In developed countries breast cancer is numerically more important than cervical cancer. Worldwide, there are almost 600,000 cases of breast cancer each year, 60% of which occur in developed countries. Breast cancer at present accounts for about 3% to 5% of all deaths from cancer in women in developed countries, but represents a smaller proportion of all cancer deaths in Africa and Asia (1% - 2% of all deaths). In most developed countries incidence is higher in urban areas than in rural areas - but emerging evidence indicates that this trend is reversing.

The risk factors associated with breast cancer are poorly understood although an increased risk is associated with a family pre-disposition, particularly breast cancer pre-menopausally in a mother or sister. Age at menarche, age at first and last pregnancy, and age at menopause are also associated with an increased risk, none of which can be easily modified through public health interventions.

There is little possibility for primary prevention strategies to reduce either incidence or mortality from breast cancer. Early detection is the main strategy for prevention. Approaches to early detection include physical examination of the breasts by trained health workers, breast selfexamination, and mammography. More randomized controlled trials are needed as there is no conclusive evidence that lives can be saved through the adoption of programmes other than those using the latter approach. Well-designed trials with a high coverage of the population at risk have shown that through screening mammography, followed by effective treatment, breast cancer mortality can be reduced by 30% in women aged 50 years and over [25]. There is as yet no clear evidence of benefit from screening programmes for pre-menopausal women [26]. A number of ethical, clinical and resource issues must however be addressed before screening programmes are implemented on a wide scale, even for older women.

The risk factors for breast cancer suggest that it will increase as development brings changes in fertility and reproductive behaviour in developing countries. Although each individual factor may make only a small contribution to increasing the risk, the cumulative effect in terms of absolute numbers will be formidable. The organization and implementation of mass screening programmes are far beyond the resources of developing countries, and breast self-examination (BSE) remains the main option. However, there is an urgent need to address the many uncertainties associated with BSE to improve its effectiveness as a means of early detection that is appropriate to the specific context of different developing countries [27].

3.2.3. Communicable disease in developing countries

Communicable diseases are still a major problem for older women in developing countries. Although in late adulthood they are no longer amongst the most common causes of death, they still account for high levels of morbidity and disability. Also important is to consider that episodes of communicable diseases earlier in life can lead to life long disabilities which aging will further accentuate. Tuberculosis, trachoma, and infectious and parasitic diseases cause significant disability [9].

Trachoma is an infectious blinding disease which tends to be particularly severe in women. Preschool children constitute the main reservoir for the micro-organism (Chlamydia) that causes trachoma. Women, being involved in child care, frequently become infected with the disease. Blinding trachoma develops slowly over many years, and thus aging women face the most severe complications leading to visual loss. The WHO Prevention of Blindness Programme reports that some 150 million people in developing countries suffer from trachoma.

The historical experience of developed countries and contemporary programmes to control tuberculosis in many developing countries show that improvements in basic living conditions and nutrition can virtually eliminate tuberculosis. The re-emergence of tuberculosis in some populations is of great concern. The adoption of essential drug programmes provides cost-effective solutions, especially in refugee situations.

Both men and women are exposed to tropical diseases - malaria, schistosomiasis, lymphatic filariasis and onchocerciasis, African trypanosomiasis and Chagas' disease, leprosy and leishmaniasis - but the personal, social and economic impact on women is known to be greater. Few, if any, studies have focused on the consequences of these diseases for older women, but in many cases, the impact grows increasingly severe with time. Skin disease and blindness resulting from onchocerciasis are cases in point, both of which are exacerbated with aging. Leprosy, too, has a particularly debilitating effect on older women, many of whom are expelled from their homes and families because of this stigmatising illness. With an effective cure for leprosy available, disability can now be prevented in the younger age groups, but for most older women, it is too late.

Aging women will be major beneficiaries of many programmes directed at controlling communicable diseases. Yet recognition of their needs is rarely the basis for implementation of such programmes, and even where they are implemented, aging women may not have access to the services provided.

3.3. Chronic disabling conditions

The most effective means of reducing chronic disability in older women is through preventative strategies initiated in mid-life. Where problems become apparent in people who already are older, secondary prevention can still contribute considerably to reducing the disabling effects of chronic illnesses.

3.3.1. Musculo-skeletal conditions

Reduced mobility has a major impact not only on the physical functioning of aging women, but also on their capacity to maintain social contact and hence their social and mental well-being. Conditions which affect mobility, such as arthritis, have major implications for quality of life. However, because they do not cause death, their effects have been inadequately addressed in health statistics.

Musculoskeletal conditions reduce mobility across a wide range of activities, and so, in turn, have a major impact on self-care. Investing in strategies to reduce musculoskeletal problems would reap a number of benefits including a general increase in the independence and well-being of aging women and a significant decrease in the cost of care and treatment.

For aging women, even those who are older, exercise is an important preventive activity against all major musculoskeletal conditions. Yet in developed countries, few older women exercise on a regular basis. Lack of exercise and inappropriate nutrition have led to an increase in the proportion of women who are overweight or obese. For older women who have already developed problems, strategies focused on rehabilitation, mobility, and other social and economic factors are needed. Aging women need encouragement and confidence to participate in safe exercise and recreation. Positive gains from participation can effectively counter negative attitudes that create barriers to many older women's involvement in physical activity. Women also need information on how to maintain appropriate nutritional intake and activity levels throughout their life.

In contrast, in developing countries, it is the excessive physical demands on women throughout their life course, including their later years, that most adversely affect physical strength and mobility. Prolonged heavy lifting, pulling and carrying loads lead to damage of the joints, particularly the vertebral column. In addition, nutritional deficiencies reduce the physical strength of women as they age. Broad development programmes are required to reduce the excessive demands for physical labour made on women throughout their lives.

3.3.2. Osteoporosis

Bone loss is a normal occurrence in both sexes after age 30, but it accelerates in women after the menopause. Osteoporosis refers to excessive bone tissue loss. Unfortunately, no measures have yet been established that provide reliable data on patterns of bone loss for more detailed population groups, or to predict bone loss for an individual woman as she ages. The causes of osteoporosis are still inadequately understood. Bone mineral loss is exacerbated by life-long lack of calcium in the diet, smoking and excessive physical activity causing prolonged amenorrhoea during earlier years.

Eighty per cent of those who have a hip fracture are women. Women in countries such as the United States and the United Kingdom have double the incidence of hip fractures than men [28]. On the other hand, older women in Asian countries who have lower bone density appear to have fewer fractures than older women in some other countries.

Osteoporosis can be a contributing factor in vertebral, ankle, wrist and hip fracture, but alone is not a cause. While hip fracture is the most severe consequence of osteoporosis, rates of fracture among older women increase markedly only in advanced old age. Decreased bone density accounts for only part of the increased risk of hip fracture among older women.

There are gaps in knowledge about the incidence of fractures in many regions, particularly those outside North America and Northern Europe. Only scant data are available from Asia, Latin America, Africa and the Middle East. The life long dietary intake of many older women in developing countries may have been deficient in the components necessary to build and protect bones, and this combined with hard physical labour throughout their lives, is more likely to damage than to protect their musculoskeletal system.

Although preventive strategies are available for osteoporosis, it is facing increasing medicalisation. Because the loss of oestrogen at menopause is associated with reduced bone density, osteoporosis is increasingly being defined as a hormone deficiency disease, a condition experienced only by women post-menopausally. This medicalisation owes much to the activities of commercial interests [29]. By playing on women's fears of aging, manufacturers of hormones and (to a lesser degree) calcium supplements have succeeded in redefining osteoporosis as symptom of menopause. This redefinition has been used to justify the routine use of hormone replacement therapy as a preventive measure despite its limitations in the prevention of osteoporosis at advanced ages [30, 31].

Many preventive strategies used for older women can also be directed at younger women who still have the opportunity to build and maintain strong bones. Such strategies include encouraging exercise and adequate calcium intake, and smoking cessation programmes. A substantial body of evidence indicates that regular exercise can reduce the risk of hip fractures by about half [32]. Stopping smoking is also important. A woman who stops smoking before the menopause will reduce her risk of subsequent fracture by about a quarter [35]. Other strategies particularly relevant for older women include modification of unsafe living environments, reduction in the high use of psychotropic drugs, and educating older women about measures they can take to prevent falls.

3.3.3. Incontinence

While there are common causes of urinary incontinence among women of both developed and developing countries, there are also differences. In developing countries frequent childbirth, poor access to facilities for the repair of birth injuries, circumcision practices, and untreated urinary tract infections can all lead to urinary incontinence. Widespread problems of this kind at younger ages in developing countries carry over to high levels of incontinence among aging women. While attention to the reproductive health of younger women will be the primary preventive solution for the future, secondary prevention is a major need for women who are aging with these problems. The onset of incontinence with increasing age is a key predictor of loss of functional independence, and can be one consequence of reduced mobility and other impairments. At its most severe, incontinence can lead to institutionalisation.

In developed countries, causes of urinary incontinence include lack of exercise, immobility, surgical intervention in childbirth and the use of specific drugs such as anti-hypertensives, diuretics, and tranquillisers. When these are the causes, there is considerable scope for primary prevention.

Incontinence can have serious personal and social consequences. It can cause anxiety, loss of self-esteem, avoidance of sexual activity, and depression. Through embarrassment, sufferers may avoid social contact and thus become socially isolated. Many sufferers do not seek help because they are too embarrassed to talk about it. As a way of overcoming this barrier, the health care professionals most usefully involved at this stage are community nurses; self-help groups are also useful.

Another factor that inhibits many aging women from seeking help is their reluctant but misinformed acceptance that little can be done about incontinence. As bladder control problems are not an inevitable consequence of aging, an important aspect of any preventive strategy is to provide information to this effect. Incontinence does not affect the majority of aging women, and a range of self-care strategies are effective in managing or correcting problems that do occur.

Self-care, involving techniques such as bladder training and exercises to strengthen the pelvic muscles, is one of three approaches that can be used to deal with urinary incontinence. The other two are medication and surgery.

Given the reluctance of many women to talk about the problem, incorporation of information about incontinence in programmes, such as those on exercise and nutrition, could prove effective. Access to health workers who are specifically trained to manage urinary incontinence is also required. In developing countries especially, education about prevention of incontinence in later years needs to be included in the training of primary health care workers who deliver other community-based health programmes such as fertility control and maternal health.

3.3.4. Multiple conditions, minor conditions, and sensory impairment

Many aging women experience a number of chronic conditions, including sensory impairments; these may be minor conditions or occur in conjunction with one of the major conditions already discussed. The effects of any one may not be severe, but their interaction can be significant in terms of reduced functioning, pain and anxiety about future health. Further, the ill-defined nature of many minor, chronic conditions poses problems for diagnosis, treatment and research, all of which tend to be oriented to specific diseases. Their effects are often attributed to the aging process, and as such are accepted by aging women as normal.

An analysis of the compounding effects of multiple conditions has shown complex interactions, with disability rising almost exponentially as the number of chronic conditions increased [33]. Prevalence and the disability impact of the 13 most common chronic conditions in the US were considered. The pairs of conditions which were most often encountered within the context of increased disability were cerebrovascular disease combined with fractured hip, diabetes or osteoporosis. Older women were found to have highest impairment levels of all groups considered: vision impairment and vision disease ranked among the most common conditions and had a marked effect on disability levels when combined with other conditions.

One of the main vision diseases and the most important cause of blindness among older women is cataracts. Some 90% of people with cataracts live in developing countries and 60% of them are elderly; in such countries unoperated cataract is a greater cause of blindness and visual disability than trachoma. The most common form of cataract is age-related, and while there is no known effective prevention, effective low technology procedures are available for restoring sight. More women than men become blind from cataract, presumably due to a longer life expectancy. In many settings gaining access to surgery is more difficult for women than men and more effective strategies such as mobile eye camps are needed in order to reach older women. Hearing loss and deafness in old age also affect negatively social interaction and mental health.

Reduction of the effects of any one of these conditions equally reduces the impact of multiple conditions. Many of these conditions are amenable to primary or secondary prevention, and early intervention can help to avoid the negative consequences that can arise when several minor conditions go unattended. The kinds of physical and social preventative strategies that apply to the major conditions which threaten the health of aging women also apply to these conditions.

3.4. Mental Health

More than any other health problem of aging women, mental health is conditioned by social and cultural factors. The definition of mental illness as well as the conditions that affect mental health are more varied than the diagnosis and causes of physical health problems. There are also strong age and gender biases in perceptions and reporting of mental health. Studies in developed countries consistently show that more older women than older men are diagnosed as having mental health problems. There are divergent explanations for such a finding. It could reflect greater stress and hardship experienced by aging women, or it could be due to the stereotypes held by the medical profession which influence their expectations and diagnosis.

The association between poverty and psychiatric illness has been well documented, and these determinants are more likely to have adverse effects on aging women than younger women or men. While there is a common misconception that there are higher overall rates of mental disorders among women than men, the prevalence of specific disorders differs for women and men. Of the two most common mental health problems experienced by older women, depression is amenable to supportive interventions but as there are no preventive measures against dementia, both care of those affected and support for their carers are required. Because of this difference in potential outcomes, and because depression and dementia can be confused, proper diagnosis is essential, yet the passive presentation of depression especially, means it may be neglected in aging women. Such neglect has particular implications for older women needing care for reasons other than depression which, if not actively addressed, can further reduce independence and compound care requirements.

The discussion that follows focuses on depression and dementia as the major mental health problems of aging women, but anxiety disorders also need to be recognised as being common among aging women. These disorders can cause aging women to limit their activities and reduce their independence. Social and psychological therapies to address these problems can restore the functions that have been adversely effected.

3.4.1. Depression

Depression can arise from the many stresses that women face as they age. Because depression can also be associated with biochemical disorders, there is need for accurate diagnosis and treatment. `Although the lifetime prevalence of any psychiatric disorder is higher for men, women are twice as likely to be depressed [34]. It has been claimed that the higher prevalence of depressive illness among aging women may be somewhat exaggerated; while mild symptoms may be common, severe illness is not frequent [35].

Mild depression is associated with the losses experienced at different times over the later life course, the most common being widowhood. Widowhood commonly brings a change in living arrangements, and it appears that control over choice is more important than the choice per se of living alone or with others. Community-based studies conducted in Brazil have indicated a considerably higher prevalence of depression among poorer older women living with a married child (usually a daughter) not by choice but because lack of economic resources preclude continued independent living. These women were also more likely to indicate a lack of a confidante and to report fewer social contacts outside the household than other women in the study [36].

In developed countries medically-diagnosed depression is most often treated with psychotropic drugs such as tranquillisers, sleeping pills and antidepressants; the use of these drugs in elderly women is considerably greater than in elderly men. This medical solution to what is often a social problem can actually cause greater problems than it solves, since drug treatment itself is not without risk nor does medication address the underlying causes of depression [37]. Depression can be alleviated through social intervention and other alternatives, and it appears that many women who experience mild forms of depression turn to these forms of support. When the social causes are recognised, approaches based on positive social interactions can be sought. There is a need to formalise more self-help approaches, including support groups, in primary care.

3.4.2 Dementia

The prevalence of dementia rises steeply with age, from less than 3% for the population aged 65 to 70 years to over 25% at age 85 and over. This gradient is remarkably constant in a number of developed countries when comparable case definition has been used [37], although social responses to dementia differ widely. Women are more likely to suffer from dementia because of their greater longevity, but there is no clear evidence of greater risk compared to men at equivalent ages. The dementias are major causes of admission to residential care in developed countries, and this likelihood is increased for older women who lack family support. There is as yet no reliable data on dementia prevalence in developing countries and culturally relevant instruments need to be developed in this respect.

Caring for a person with dementia places enormous demands on the carer, frequently for years. Most of those caring for people with dementia are aging women, either spouses or adult daughters. Gaining recognition and securing support for carers has been one of the main efforts of Alzheimer's Disease International, which is now established in a number of developing as well as developed countries. In addition to offering self-help approaches, such organizations have successfully lobbied governments in countries as diverse as Mexico and Australia. Support for carers is one of seven key components of Australia's National Action Plan for Dementia Care launched in 1992 [38].

The volume of research into dementia has grown exponentially in recent years, but no causes have yet been identified or treatments established. Most research has been undertaken in developed countries, and while projections of dementia have been based on population projections, no cohort studies have been made to establish whether there is any evidence of changing prevalence in successive cohorts.

3.5. Different problems - common solutions

It is apparent that there are common factors contributing to each of the conditions affecting the health of aging women. It follows that broad-based strategies which address these common causes will have far more widespread and beneficial outcomes than specific disease-focused strategies. For example, the adverse effects of smoking, poor nutrition and poor physical condition (the latter due either to lack of exercise or the damaging effects of excessively arduous physical labour) have been repeatedly identified as causes of the major health problems reviewed above. Preventive population strategies in these fields would achieve positive outcomes in several problem areas simultaneously. In addition there is an urgent need to provide more information to older women about normal aging, and about primary health care and self-care approaches to problems that do arise. Information that is accessible and acceptable is the basis of health promotion and prevention strategies and will be best developed by involving older women directly.

Another broad-based strategy is the training of primary health care workers who can respond to older women's health care needs. With basic training, aging women themselves can also take on many education roles, leading self-help groups and advocating on behalf of aging women.

Careful consideration should also be given to the risk of over-medicalisation of health problems of aging women, exposing them to unnecessary, inappropriate, and costly interventions. Preventive strategies can provide a strong counter to this development, including avoidance of an inappropriate use of drugs as noted in several of the problem areas.

Finally there is a need to strengthen and support non-governmental organizations active in the area of women's health, in particular, encouraging close links with existing family health services and maternal and child health programmes.

The major health problems of older women world-wide stem from non-communicable diseases. Primary and secondary prevention strategies offer several advantages in addressing these health problems because they:

* give women the opportunity to avoid many` health problems that might otherwise arise as they age, and to be involved in managing the problems they do experience;

* provide a low cost, population-wide means of reducing the prevalence of sickness and disability in the future;

* present an approach to health that aging women can identify with and participate in, whether at an individual, community, or wider policy level.

The most feasible and valid approach to prevention in both developed and developing countries is through primary health care.

Strategies to address the identified health priorities of aging women from several perspectives include:

* a focus on prevention of major avoidable health problems of aging women by recognising that:
  - heart disease and stroke are priorities for aging women as much as for aging men;
  - smoking is as much an issue for future cohorts of older women as current cohorts, and concerns equally developing and developed countries;
  - cervical and breast cancer are even more important problems for older women than younger women;
  - non-communicable diseases are the major causes of ill-health among aging women everywhere; and
  - communicable diseases are a continuing threat to the health of aging women in developing countries.

* the encouragement of broad-based preventive programmes that will simultaneously address several priority health areas by:
  - developing disease prevention and health promotion strategies for non-communicable diseases (heart disease and stroke in particular) by supporting nutrition programmes and encouraging better physical fitness as part of healthy aging. In developing countries this means reducing the adverse effects of hard physical labour, and in developed countries, promoting exercise and making available information on other self-care activities;
  - stressing the health benefits over the life course of not smoking; encouraging antismoking programmes targeted at younger women and giving more attention to smoking cessation and other prevention programmes among aging women. This will require support to halt the spread of the tobacco-related epidemics in

developing countries and to introduce comprehensive legislation controlling cigarette smoking;

- ensuring that population programmes for the early detection of cervical cancer cover post-menopausal women, and that breast cancer screening programmes are directed to post-menopausal women, with no upper age limits imposed.

* the use of health promotion to counter the over-medicalisation of health care for aging women, by providing women with information on normal aging and self-care approaches to maintaining health;
* the training of relevant primary health care workers to enable them to respond to the health care needs of aging women, and to train older women themselves to promote self-care;
* the use of the WHO Aging and Health Programme as a vehicle for consolidating and exchanging information on model initiatives taken so far so that small initiatives become system wide, and the inclusion of experts in the health of older women on relevant committees and working groups;
* the Aging and Health Programme working with WHO Regional Offices and older women's organizations at national level to identify best practice in local programmes and to develop packages of locally relevant resource materials to advance the strategies proposed by the WHO Global Commission;
* undertaking critical appraisals of existing protocols and guidelines for population screening programmes of relevance to aging women to ensure they are based on sound epidemiological evidence, and promote cost-effective approaches to prevention.

IV - DETERMINANTS OF OLDER WOMEN'S HEALTH

In common with any other population group, the major health problems of aging women are readily seen to stem from economic, social, cultural and political factors, as well as biological factors. This section will focus on major economic, social, political and cultural determinants of health of specific relevance to aging women, as depicted in Figure 4.1.

While these factors are common to developed and developing countries, there are substantial variations in the scale and spread of their effects across the population of aging women. The differentials in health status of women compared to men, and older people compared to younger people are attributable to multiple disadvantages. For many women, the effects of these disadvantages are felt throughout their whole life, and the health status of aging women reflects the compounding effects of these age and gender differences. Girls' nutrition, for example, will have long-term effects on bone strength, as reproductive health and sexually-transmitted diseases will affect the likelihood of cancers of the reproductive organs.

Figure 4.1
Social determinants of health

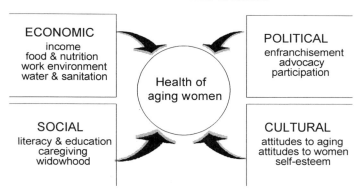

While admitting the negative lifelong effects of these factors on the health of some aging women, it has to be recognised that there are many aging women in good health. Positive economic, social, cultural, political and environmental circumstances have contributed to good health for these women, just as negative circumstances have resulted in poor health for others.

The aim of reviewing the economic, social, cultural and political determinants of health of aging women is to identify correlates of both positive and negative outcomes as a basis for improving and maintaining the health of women as they age. It is also recognised that much of the health of older women reflects the circumstances of their earlier lives, and that particular groups of older women will have special needs. The papers on adolescent health and women's health prepared for the WHO Global Commission on Women's Health set the scene for the discussion of determinants of healthy aging for women, and improvements in the health of aging women can be taken as signifying improvements in the health of women at all stages of their life.

4.1. Economic determinants

4.1.1. Adequate income

Poverty in old age often reflects poorer economic status earlier in life; many older women exist in conditions of relative if not absolute economic poverty, unable to meet minimal needs in many areas such as nutrition and shelter [8]. Even in developed countries, many older women lack independent economic security; retirement income is almost always lower for women than it is for men.

Social security systems have been, and still are to a large extent, based on three key assumptions: that children are not born out of wedlock; that marriages last forever ; and that the socially desirable role of a woman is that of housewife and mother, without paid work, and dependent on her husband. The social security systems in the United States and the United Kingdom, for example, while redistributive to women as a group, tend to treat women as dependents of their husbands rather than individuals who make a worthwhile contribution in their own right. Societies have changed. There is a much greater diversity and volatility of marriage arrangements, greater participation by women in the paid work force, and a greater emphasis on individual independence within marriage. Figure 4.2 shows the extent to which the social security systems in different countries are successful in ensuring a fair and adequate retirement income for all women, especially those living alone.

Health care for older people is usually financed in tandem with social security systems. Current transformations and the radical reshaping of some health systems suggest a move away from universal health provision in favour of various "safety nets" in both health and social welfare provision. The negative impact of reductions in benefits, tighter eligibility criteria, increased charges for health care and reduction in the access to health services will be felt mainly by aging women.

The insecurity of social "security" for aging women is especially evident in Eastern Europe. Notwithstanding high levels of participation in the paid workforce at earlier ages, the level of benefits available on reaching retirement age has generally been low, and recent economic changes have further reduced purchasing power. The loss of men in the Second World War also means that many of these women did not marry and so are not able to call on family support but have to rely on whatever public support is forthcoming.

Figure 4.2
Percentage of elderly (65 years & over) households below 50 % of
median household income (1987)

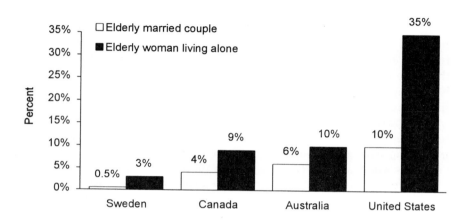

While most elderly women in industrialised countries receive some sort of social insurance or occupational benefit, very few elderly women in developing countries receive pensions. Where pension schemes exist in developing countries, they are almost entirely limited to public sector employees, the great majority of whom are men. The prospect of wider systems developing in the future is extremely limited. In the absence of publicly-funded social security schemes, aging women in developing countries must rely on the family which becomes the main source of security and shelter.

The great majority of aging women lack the means to pay for even basic health care. Using part of their limited income to meet the cost of health care would exacerbate the deprivations that contribute to their poor health. As shown in Box 4, lack of financial autonomy and reliance on children places older women in rural areas in particular, in a dependent position.

BOX 4: 21.5 million elderly widows in China

China will experience a fast aging process because of the official one child per family policy established in 1979, which has rapidly lowered the total fertility rate [12] Two thirds of women 65 years and over are widowed (an estimated 21.5 million in 1990); 80% of these widows in villages and 40% in cities depend on the support of their children. Only one woman in 10 aged 60 years and over can read or write; this potentially raises intergenerational conflict when younger age groups have had greater educational possibilities [12].

Increasing urbanisation contributes to deteriorating living conditions for aging women, both those who have been left behind in rural areas to face increasing responsibility for cultivation of crops and those who migrate to urban areas only to find traditional roles and reciprocal support no longer available to them. For most of those who remain in rural areas, health services are scarce, while in urban areas, doctors and medically-orientated services make little provision for migrant women from rural areas to share their traditional knowledge and experience. At the same time, the increasing number of younger women living in cities is creating future cohorts of aging women in urban settings who will have different needs.

International labour and social security organizations have longstanding interests in retirement incomes, and are taking an increasing interest in issues of gender equity. The ways in which social services such as health care and housing relate to employment opportunities and working conditions are also being addressed. It is through liaison with these agencies that issues of health of aging women can be taken up in an intersectoral framework.

4.1.2. Adequate basic resources: food and nutrition

In developing countries, the nutritional deficiency of the general population is even more pronounced in aging women. Famine, war and migration disrupt food distribution for everyone. But even under normal circumstances, poor nutrition is exacerbated by such problems as bad teeth, food of low nutritious quality, and chronic digestive disturbances including parasitic infections. The health of aging women in these countries reflects the cumulative effects of these problems. For example, years of child bearing and sacrificing her own nutrition for that of her family often leads to chronic anaemia.

The nutritional problems of poor rural women have common roots in many countries and regions. In a variety of different settings the same themes emerge: in poor households and communities, women work harder than men but eat less, and men contribute less to family prosperity, health and well being although they earn more. The high cost to women of a heavy workload, combined with insufficient nutrition, is reflected in poor health and lack of well-being in old age. Particular manifestations are injuries to necks and backs from carrying heavy loads (Box 5).

BOX 5: Hard labour

In the remote Himalayan villages 600 kilometres north of New Delhi, women walk an average of 10 kilometres three days out of four, for an average of seven hours at a time. They bring back about 25 kilos of wood with each load. All women, young and old and even pregnant, participate in this activity. When the men in one small village wanted to sell off the nearby community forest to the government to turn it into a farm for seed potatoes, the women protested. If the forest had been cut down, the women would have had to spend several more hours every day to fetch the family's daily requirement of food and fuel [39].

Behind most food security policies lies the assumption that once a household obtains sufficient food, all its individual members will be adequately nourished. However, improving a household's access to food does not guarantee that the older women in the family will receive sufficient food. Some development initiatives ignore women, some fail to recognise their particular problems, and some even worsen their situation.

In developed countries malnutrition is usually restricted to the poor and underprivileged and is often manifested as over-nutrition through diets rich in carbohydrates and fat. Some nutritional problems in aging women are a consequence of lifelong habits and others are imposed by poverty, often compounded by social circumstances such as living alone.

Finally, in situations of conflict, older women may be at even greater risk of not receiving adequate food, as reported in a recent survey in Bosnia Herzegovina [40].

4.1.3. Adequate living environments: water, sanitation and shelter

Another determinant of health is an adequate living environment, especially access to safe water and sanitation. In rural areas of developing countries less than two-thirds of the population have access to safe water; less than half have access to sanitation. For example, only 10-15% of people in rural areas of the Lao People's Democratic Republic have access to a safe, sustainable water supply and as few as 1-2% have access to properly constructed latrines. Overall figures of this kind emphasize the plight of many aging women who have been left in small villages when younger people move to urban areas.

Lack of safe drinking water affects women more than men in terms of their health. Because of the gender-based division of labour (particularly domestic chores) women are more frequently in contact with polluted water and therefore at greater risk of infection from this source. Regular carrying of heavy loads may aggravate musculo-skeletal problems, prolapse of the uterus and acute malnutrition. In Indonesia, for example, the most frequently reported physical disability affecting aging women is caused by fetching water.

While educating women about safe water management practices has a part to play, its effectiveness will be limited unless there are also changes in heavy agricultural responsibilities and the risk of infection from contaminated water in the fields. The provision of piped water is one such change that alleviates other problems. Other environmental hazards that threaten the health of older women include lifelong exposure to agricultural pesticides and indoor air pollution from smoky kitchens.

4.2. Social determinants

Three social determinants have significant effects on the health of aging women. The first, education and literacy, is part of earlier life experience. The second and third are major and widely-experienced events that occur in the later life course: the likelihood of caring for a disabled spouse or relative; and widowhood. These experiences can be regarded as normal insofar as there are social and cultural norms that govern roles and expectations. These events can have both positive and negative impacts on health, and the individual experiences of older women vary widely even within the same society. Other events that may occur in later life, such as violence and abuse, can be seen as abnormal and can only have negative effects on the health of aging women. Fear of these events as well as actual experience can add to their vulnerability. The diversity of experience of aging women, and their general disadvantage compared to aging men with regard to literacy and widowhood, are seen in Table 4.1.

The current cohort of older women includes women born in the 1890s and those born in the 1930s. This very wide age range presents considerable contrasts not only in education and occupational opportunities, but also in social experiences and major life events. The next century's aging women were born post-World War II. Their expectations about their future life will be different from current cohorts of older women. The health status of current cohorts of older women reflects social conditions many years ago, whereas the health of future aging cohorts will reflect recent, current and future social and economic conditions. It is not easy to predict the future health effects of these factors.

4.2.1. Literacy and education

Education is one of the more readily modifiable social determinants of health. The relationship between education and health is well established, with higher educational levels being associated with good health. People with greater education consistently show less disability and better chances of recovery after illness.

Levels of literacy and education among current cohorts of aging women are low in many developing countries. Improvements in education of girls will result in better educated future cohorts. Achieving basic literacy for aging women is a prerequisite to promoting their participation in increasingly literate societies. Just as education of younger women has been a central factor in improving maternal and child health, so increased literacy for older women can be expected to bring health improvements for them.

If attention is not given to literacy, older women will be even further marginalised. In developed countries, the high level of involvement of older women in continuing education indicates their desire to "catch up" on missed opportunities. The current shifts in work force participation of young and mid-aged women, together with their improved education and work experience, will create a potentially large group of aging women in the future who will wish to be involved not only in the work force but in other aspects of public life, in both the formal and informal sectors.

Table 4.1

Illiteracy and widowhood among aging women and men (60+ years) [44]

Country	% illiterate		% widowed	
	Women	Men	Women	Men
Sub-Saharan Africa				
Mozambique	99	86	55	19
Burkina Faso	99	94	50	8
South Africa	37	4	48	10
India	92	65	64	19
China	95	61	58	27
Other Asia and Islands				
Bangladesh	96	70	66	8
Philippines	51	42	41	15
Thailand	70	34	53	17
Korea	71	32	64	13

Middle Eastern Crescent				
Egypt	95	77	60	12
Turkey	85	50	50	15
Latin America				
Brazil	56	44	47	12
Mexico	45	33	38	12
Argentina	14	11	44	13
Former Socialist Economies of Europe				
Romania	u	u	50	16
Poland	5	3	52	14
Hungary	3	1	52	16
Established Market Economies				
United States	7	9	26	6
Spain	22	9	42	14
Australia	u	u	43	12
France	u	u	45	13
Japan	u	u	49	12

Note: u = lliteracy reported as universal

4.2.2. Aging women as caregivers

WHO has recognised the importance of informal caregiving in both developed and developing countries [5]. Since in industrialised countries the age range above 60 spans more than a generation, it contains a great variety of life styles and living arrangements. A striking feature is the proportion of older women who are carers. Support within the family largely rests on the spouse; aging women are more likely to care for their older husbands than the reverse. When a spouse is unavailable, it is largely women (usually adult daughters and daughters-in-law) who fill this role; many of these women are themselves aged 50 years and over, caring for parents (usually mothers) who are in their late 70s or 80s. Aging women also act as caregivers for disabled adult children and for younger children; a case in point here is AIDS, where grandmothers are increasingly assuming the role of caregiver as shown in Box 6. "Family care" generally means care provided by women. Conversely, in developed countries, it is the relative absence of family support for older women that underlies their greater use of residential care.

Providing assistance for caregivers is appropriate, and regular relief from caregiving responsibilities is essential. Caregiving women need options. While there are many positive aspects to the caring role, a growing literature has documented the adverse emotional and physical effects of caring for a disabled older adult over extended periods. Severely disabled people now live for many years, even decades. The value placed on the role of wife or daughter as the primary caregiver is such that providing them with support may be more appropriate than relieving them of caregiving. The social value placed on caregiving is a potent force shaping the nature of assistance provided, and public recognition of this value is fundamental to the provision of public funds to support carers.

> BOX 6: AIDS: the grandmothers' burden in an African community; a statement from HelpAge International
>
> *"The continuing burden of AIDS may well fall most heavily upon the grandmothers in certain developing countries. This assertion is probably contrary to most received knowledge on AIDS. In a family situation where both parents and some of the children are dying of AIDS, the surviving responsible person is likely to be the grandmother who is likely to be the most active, fit and competent person to manage the family affairs .... In a society where there are no adequate medical, hospice or counselling facilities, the grandmother is required over a long terminal period to nurse patients suffering from a disease which is unfamiliar, or even still unknown within the local culture. It is a disease which is dangerous to the uninitiated grandmother-nurse herself. It is a disease for which local traditional remedies have no application and no effect. It is a disease for which the grandmother may have no access to prognosis or advice on palliative treatment and preventive action.*
>
> *In addition to the nursing responsibility, the grandmother will have the domestic care and the preventive health responsibilities for the surviving infants. More than that, it is likely that the family sources of income and the family's ability to produce or procure food supplies will have been cut off. The grandmother will have to become the wage earner or food producer. "* [41]

The entry of more women into the paid work force in developed countries has often been seen to be eroding the availability of family caregivers. The scale of this trend is limited by the low degree of participation of women over 50 in the paid work force, although younger working women caring for elderly relatives are a small but special minority of carers. The rapidly industrialising countries of Asia are currently undergoing major transformations in women's work force participation. The impact on intergenerational relationships, and the extent to which benefits of development are shared across generations, are not yet apparent. Rather than overstating the impact of increased work force participation on the availability of carers, it is more important that a range of options be developed to enable women to choose the balance of work and caring responsibilities that best meets their particular circumstances.

4.2.3. Widowhood

Aging women everywhere are far more likely to be widowed than older men, but some countries have greater numbers of widowed women than others. The marked differences in the proportion of men and women over age 60 who are widowed in developing countries is due as much to high remarriage rates of men as to women's better life expectancy, which is the main factor in developed countries.

Although social norms that sanction men remarrying, or marrying younger women make widowhood far less likely for men, most women can expect widowhood to be part of their normal adult life. However few older women are prepared for this role. Social norms of widowhood generally mean restrictions of independence, as widowhood triggers a series of adjustments including changes in living arrangements and financial security as well as in personal relationships affecting companionship and intimacy. The great majority of older women in developed countries cope with these adjustments without any ill effects on their health, but for a small minority there are significant consequences for mental health.

The vast majority of aging women in developing countries live in extended family households, as much by necessity as by choice. In addition to urbanisation which can leave widows isolated in rural areas, growing mega-cities are giving rise to ever expanding urban slums, where often there is a lack of support from the extended family. Even when the widow has access to family support and the opportunity to contribute to the household in practical ways, this situation can result in dependency on the younger family members. In some countries, as shown in Box 7, widowhood practices pose a real threat to the health and well-being of these widows.

The situation of widows in developed countries presents a different picture of economic resources and dependency. While it is a degree of independence that enables widows to live alone, living alone may also make them more vulnerable to isolation, a vulnerability that is compounded if health declines.

BOX 7: Widowhood practices in Nigeria

In Nigeria, family law permits certain widowhood practices which discriminate against women, particularly women married according to customary rather than statutory law. Some of the negative practices derive from the belief that "the beauty of a woman is her husband ". At his death, she is seen as unclean and impure, and the customs she must observe in the weeks following her husband's death can undermine her health. If she has no adult male children, she may be ejected from her husband's house as both it and his land will have been inherited by his oldest brother. In most cases, the husband's kin do not provide the widow with any economic support, particularly if she will not accept the status of additional wife to one of her husband's brothers.

In a study in Imo State, Nigeria, interviews and discussions were held with traditional rulers, leaders of women's organizations and widows. Five factors impacting on the health and economic status of widows were identified: long period of incarceration during mourning, obligatory poor standard of hygiene, deprivation of the husband's property and maltreatment by his relatives, enforced persistent wailing, and the practice of demanding that a widow sit in the same room with her husband's body until burial [42].

Independent relationships with adult children and younger generations provide great support to widows, but dependence on children can cause a conflict of cultural and intergenerational values. As values change, aging women are in an increasingly vulnerable social position. "To be old, used to be the best part of life." This statement from a Kenyan woman refers to a time when older women were respected for their great age and wisdom and played important roles in society as judges, teachers, and community leaders. Aging women in many such cultures no longer automatically have a central role in the community and the spread of western education and values has diminished the respect previously given to the traditional knowledge possessed by older people.

4.3. Political determinants

Women have traditionally been dependent on men as decision-makers to address their needs, including health needs. This subservience has resulted in a lack of attention to their needs which differ from those of men. The entry of women into political life has the potential to reverse this historic neglect.

4.3.1. Participation and protection of citizenship

The growing participation of women in political life is seen in their enfranchisement and mobilisation for action, including action on health.

Women have only recently had access to political power and progress has been uneven over time and between countries. New Zealand was the first country to grant women the franchise (in 1893), yet the first woman was not elected to Parliament until 40 years later and it took 100 years before a woman was elected leader of a political party. Women in many countries, including France, Japan, Italy and Hungary, did not gain the vote until after the Second World War. In South Africa, many older women voted for their first time in their lives in 1994. Women are still not fully enfranchised in some developing countries.

The greater participation of women in the public life of many nations is partly the result of the political mobilisation of women through the international women's movement of the last 25 years; 1995 is the end of the United Nations designated second International Decade for Women.

"The pioneers of the second wave of feminism are advancing into middle age or beyond. In fact the whole postwar baby-boom generation is moving into midlife, which means that this will be an age group to reckon with in every sense of the word. " [43]

The rights and protection usually afforded by citizenship are threatened in situations of political conflict, when the role of the State and legal system break down. They are lost altogether to refugees. Women are more likely to be the victims of these circumstances. The loss of life in conflict also robs many older women of the support of their spouses and children that they could normally have expected in old age. The impacts of war on older people that have been reported in former Yugoslavia [44] are experienced in many other parts of the world.

4.3.2. Health advocacy

There are already signs that a politicised cohort of older women is emerging, and that health is one of the major causes behind the political mobilisation of aging women. Increasing numbers of aging women hold positions in which they can voice their interests in the decision-making process. There will be more advocates for aging women's health and needs in the future.

An example of advocacy for aging women is the Boston Women's Healthbook Collective which published the first self-help health manual for women in 1971. This became a landmark in efforts to disseminate and reinterpret issues that medical knowledge had rarefied. The manual had a resounding impact and the Collective became a key promoter of the women's self-help movement in many diverse countries including Puerto Rico and Mexico [45]. Members of the Collective, themselves in mid-life, supported the publication of a book for older women

"Ourselves, Growing Older" [47]. This book, which sold more than 100,000 copies, was written by women aged from 40 to over 90. Those who carried out this project are also involved in initiatives to educate aging women and their health care providers about a variety of health issues, for example, urinary incontinence.

In both developed and developing countries, positive examples of health advocacy can be found in non-government organizations and informal groups, many of which are highly developed and provide strong leadership. Empowering and mobilising women around the issues of health and aging is a central strategy for action. The collective nature of such action itself provides a significant opportunity for participation. It also helps women to know the value of antidiscrimination legislation as a tool for equality. Even where such legislation exists, however, there is a need to ensure that principles are put into practice and that *de jure* rights are not simply taken as meaning that *de facto* rights operate.

4.4. Cultural determinants

How women experience aging and their health status as they age will be profoundly influenced by the cultural context in which this occurs. Attitudes of others towards older women, attitudes of aging women towards themselves and attitudes towards menopause and aging in women all influence expectations of health in later years. Fostering positive attitudes to aging women is critical to maintaining positive public policies.

4.4.1. Attitudes towards older women

The status accorded to older women varies tremendously in different cultures. In pre-industrial societies, status was sometimes high with opportunities to gain prestige and authority with age; such opportunities to gain empowerment with age have usually diminished with modernisation and development [46]. Nevertheless, recent work of the European Commission reports positive attitudes to older people in a number of northern European countries where older people have achieved independent and active roles in post-industrial society. In southern European countries however, there was recognition that while the traditional status of the elderly has been lost, no new positive roles have yet emerged [47].

Women experience discrimination on the basis of age earlier than men. Age discrimination compounds the disadvantages of gender discrimination. Women are considered old at an earlier age than men. Further, they are perceived as weak, dependent, vulnerable, and lacking in femininity and sexuality. Such negative images contribute to rendering older women invisible and negate their significant diversity and resourcefulness. Such low status of aging women is not inevitable.

As shown in Box 9, in many societies positive roles are available for women as they grow older, which may involve the accumulation of status and authority. These roles include mother-in-law, grandmother, keeper of the lineage, leader in religion and ritual, master craftswoman, councillor and political leader. Many older women also enjoy greater freedom in movement and personal behaviour [51].

BOX 9: Maori women: honour with age

Maori, the indigenous people of New Zealand, offer different definitions as to when a Maori woman becomes a *kuia* (the term to denote respect accorded to an older woman). Being a grandmother is seen as one qualification, yet many Maori women reach this status before their 40th birthday. Another definition (probably the most widely accepted) concerns that stage in her life cycle when a woman passes menopause and is no longer of childbearing years. A third perspective of being a *kuia* is the role itself. The title is given in association with acceptance of any mantle of leadership.

"The honour is usually received humbly and not without some reluctance, not only because it is a public admission of being old, but because of the responsibility that the role carries: a keeper of tribal lore, arbiter of disputes, source of wisdom and the link with the past all rolled into one. She is the personification of the tribe." [48]

Even today, in rapidly changing times, the role of the *kuia* has been maintained as a profound expression of traditional Maori values and customary practice [49].

4.4.2. Attitudes of older women towards themselves: self esteem

The relationships between aging, health and self esteem are multi-faceted. Self esteem reflects a sense of self worth and being valued by others. Just as self esteem can contribute to both mental and physical health, which in turn enhance self esteem, lack of self esteem can affect health adversely, particularly mental health. Traumatic events earlier in a woman's life are especially likely to have a negative effect on the establishment of her identity and self confidence, with long lasting effects. In extreme cases, these events can include sexual violence and bodily mutilation, but many other lesser events can also lower self esteem.

In some developed countries, aging women face a difficult choice of either ceding to fashionable trends by trying to remain "forever young", or accepting the stereotyped and circumscribed roles assigned to older women. Yet the roles of grandmother, carer or widow can bring new value and meaning to the lives of older women as their relationships with family and close associates are restructured. Where widowhood and other changes in extended family relationships involve losses, contact with peers is likely to be especially important in giving aging women a valued role in their immediate social group. In establishing new social norms for the transitions of later life, peer support can reduce social isolation and depression, and the over-medicalisation that otherwise frequently accompanies these events in developed countries.

In developing countries where the breakdown of extended family relationships has eroded the status once accorded to older women in traditional society, peer support is likely to play an increasingly important part of the lives of aging women. The balance of creating new roles and maintaining traditional roles in rapidly changing societies is a major task that aging women themselves are best placed to undertake. Initiatives that will strengthen the capacity of these women to advocate and act on their own behalf become the major means of overcoming the barriers posed by low self esteem and lack of personal resources, including illiteracy.

In all countries, fostering positive attitudes to their own aging among older women and enhancing their self esteem are keys to them controlling their lives and maintaining social participation. The benefits to mental and physical health that flow from this in turn enable continuing personal development and involvement in the wider society. The popular media in all societies have a major part to play in presenting the achievements and appearance of aging women in ways that are positive and accurate rather than sustaining negative and unrealistic stereotypes.

Finally, older women are frequently the guardians of religious and spiritual culture, and these values become more important to many women as they age. Respect for older members of society is often part of these values, and older women can play a significant role in preserving these mores and transmitting them to other generations.

4.5. Better lives - better health

The multi-dimensional determinants of health of older women mean that any strategies to improve and maintain health must be equally broad based. Multisectoral action is required not only to address the disadvantaged status of many aging women, but also to recognise and support their continuing contribution, taking into account changing social situations in both developed and developing countries.

Several strategies can be proposed to address underlying determinants of the health of aging women. These strategies concern policy development to improve the well-being of aging women and advocacy to foster their participation in decision-making and self-help activities, including support for carers.

Strategies proposed to these ends are:

* the adoption of a life course perspective on health, which recognises that the most powerful determinants of the health of aging women (living conditions and social roles) are the same as determine health at earlier stages of the life course;
* availability of affordable primary health care, to ensure that aging women are not denied access to health care because of their inability to pay. Given the very low incomes of aging women in many parts of the world, strategies must focus on the provision of health care either free or at low direct cost to the consumer;
* extension of basic literacy programmes to aging women so that they may reap the same health benefits from education as younger women and enhance their capacity for continued participation in increasingly literate societies;
* recognition of the role of aging women as caregivers and the provision of support for caregivers as part of community-based primary health care services;
* promotion of positive models of healthy older women participating in all avenues of society; and self-help groups which enable elderly women to use their collective resources and strengthen older women's networks;
* establishment of consultative mechanisms at national and local level to give older women a voice in the development of policy and programmes for the health of aging women and opportunities to advocate on behalf of all older women; and
* non-discrimination against older women's access to health care on the grounds of age or sex through enfranchisement and the development of legislation that protects their rights.

V - A FRAMEWORK AND STRATEGIES FOR ACTION

5.1. A Framework for Action

5.1.1. Role of the WHO Global Commission on Women's Health

The WHO Global Commission on Women's Health is ideally placed to reinforce the Organization's advocacy for the adoption and implementation of effective strategies to ensure that aging women's health issues are firmly placed on national and international agendas. This report to the Global Commission might be used as the basis for such advocacy by providing guidance and motivation to Member States and other international agencies. One means to this end is the widespread dissemination of this report.

In addition, the Global Commission on Women's Health, by its very mandate, has an important role within WHO to accelerate the recognition of aging women in the work of all WHO programmes. The Aging and Health Programme is a vehicle to this end, and the WHO Fourth International Conference on Health Promotion in 1997 and the International Year of the Older Persons in 1999 provide key points for advancing strategies and reporting progress in the short to medium term.

5.1.2. Health for all aging women

The framework for improving health for all aging women is the same as that for improving the health of all members of society. This framework incorporates the principles of the Ottawa Charter and focuses on strategies that address the determinants of health at a population level rather than the consequences of ill health at an individual level.

The Ottawa Charter called for goal-setting and development of action strategies to achieve WHO's goal of Health For All, with particular reference to equity, health promotion, reorientation of health services to strengthen primary health care, community action and participation, healthy public policy, intersectoral cooperation to develop supportive environments, and international cooperation. The initiatives lauched by the Ottawa Charter have been furthered through a number of international conferences on health promotion. The fourth such conference is to take place in Delhi in 1997, with the theme "Moving Health Promotion into the 21st Century". Women's health and aging have been identified as two priority health promotion issues to be addressed.

Based on projected outcomes of current demographic trends, strategies are proposed through which Member States and organizations can take action appropriate to the needs of aging women. In implementing these strategies it must be remembered that the diversity of the health status of aging women means it is not practicable to target narrow groups defined by age alone. Rather, a life course perspective is needed which looks to the cumulative health benefits that will accrue to aging women through the improvement of women's health at all ages. The improvement in the health of older women will itself be an indicator of the extent to which this strategy has been successful.

5.1.3. WHO programmes and regional developments

The reactivation and reorientation of the WHO Aging and Health Programme presents a major opportunity to sharpen the focus on issues affecting the health of aging women, and to further the strategies proposed here. The Programme acts as a catalyst at three levels: within all WHO programmes, through WHO Regional Offices, and through inter-agency initiatives, involving government and non-government agencies.

The network of WHO Regional Offices serves to transfer general strategies to specific regional, national and local settings. The Regional Offices have a particularly critical part to play in identifying programmes that offer models of good practice for promoting health of aging women. Given that resources and expertise are especially limited in developing countries, it is essential that duplication of effort be minimised. Most initiatives for improving the health of aging women will occur within existing structures and programmes, and Regional Offices are well placed to facilitate exchange of information and sharing of practical experience. The great diversity of the latter offers a foundation for further initiatives with an increased focus on aging women.

By combining a review of past developments with information on models of good practice, simple but effective guidelines for enhancing the focus on health of aging women in future planning and programmes can be developed. Input from agencies concerned with women's health can be sought in developing these materials, which can in turn be made widely available to other agencies. The Regional strategy on health care of the elderly [50] and the manual for primary health care workers prepared by the WHO Regional Office for the Eastern Mediterranean provide models of the kind of guidelines that can be developed for aging and health promotion, with specific strategies focused on the special needs of aging women. Another example of widely-applicable material is the training manual on quality health care for the elderly produced by the Western Pacific Regional Office [51].

Ensuring that experts in women's health and aging from all Regions are involved in WHO activities related to aging and health will be an important means of advancing the strategies proposed in this report, both within the Organization and in interaction with other international, national and non-governmental agencies.

5.2. Strategies for action

The action strategies proposed are in accord with the key components of the WHO Aging and Health Programme, and the work of the Programme will in turn support their adoption and implementation by Member States and other organizations.

5.2.1. Policy

Policy strategies are fundamental in expressing a commitment to improving the health of aging women and addressing the underlying determinants of health. The policy strategies proposed are that:

* Member States undertake a review of national health goals and targets to ensure that health of aging women is fully addressed. Such reviews are best undertaken by adopting a life course perspective which recognises that the most powerful determinants of the health of aging women are the same factors associated with living conditions and social roles that determine health at earlier ages;

* Member States develop intersectoral policy initiatives aimed at reducing the differences in life expectancy between groups of older women within each country. Such initiatives will eventually contibute to reduce life expectancy differences between older women in developed and developing countries;

* Affordable primary health care be made available to ensure that older women are not denied access to health care because of their inability to pay. Given the very low incomes of older women in many parts of the world, strategies must focus on the provision of health care either free or at low direct cost to those who cannot afford full payment.

5.2.2. Programme development

Population-based health promotion strategies are the only feasible means of addressing the underlying common causes of the major health problems that adversely affect the health of aging women. Small scale programmes have been established addressing these problems in some countries, and the coverage of such approaches needs to be widened. Programme development will best be advanced through strategies that:

* Focus attention on major preventable health problems of aging women by recognising that:
  - heart disease and stroke are as much priorities for aging women as for aging men;
  - smoking is equally an issue for current and future cohorts of older women in developing countries as well as developed countries;
  - older women are at greater risk of cervical cancer and breast cancer than younger women;
  - non-communicable diseases are the major cause of health problems for aging women in all countries;
  - communicable diseases continue to affect negatively the health of aging women in developing countries; such diseases, often experienced early in life, may lead to lifelong disabilites further aggravated by the aging process.

* Develop broad-based preventive approaches that simultaneously address several priority health areas by:
  - developing programmes to promote prevention of non-communicable diseases (heart disease and stroke in particular) such as nutrition programmes and encouragement of improved physical fitness. In developed countries this means promoting appropriate exercise while in developing countries it means reducting the adverse effects of hard physical labour;
  - stressing among younger women the benefits to health over the life course of not smoking and giving more attention to aging women in smoking cessation programmes. Global efforts to halt the spread of the tobacco-related epidemics in developing countries and to introduce comprehensive legislation controlling the sale of tobacco products are important endeavours in this respect;
  - ensuring that population programmes for the early detection of cervical cancer include post-menopausal women, and that breast cancer screening programmes are directed to post-menopausal

women.

* Extend basic literacy to aging women so they can benefit from health and other education programmes and enhance their capacity for continued participation in increasingly literate societies;
* Recognise the role of aging women as caregivers and provide support for caregivers as part of community-based primary health care services.

5.2.3. Advocacy

In order to advance the health of aging women, older women need to be empowered to participate in the development and implementation of policies and programmes. Ways to equip them for this participation include:

* Presentation in the popular media of positive models of healthy older women participating fully in society;
* Providing women with information on normal aging and self-care in order to counter the trend to over-medicalize health care of aging women;
* Establishment of consultative mechanisms at national and local level to give older women a voice in the development of policy and programmes related to their health, and to create opportunities for them to advocate on behalf of other older women;
* Promotion of self-help groups that enable elderly women to use their collective resources and strengthen older women's networks;
* Ensuring that older women are not discriminated against in access to health care on the grounds of age or sex, through enfranchisement and the development of legislation that protects their rights;
* Including representatives with expertise in health of aging women on different WHO Expert Committees, such as that of the Aging and Health Programme.

5.2.4. Information

Information is required at several levels: for aging women themselves, for policy makers, and for those who plan and develop health care and services for older people. This can be provided in a number of ways, e.g.:

* Dissemination of information on normal aging (including facts about the menopause and incontinence, nutrition, mental health and physical activity) showing the diversity of experience of healthy

aging;
* The WHO Aging and Health Programme provides the framework for consolidating and exchanging information on model initiatives taken so far, encouraging the involvement of older women's organizations and other NGOs to develop packages of locally relevant resource materials in agreement with the Global Commission's recommendation;
* Adoption of age and sex specific life expectancies in conjunction with life expectancies at birth as basic indicators for monitoring changes in the later life course.

5.2.5. Training and Research

The reorientation of health services to focus on primary care can be advanced through strategies that train relevant groups of primary health care workers to enable them to respond to the health care needs of aging women, and train older women themselves to promote self care.

WHO can play a leading role in shaping the direction of research that will contribute to improving the health of aging women. Suggested research strategies that can be pursued through the Aging and Health Programme include:

* Promotion of the involvement of older women in indicating research that addresses their concerns;
* Development of appropriate and relevant indicators of older women's health, involving both the critical analysis of the current global measures of health status from the perspective of older women, and taking account of the way in which aging women perceive their quality of life and value their health; and
* Critical appraisal of existing protocols and guidelines for population screening programmes of relevance to the health of women to ensure they are realistic and based on sound epidemiological evidence, thereby promoting cost-effective approaches to prevention.

5.3. Global Framework - Local Action

In addition to the above strategies which are closely linked to the Aging and Health Programme, the Global Commission on Women's Health is itself in a unique position to take action to promote international cooperation to advance the health of aging women. Other

WHO programmes such as Human Resources for Health (HRH), Strengthening of Health Services (SHS), Epidemiological Surveillance and Health Situation and Trend Assessment (HST), Intensified Cooperation with Countries (ICO), Noncommunicable Diseases (NCD), and Mental Health (MNH) should be involved in promoting these strategies. Such action could be very influential in strengthening political commitment to improving the health of older women. To ensure that the work of the Global Commission has a lasting impact, it is proposed that:

* This report be widely disseminated at the Fourth World Conference on Women, to Member States, international organizations and non-governmental organizations (particularly women's organizations) to raise awareness and recognition of older women's perspectives in all health policy and programmes; and
* That a task force of the Global Commission on Women's Health be reconvened in 1999, the International Year of Older Persons, to report on the progress that has been made in advancing the health of older women.

REFERENCES

1. du Guerny J. Social policies and planning for midlife and older women in Latin America: an international approach. In: Midlife and older women in Latin America and the Caribbean. Washington, DC, Pan American Health Organisation and Amer. Ass. Of Retired Persons, 1989.
2. World Health Organization Global Commission on Women's Health. Women's Health: Towards a Better World. Geneva, World Health Organization, 1994.
3. The uses of epidemiology in the study of the elderly. Report of a WHO Scientific Group on the Epidemiology of Aging. (WHO Technical Report Series, No. 706). Geneva, World Health Organization, 1984.
4. Kane RL, Evans JG, Macfadyen D. (eds), Improving the health of older people: a world view. New York, Oxford University Press on behalf of the World Health Organization, 1990.
5. Kendig H, Hashimoto A, Coppard L. (eds), Family support for the elderly: the international experience. New York, Oxford University Press on behalf of the World Health Organization, 1992.
6. Mylander M. Continuities and discontinuities. Women and Health 1979;4:322.
7. United Nations Development Programme. Human Development Report 1994. New York, Oxford University Press, 1994.
8. Health in development: prospects for the 21st century. Geneva, World Health Organization, 1994.
9. Kinsella K, Taeuber CM. An Aging World II. (International Population Reports, P95/92-3). Washington DC, US Government Printing Office for US Bureau of the Census, 1992.
10. Peto R, Lopez AD, Boreham J, Than M, Heath C. Mortality from smoking in developed countries 1950-2000: indirect estimates from national vital statistics. Oxford, Oxford University Press, 1994.
11. Murray CJL, Lopez AD, Jamison DT. The global burden of disease in 1990: summary results, sensitivity analysis and future directions. Bull WHO 1994;72:495-509.
12. Development of indicators for monitoring health for all by the year 2000. Geneva, World Health Organization, 1981. (WHO Health Series No. 4).
13. Mathers CD, Robine J-M. Health expectancy indicators: a review of the work of REVES to date. Australian Institute of Health and Welfare and INSERM, 1993; 226: 1-21.
14. Murray CJL. Quantifying the burden of disease: the technical basis for disability-adjusted years. Bull WHO 1994;72:429-45.
15. Nord E. Methods for quality adjustment of life years. Soc Sci Med 1992;34:559-69.

16. Kalache A., Aboderin I. Stroke: the global burden. Health Policy and Planning, 1995; 10:1 -21.
17. Beaglehole R, Bonita R. Cardiovascular disease in elderly people: epidemiology and prevention. Cardiovasc Risk Factorsint J 1993; 4:279-89.
18. Epidemiology and prevention of cardiovascular diseases in elderly people. Report of a WHO Study Group. Geneva, World Health Organization, 1995.
19. Rose G. Sick individuals and sick populations. Int J Epidemiol 1985; 14:32-8.
20. Milio N. Nutrition policy for food-rich countries: a strategic analysis. Baltimore Johns Hopkins University Press, 1990.
21. Crofton J. Smoking and health in China. Lancet 1987; 2:53.
22. World Health Organization. Control of cancer of the cervix uteri: A WHO meeting. Bull World Health Organ 64:607-618.
23. Restrepo HE. Cancer epidemiology and control in women in Latin America and the Caribbean. In: Gomez EG, (ed). Gender, women and health in the Americas. Washington, DC, Pan American Health Organisation, 1993; 90-103.
24. Day NE. The epidemiological basis for evaluating different screening policies. In: Hakama M et al, (ed). Screening for cancer of the uterine cervix. Lyon, IARC, 1986. fScientific Publication, No. 76).
25. Fletcher SW, Black W, Harris R, Rimer BK, Shapiro S. Report of the international workshop on screening for breast cancer. Journal of the National Cancer Inst 1993; 85:1644-56.
26. Elwood JM, Cox B, Richardson A. The effectiveness of breast cancer screening by mammography in younger women. Online J Current Clin Trials 1993; Feb25:32.
27. Kalache A. Risk factors for breast cancer, with special reference to developing countries. Health Policy and Planning, 1990; 5: 1 -22.
28. Cummings SR, Kelsey JL, Nevitt M, O'Dowd KJ. Epidemiology of osteoporosis and osteoporotic fractures. Epidemiol Rev l985; 7:178-208.
29. Coney S. The menopause industry: how the medical establishment exploits women. New York, Spinifex, United States of America, 1994.
30. Felson D, Zhang Y, Hannan M, Keil D, Wilson P, Anderson J. The effect of postmenopausal estrogen therapy on bone density in elderly women. New Eng J Med 1993 ; 329: 1191 -3.
31. Ettinger B, Grady D. The waning effect of postmenopausal estrogen therapy on osteoporosis. New Eng J Med 1993; 329: 1192-3.
32. Law MR, Wald NJ, Meade TW. Strategies for prevention of osteoporosis and hip fracture. Br Med J 1991; 303:453-9.
33. Verbrugge LM, Lepkowshi JM, Imanaka Y. Comorbidity and its impact on disability. The Milbank Quarterly 1989; 67:450-484.
34. Paltiel FL. Mental health of women in the Americas. In: Gomez EG (ed). Gender, women and health in the Americas. Pan American Health Organisation Scientific Publication No 541, Washington, DC, World Health Organization, 1993.
35. Robson PJ. Self-esteem: a psychiatric view. Br J Psychiatry 1988; 153:6-15.
36. Veras R, Murphy E. Community based surveys in developing countries on ageing adults. Int J Geriatric Psychiatry. The Milbank Quarterly 1989; 67:450-84.
37. Preston GAN. Dementia in elderly adults: prevalence and institutionalisation. J Gerontol Med Sci 1986; 41:271-6.
38. Department of Health and Community Services. Putting the pieces together: a national action plan for dementia care. Canberra, Australian Government Publishing Service, 1994.
39. Waring M. Counting for nothing: what men value and what women are worth. United States of America, Allen and Unwin, 1988.
40. Vespa J, Watson F. Who are the nutritionally vulnerable in Bosnia Herzegovina? London, Institute of Child Health, 1995.
41. Beer C. ageACTION 1990/1;2:4.
42. Amadi IR. Women and widowhood practices in Imo State, Nigeria. Geneva, World Health Organization, 1994. (Unpublished paper cited in Anthology on Women, Health and Environment, (EHG, 94.11)).
43. Doress-Worters PB, Laskin Siegal D. Ourselves growing older: women aging with knowledge of power. New York, Simon and Schuster, 1994.
44. Seroka, JH. The elderly in Yugoslavia: A forgotten group in time of crisis. In L Katz Olsen (ed). The graying of the world: Who will care for the frail elderly? Binghampton New York, Haworth Press, 1993: 189-314.
45. Portugal AM, Matamala MI. Women's health movement: a view of the decade. In: Gomez EG, (ed) Gender, women, and health in the Americas. Washington, Scientific Publication No 541, Pan American Health Organisation, Regional Office of the WHO, 1993; 269-80.

46. Chaney EM (ed). Empowering older women: cross-cultural views. A guide for discussion and training. Women 's Initiative of the American Association of Retired Persons in cooperation with the International Federation on Ageing, 1990.

47. Commission of European Communities. Age and attitudes: main results from a Eurobarometer survey. Brussels, The Commission 1994.

48. Maaka R. Te Ao o te Pakeketanga: The world of the aged. In: P Koopman-Boyden (ed), New Zealand 's Ageing Society: The Implications. Wellington, Daphne Brasell, 1993; 213-54.

49. Coney S. Standing in the Sunshine: the History of New Zealand since Women Won the Vote. New Zealand, Viking Press, 1993.

50. Health Care for the Elderly: a manual for primary health care workers. Alexandria, World Health Organization Regional Office for the Eastern Mediterranean, 1994. (WHO Regional Publications, Eastern Mediterranean Series, No. 10)

51. Quality health care for the elderly: a manual for instructors, for nurses and other health workers. Manila, World Health Organization Regional Of fice for the Western Pacific, 1995. (Western Pacific Education in Action Series No 6)

THE JOURNAL OF NUTRITION, HEALTH & AGING

Edited by B.J. VELLAS, M.D., Ph.D.; Wm.C. CHUMLEA, Ph.D.; D. LANZMANN, M.D.

The Journal of Nutrition, Health & Aging

Springer Publishing Company and Serdi Publisher
Volume 1, Number 2, 1997

MISSION AND EDITORIAL POLICY

There is an increasing scientific and clinical interest in the interactions of nutrition and health as part of the aging process. This interest is due to the important role that nutrition plays throughout the life span. This role affects the growth and development of the body during childhood, affects the risk for acute and chronic diseases, the maintenance of physiological processes and the biological process of aging. A major aim of "The Journal of Nutrition, Health & Aging" is to contribute to the improvement of knowledge regarding the relationships between nutrition and the aging process from birth to old age.

1998 SUBSCRIPTIONS INFORMATION

❏ Institution: $120.00 per year in U.S. ; $140.00 per year elsewhere (for subscriptions outside North America, please add $20.00 for air freight)
❏ Individual: $80.00 per year in U.S. ; $ 95.00 per year elsewhere (for subscriptions outside North America, please add $20.00 for air freight)
❏ Check
❏ Charge my ❏ American Express ❏ VISA
❏ MasterCard 4-digit interbank # _____

Card # _____ Exp. date _____
Signature_____
Name (please print)_____
Address _____
_____
City/State/Zip/Country _____
Send order and payment to:
• For North America : Springer Publishing Company, 536 Broadway, New York, NY 10012-3955, USA. Fax: (212) 941 7842
• For Europe : Serdi Publishing Company, 320 Rue Saint-Honoré, 75001 Paris-France. Fax: (33) 5 61 75 11 28 • E-mail: 100775.1315@CompuServe.com

CALCIUM AND OSTEOPOROSIS: TIME TO THINK AGAIN *

R.P. HEANEY

Creighton University. Omaha, USA

Several well-controlled triais have demonstrated impressive fracture reduction in the elderly when their diets were supplemented with calcium. For this reason the National Institutes of Health in the United States, at a 1994 Consensus Conference on Optimal Calcium Intake, recommended an intake of 1500 mg/day for all estrogen-deprived women, and after age 65, for everyone, men and women, estrogen-replete and estrogen-deprived [1]. Two years earlier the Food and Drug Administration in the United States had permitted a health claim for calcium-rich foods. These official actions, by agencies of a major Westem nation, would seem to have settled the relationship between calcium and bone health.

However, it may be that we have been too cautious. 1500 mg Ca/day may not be sufficient. McKane and colleagues at the Mayo Clinic (Rochester, MN) recently reported studies of elderly women who had been maintained on 2400 mg Ca/day for three years, and compared them with age-matched controls whose intake had been 800 mg/day [2]. (800 mg/day is the current RDA in the US and is at or above the corresponding RDA values for most Western nations). They found that the women maintained on 800 mg/day had elevated levels of parathyroid hormone (PTH), exaggerated parathyroid gland secretory response, and elevated levels of bone remodeling. The most important finding, however, was that the women maintained on 2400 mg/day had a complete normalization of all of the hormonal changes: PTH levels were clown at young adult normal levels, PTH secretory response was reduced, and bone remodeling was also reduced to young adult normal values. Thus, all of the abnormalities of the calcium economy in the elderly, previously thought to be due simply to aging, must be recognized for what they are: signs of calcium privation. The reasons are lifelong low calcium intake, deteriorating calcium absorption efficiency in the elderly, and often a decreasing calcium intake as well.

In addition to nearly universal calcium deficiency, many elderly individuals ingest insufficient quantifies of protein and phosphorus as well. All of these nutrients are necessary for maintenance of normal musculoskeletal status and for protection against fracture.

For most elderly individuals, the best way to get all three nutrients is in the form of milk. One liter of milk contains about 1300 mg calcium, 1000 mg phosphorus, and 35 g protein. If calorie intake is a concern, non-fat, or low-fat milk should be used instead of whole milk. The same liter of non-fat milk contains only 360 kCal.

As professionals concerned with the optimization of bone health in the elderly in our populations, our goal should be one full liter of milk per day per person (or the equivalent in other dairy foods). The good news, in this regard, is that this preventive regimen has a negative cost, that is, the milk substitutes for other foods with less nutritional value and higher cost. Thus it turns out that it actually costs society less to provide the elderly with these essential nutrients than not to provide them.

Biomedical scientists have been reluctant to embrace this conclusion heretofore, in part because of concern that we might be perceived as having been co-opted by the dairy industry. But all of the Western nations face a growing epidemic of osteoporotic fractures, with staggering economic and human costs. It is time that we face reality. We have been overlooking an obvious, inexpensive, effective preventive agent for too long. We need to let the policymakers know that a major increase in milk intake will produce an immediate benefit for their aging populations.

*   Abstract International Symposium "Nutrition and Aging" (CERIN) Paris 6-7 December 1996 in "Nutrition et Personnes Agées" 1997 Centre de Recherche et d'Information Nutritionnelles, 89 rue d'Amsterdam 75008 Paris.

REFERENCES

1.   NIH Consensus Conference: Optimal Calcium Intake. JAMA 1994;272:1942-1948.
2.   McKane WR, Khosla S, O'Fallon WM, Robins SP, Burritt MF, Riggs BL A high calcium intake reverses the secondary hyperparathyroidism and increased bone resorption of elderly women. J Bone Miner Res 1995;l0:S451.

VITAMIN D SUPPLEMENTATION: A CRITICAL APPRAISAL *

P. LIPS

Departement of Endocrinology, Free University Amsterdam, Pays-Bas

Vitamin D deficiency is commonly observed in the elderly in northwestern European countries. Elderly people do not stay often outside in the sunshine. The ability of the skin to produce vitamin D^3, when exposed to sunshine decreases with aging. The dietary vitamin D intake in the elderly is not sufficient to compensate for the decreased synthesis in the skin. Vitamin D status can be assessed by measurement of serum 25-hydroxyvitamin D concentration. This is usually low in the elderly, and especially in the institutionalized and in patients with hip fracture.

Vitamin D deficiency leads to a decreased absorption of calcium from the gut. This results in secondary hyperparathyroidism, leading to high bone turnover and cortical bone loss. In this way vitamin D deficiency can aggravate osteoporosis and contribute to the pathogenesis of hip fractures. Severe long-standing vitamin D deficiency can lead to osteomalacia, characterized by an increased quantity of unmineralized bone tissue (osteoid) which decreases bone strength and also may cause (hip) fractures. The effects of vitamin D deficiency also depend on dietary calcium intake. A high intake leads to higher calcium absorption and lower activity of the parathyroid glands. On the other hand, a low calcium intake may aggravate the effect of vitamin D deficiency.

Vitamin D supplementation increases serum concentrations of 25-hydroxyvitamin D and 1,25-dihydroxyvitamin D (the active metabolite) in vitamin D deficient elderly, and decreases the concentration of parathyroid hormone. In vitamin D replete elderly, however, vitamin D does not decrease parathyroid hormone. Vitamin D supplementation 400 lU/day decreased wintertime bone loss from the lumbar spine in postmenopausal women.

Large scale prevention studies were done in Lyon and Amsterdam. In Lyon, 3270 women in nursing homes received either vitamin D^3, 800 lU/day and calcium 1200 mg/day or double placebo. The combined treatment led to a significant decrease of hip fractures and other peripheral fractures. The main advantage occurred during the first 18 months of treatment. In Amsterdam, 2578 elderly received either vitamin D3, 400 lU/day or placebo. The bone mineral density of the femoral neck increased 2.2% in the vitamin D group compared with the placebo group. However, the incidence of hip and other peripheral fractures was similar in the vitamin D and placebo group. The two studies differed in several aspects: the French elderly were older, and had a much lower calcium intake than the elderly in Amsterdam. The combined treatment in Lyon resulted in a greater suppression of parathyroid hormone and a greater increase of bone mineral density in the hip than the vitamin D^3, treatment in Amsterdam.

It can be concluded that vitamin D treatment improves vitamin D status, suppresses parathyroid activity and may increase bone mineral density. Vitamin D in combination with calcium supplements may decrease fracture incidence in frail elderly with severe vitamin D deficiency and low dietary calcium intake. Vitamin D supplementation should be recommended in risk groupe, such as nursing home residents, but generalized supplementation of all elderly is not indicated.

*   Abstract International Symposium "Nutrition and Aging" (CERIN) Paris 6-7 December 1996 in "Nutrition et Personnes Agées" 1997 Centre de Recherche et d'Information Nutritionnelles, 89 rue d'Amsterdam 75008 Paris.

PROTEIN INTAKE AND HIP FRACTURE *

J.-P. BONJOUR, M.-A. SCHURCH, R. RIZZOLI

Division of Clinical Pathophysiology, WHO Collaborating Center for Osteoporosis and Bone Disease, Department of Internal Medicine, University Hospital (Genève, Suisse)

In many countries osteoporosis represents a major health problem in terms of both morbidity and financial burden for the community. Taking into account both the consequences of all other osteoporotic fractures and the progressive aging of the population, it appears imperative to rapidly implement prevention programs aimed at reducing the dramatic consequences of osteoporosis. Many studies have focused on the hormonal deprivation occurring at the menopause. However, deficiency in nutritional elements could play a major role in the pathogenesis of osteoporosis and of fractures in elderly. There is now clearcut evidence that correction of an inadequate supply in both calcium and vitamin D can reduce bone loss and fracture incidence in elderly subjects. In addition, several studies point to the existence of a tight connection between the protein intake and bone metabolism. Protein intake below RDA could be particularly detrimental for both the acquisition of bone mass and the conservation of bone integrity with aging. In a survey made in hospitalized elderly patients our clinical research team observed that reduced protein intake was associated with lower femoral neck bone mineral density (BMD) and poor physical performance. This observation is in keeping with several studies in which a stase of malnutrition or undernutrition was documented in elderly patients with hip fracture. In these patients, in whom we detected very low femoral neck BMD at the level of the proximal femur, the self-selected intake of protein and energy was insufficient during their hospitalization. It is now well established that the clinical outcome after hip fracture can significantly be improved by daily nutritional supplementation, as documented by a reduction in both complication rate and median duration of hospital stay. That normalization of the protein intake, independently of that of energy, calcium and vitamin D, was responsible for this more favourable outcome has now been adequately documented. Furthermore, very recently we observed that in undernourished elderly subjects an increase in the protein intake, from low to normal, can be beneficial for bone integrity. This effect could be mediated by a positive influence on IGF-1, a bone anabolic growth factor. The plasma concentration of IGF-1 decreases with advancing age. Dietary protein positively influences the hepatic production and plasma level of IGF-1. Experimental studies indicate that IGF-1 has the capacity to enhance bone formation, by a direct action on osteoblastic formation and probably also by exerting an indirect effect at the kidney level. IGF-1 increases renal functions important for calcium-phosphate homeostasis, namely 1,25-dihydroxyvitamin D production, which plays a key role in the intestinal absorption of bone mineral, and the tubular reabsorption of phosphate which controls the level of the phosphatemia. In adult animals we have recently shown that administration of IGF-1 can also affect positively bone mass and increase the resistance to mechanical stress. Therefore these experimental and clinical observations sustain the hypothesis that protein replenishment by acting on the production and maybe also on the bone action of IGF-1 can favourably influence the incidence of osteoporotic fractures. Further research should be aimed at better understand the cellular and molecular mechanisms by which nutrients such as proteins can affect bone anabolism and the risk of fracture in elderly.

*   Abstract International Symposium "Nutrition and Aging" (CERIN) Paris 6-7 December 1996 in "Nutrition et Personnes Agées" 1997 Centre de Recherche et d'Information Nutritionnelles, 89 rue d'Amsterdam 75008 Paris.

REFERENCES

Ammann P, Rizzoli R, Müller K, Slosman D, and Bonjour JP (1993) IGF-1 and pamidronate increase bone mineral density in ovariectomized adult rats. Am. J. Physiol. 265:E770-E776.

Bonjour JP and Rizzoli R (1995) Inadequate protein intake and osteoporosis: possible involvement of the IGF system. In Nutritional aspects of Osteoporosis '94, Burkhardt P, and Heaney RP eds. Challenges of Modem Medicine, vol. 7. Roma, Ares-Serono Symposia Publications 1995:399-408.

Caverzasio J, Montessuit C, and Bonjour JP (1990) Stimulatory effect of insulin-like growth factor-1 on renal Pi transport and plasma 1,25-dihydroxyvitamin D3. Endocrinology 127:453-459.

Chevalley T, Rizzoli R, Nydegger V, Slosman D, Tkatch L Rapin CH, Vasey H, and Bonjour JP (1991) Preferential low bone mineral density of the femoral neck in patients with a recent fracture of the proximal femur. Osteoporosis Int. 1:147-154.

Delmi M, Rapin CH, Bengoa JM, Delmas PD, Vasey H, and Bonjour JP (1990) Dietary supplementation in elderly patients with fractured neck of the femur. Lancet i:1013-1016.

Froesch ER, Schmid C, Schwander J, and Zapf J (1985) Actions of insulin-like growth factors. Annu. Rev. Physiol. 47:443-467.

Geinoz G, Rapin CH, Rizzoli R, Kraemer R, Buchs B, Slosman D, Michel JP, and Bonjour JP (1993) Relationship between bone mineral density and dietary intakes in the elderly. Osteoporosis Int. 3:242-248.

Hammerman MR (1987) Insulin-like growth factors and aging. Endocrinology and Metabolism Clinics 16:995-1011.

Orwoll ES (1992) The effects of dietary protein insufficiency and excess on skeletal health. Bone 13:343-350.

Thissen JP, Triest S, Moats-Statts, Underwood LE, Mauerhoff T, Maiter D, and Ketelslegers JM (1991) Evidence that pretranslational and translational defects decrease serum IGF-1 concentrations during dietary protein restriction. Endocrinology 129:429-435.

Tkatch L Rapin CH, Rizzoli R, Slosman D, Nydegger V, Vasey H, and Bonjour JP (1992) Benefits of oral protein supplement in elderly patients with fracture of the proximal femur. J. Am. Coll. Nutr. 11:519-525.

CHANGES IN B
WITH AGING ,

WM.C. CHUMLEA , S.S. GUO , D. VELLAS

*Department of Community Health, Wright State University School of Medicine (Dayton, Etats-Unis).
** Service de médecine Interne et Gérontologie Clinique, CHU Purpan-Casselardit (Toulouse, France).

Significant quantitative and qualitative changes occur in the body's composition during the aging process. Among the elderly, increases in functional differences and in the rates of aging among individuals and among physiological systems within individuals increase inter-individual heterogeneity, because muscle and adipose tissues play a significant role in detemmining levels of functional status and health outcomes in the elderly. Fat free mass (FFM) is the single most important predictor of survival in critical illness and is a significant predictor of outcome in malignancy, and other acute illnesses. A significant loss of FFM (40% or more) is life threatening because of the reduction in body cell mass below the minimum level necessary to maintain physiologic functions. Normal physiologic function in severe illness is not regained until body composition levels return to normal. A significant part of loss of weight with age is due to a decrease in body water, which is reflected in a reduced muscle cell mass, and in body cell mass in general.

Reliable valid assessments or indices of body composition are necessary to determine the degree and prevalence of wasting or sarcopenia and the identification of risk factors associated with weight-related health conditions so as to be able to screen for those elderly persons at risk for a loss body composition profile and its health sequalae. Determining the relationship of changes in body composition during aging to morbidity and mortality is complicated by several de the accuracy and reliability of the methods of composition and the effects of age, sex, race, genetic, factors. These covariables not only affect the level of, and body composition, but are also associated with the onset and chronic comorbidity.

deposits are found between and within the muscles to a greater nt in the older men as muscle tissue is replaced by intramuscular fat, ut this marbling of muscle is not reflected in a subcutaneous fat measurement by anthropometry. After age 65 years, there can be continued increase in percent body fat in both men and women with a loss of muscle but not of body weight. Adipose tissue is redistributed as infra-abdominal adipose tissue increases and subcutaneous fat thickness on the limbs decreases. Imaging scans of middle-aged and elderly men have demonstrated that there was less subcutaneous adipose tissue and significantly more infra-abdominal adipose tissue in the older men than in the younger men at the same levels of fatness.

Weight and body mass index (BMI) are useful measures to describe levels of obesity indirectly in large samples, but for an individual, the amount and distribution of total body fat is independently related to cardiovascular disease risk factors. High and low levels of BMI are associated with increased risks of disease, and the relationship of BMI with all-cause mortality is reportedly U-shaped. To a great degree, the paradox of a high BMI associated with a high risk of mortality in middle age as characterized by a U-shaped curve, but a low weight associated with a high mortality some 20 years later in old age has been explained. The key to understanding this paradox is the change in weight from middle to old age in conjunction with a decline in health status. Thus, these was a loss of weight with age as a result of worsening health conditions with age in those persons who tended to have the greatest weight in middle age. If health is maintained, then a low body weight is not an important risk factor. These investigators recognize the limitations of this study in that the weight-related data were self-reported and the analysis limited to age 70 years. The changes in weight from middle to old age can not be quantified into lean and fat, and so the interaction with health conditions and specific components of body composition are unknown.

The relationships among body composition variables can have different statistical and biological associations, depending upon the health and nutritional status of the subjects. The fact that the skinfolds and midarm muscle area were more highly correlated with body weight, BMI and Wt/Kh in ill and malnourished groupe of elderly may be, in part, a function of errors. Measurements of skinfolds and circumferences of the limbs of the elderly are prone to measurement errors which are not random, but a function of the amount of subcutaneous adipose tissue. Thus, anthropometric variables are affected by the physical, functional, health and nutritional status, and age of the elderly subjects to be studied. For example, skinfolds are not that informative in the healthy elderly because skinfolds and circumference measurements from the limbs decrease with aging, in association with changes in fat and muscle distribution. As a result, circumferences of the trunk provide more information regarding stores of body fat and risk factors for cardiovascular disease in the healthy elderly than do skinfolds, while circumferences of the limbs are more infommative of changes in muscle mass in the sick or frail elderly.

In summary, the body's composition is an interdependent, multifaceted quantity. We are not yet capable of describing and quantifying the tissues in the body with consistent levels of accuracy. We are, however, capable of determining when the amount of FFM starts to decrease or determine when the distribution of tissues in the body's composition shifts toward a greater than normal level of fat or adipose tissue. In an individuel with these condiffons, the risk for disease and early death increases, but the magnitude of the changes relative to the threshold for the increased Rsk are affected by the age, sex, race and living habits of the individual. Some of this change may be a normal manifestation of age, but it is evident that a loss of FFM or an increased amount of internal adipose tissue in the abdomen place one at the increased health risk.

---

*   Abstract International Symposium "Nutrition and Aging" (CERIN) Paris 6-7 December 1996 in "Nutrition et Personnes Agées" 1997 Centre de Recherche et d'Information Nutritionnelles, 89 rue d'Amsterdam 75008 Paris.

DIETARY FAT AND BLOOD LIPID RESPONSES: A META-ANALYSIS *

D.J. MCNAMARA

ENC (Washington DC, Etats-Unis)

A meta-analysis was undertaken to develop predictive equations in order to estimate the extent to which current dietary guidelines would be expected to alter blood lipid and lipoprotein levels in the population. Human diet intervention studies (n=227, published between 1966 and 1994) were collected and analyzed to determine the effects of dietary fat type and amount and of dietary cholesterol on plasma cholesterol and triacylglycerol levels and plasma lipoprotein cholesterol concentrations. Data involving 23,686 study subjects (70% male, average age 37 yrs) in 370 independent groups indicated that 76% of the variance in senum cholesterol levers (ΔSC, mg/dl) is accounted for by changes in the percent of calories from saturated fat (ΔSFA,% energy) and polyunsaturated fat ($\Delta PUFA$, % energy) and the amount of dietary cholesterol (ΔC, mg/day): $\Delta SC = 1.92 \, \Delta SFA - 0.90 \, \Delta PUFA + 0.022 \, \Delta C$

The data indicate that for every 1% reducffon in saturated fat calories plasma cholesterol levels are reduced 1.9 mg/dl; for a 1% increase in polyunsaturated fat calories plasma cholesterol levels decrease 0.90 mg/dl, and a 100 mg/day decrease in dietary cholesterol results in plasma cholesterol being lowered 2.2 mg/dl. The analyses also indicated that dietary fat unsaturation and amount (ΔFAT, % energy), as well as dietary cholesterol, accounted for 36% of the dietary effects on plasma triacylglycerol levels (ΔTAG, mg/dl): $\Delta TAG = 0.014 \, \Delta C - 1.07 \, \Delta PUFA - 0.92 \, \Delta FAT$

The predictive equation indicates that as dietary fat calories are reduced, plasma triacylglycerol levels increase with the exchange of carbohydrate calories for fat calories.

Specific dietary lipid effects on plasma lipoprotein cholesterol levels could also be estimated using the results of the meta-analyses. 65% of the variance in LDL cholesterol (ΔLDL, mg/dl) is accounted for by calories from saturated and polyunsaturated fat: ΔLDL = 1.81 ΔSFA- 0.50 ΔPUFA

Predicted LDL cholesterol changes are 1.8 mg/dl per 1% saturated fat calories and 0.5 mg/dl per 1% polyunsaturated fat calories; the dietary cholesterol contribution to LDL levels was not significant.

Dietary saturated and total fat accourt for 41% of the variability in responses of plasma HDL cholesterol to dietary changes: ΔHDL = 0.29ΔSFA + 0.19ΔFAT

A 1% reduction in total fat (as saturated fat) intake results in a 0.4 mg/dl reduction in HDL cholesterol. There was no evidence that polyunsaturated fat intake lowered plasma HDL levels in humans.

There were no significant statistical improvements in the predictive models when interactive effects of dietary components were included in the equations nor was there evidence for differences due to baseline diets, duration of treatment, gender or age. The data did not support an exponential relationship between initial and final dietary cholesterol intakes with changes in plasma cholesterol levels nor a threshold relationship for the plasma cholesterol response to changes in dietary linoleic acid intake.

Based on these data, bringing the average American diet (37% calories FAT, 13% SFA, 7% PUFA, 450 mg cholesterl/day) in fine with the National Cholesterol Education Program Step I dietary guidelines (30% FAT, 10% SFA, 10% PUFA, 300 mg cholesterol/day) is predicted to reduce plasma total cholesterol levels by 11.8 mg/dl (an average of 6%) and LDL cholesterol levels by 6.9 mg/dl (average of 5%). The recommended diet would also result in a 2.2 mg/dl decrease in plasma HDL cholesterol and no significant change in plasma triacylglycerol levels. Not only are these effects of the dietary change on plasma lipids relatively modest, the corresponding changes in cardiovascular disease risk would be highly dependent on the initial plasma lipoprotein profile and may not be relevant to all populaffons. One concem of such dietary changes in an older population is the evidence that pasma HDL cholesterol levers are a better estimator af cardiovascular disease risk than total or LDL cholesterol levels. In addition, the effects of the recommended dietary changes on pasma insulin and glucose levels in the elderly remain unclear.

---

*   Abstract International Symposium "Nutrition and Aging" (CERIN) Paris 6-7 December 1996 in "Nutrition et Personnes Agées" 1997 Centre de Recherche et d'Information Nutritionnelles, 89 rue d'Amsterdam 75008 Paris.

BLOOD CHOLESTEROL AND MORTALITY RISK IN THE ELDERLY *

R.A. KRONMAL

School of Public health and Community Medicine, University of Washington (Seattle, Etats-Unis).

INTRODUCTION

There have been many studies of the elderly relating blood lipid levels to the risk of all-cause, coronary heart disease (CHD) and non-CHD mortality. Some studies show a positive relationship between total and LDL-C cholesterol and CHD mortality; others show no relationship. For all-cause mortality, most studies show little or no relationship to LDL-C or total cholesterol levels. However, a few studies report an increased mortality in those with low total cholesterol or LDL-C. For HDL-C there is more consistency. Most studies show a negative relationship between HDL-C levels and CHD and all-cause mortality. Complicating the issue further are differences in results as a function of age and gender. Accounting for the effects of prevalent CHD and other diseases adds additional complexity to the interpretation of findings.

In this paper we present findings that clarify each of the above issues and provide evidence supporting a unified explanation for the diverse results reported in the literature. This is accomplished by focusing on the effects of blood lipid levels on CHD and non-CHD mortality, separately, and by carefully incorporating the effects of age and gender.

The Cardiovascular Health Study (CHS) cohort provides data that are well suited to study these issues. This large cohort of 5201 persons, 65 years of age and older, was selected to be a representative sample of elderly in four US communities. This study has the unique advantage of having measured many variables that allow determination of the presence of subclinical CHD. This information makes it possible to account for the presence of subclinical CHD in modeling the risks associated with lipid levels. In addition, CHS has collected self-assessed health status of the participants. This variable can be used to adjust for the possible confounding effect of undiagnosed illness. Further, the wide age range (65-99 years) and the almost equal numbers of men and women, provides the opportunity to characterize the effects of both age and gender on the relationship between the lipid levels and mortality.

METHODS

Description of Cohort

Recruitment for CHS took place in four U.S. Communities. In this report, we restrict attention to the 3500 participants who were free of prevalent CHD at study entry. All participants with angina, a history of myocardial infarction, coronary bypass surgery or angioplasty were excluded. Follow-up is for five years. The cause of death was classified by a committee of physicians based on a thorough review of the participants medical records. Death due to CHD is defined by the ICD-9 codes of 410-414. All lipid determinations were done by a central laboratory, which was subject to extensive quality control procedures.

Statistical Analysis

Proportional hazards regression is used to adjust for factors that may be confounders of the relationship of the lipid levels to mortality. Statistical tests for the effect of the lipid levels in five categories test the hypothesis of equal risk across the categories.

RESULTS

The sample consisted of 1393 men and 2107 women with mean ages at enrollment of 73.3 and 72.4, respectively. The total mortality rate was 27.4/1000 person-years for men and 12.5/1000 person-years for women during the average of 4.34 years of follow-up.

The CHD mortality rate was remarkably low. There were only 55 CHD deaths, with rates of 6.3/1000 person-years in men and 1.8/1000 person-years in women. Total cholesterol level was not associated with CHD mortality in either men or women. While there was no statistically significant association of HDL-C with CHD mortality, there was a trend towards increased mortality associated with low HDL-C levels. Adjustment for risk factors for CHD, subclinical CHD and self-assessed health did not affect these relationships.

There was a statistically significant inverse association of total cholesterol with non-CHD mortality in women (p<.01). The non-CHD death rate for women with total cholesterol levels less than 4.78 mmol/L was 24.6/1000 person-years compared to 11.6/1000 person years for women with levels between 5.31 to 5.78 mmol/L. This corresponds to a relative risk of 1.67, after adjustment for significant prognostic factors.

There was no association of total cholesterol with non-CHD mortality for men. Nor was there any relationship of HDL-C with non-CHD mortality for either men or women.

CONCLUSIONS

For CHD mortality, the findings of this study are consistent with what has been observed in other studies. Total cholesterol levels were not associated with CHD mortality, while HDL-C followed the expected pattern of higher CHD mortality associated with low HDL-C levels.

Low total cholesterol in women was associated with increased non-CHD mortality. This association persisted even after adjustment for variables that reflect the participants health and risk status. Thus our results do not support the hypothesis that poor health is the cause of the association of low total cholesterol with non-CHD mortality.

*   Abstract International Symposium "Nutrition and Aging" (CERIN) Paris 6-7 December 1996 in "Nutrition et Personnes Agées" 1997 Centre de Recherche et d'Information Nutritionnelles, 89 rue d'Amsterdam 75008 Paris.

DISABILITY IN OLDER WOMEN:
ITS CHARACTERISTICS AND IMPACT

L. P. FRIED, J. M. GURALNIK, E. SIMONSICK, J. D. KASPER,

Drs. Fried and Kasper: The Johns Hopkins Medical Institutions, Departments of Medicine and Epidemiology (Dr. Fried) and Health Policy and Management (Dr. Kasper) Baltimore USA ;Drs. Guralnik and Simonsick: National Institute on Aging, Epidemiology, Demography and Biometry Program.

INTRODUCTION

Physical disability is an age-associated burden that is highly prevalent in older adults. Overall, 40 percent of people age 70 years and older in the U.S. report limitations in theirability to carry on their usual activities [1]. According to the 1990 U.S. Census, 16 percent of adults age 65 and older have difficulty with basic mobility-related activities such as walkingshort distances, and 12 percent have difficulty with basic self-care tasks [2]. Five to eight percent of community-dwelling adults age 65 and older receive help with one or more activities ofdaily living (ADLs) [3]. An additional 7 percent of adults age 65 years and older reside in nursing homes, of whom, 90 percent are dependent in one or moreADLs [4]. Physical disability in older adults is associated with poor quality of life, dependence on formal and informal careproviders, and substantial medical and long-term care costs. The high health care costs mayresult from the diseases that underlie disability, the severity of disease, and/or the presence ofcomorbid conditions [5,6]. In addition, disability itself is associated with high risk of superimposed acute illnesses and injuries. To promote the health and well-being of olderadults, it is important to have a substantive understanding of the impact of disability on aperson"s quality of life. The goal of this article is to add to insight into the characteristics ofdisablement and its impact on daily life in the one-third most disabled older women living inthe community, using data from the Women"s Health and Aging Study (WHAS).

I - METHODS: THE WOMEN'S HEALTH AND AGING STUDY

The Women's Health and Aging Study is a prospective, observational study of 1,002community-dwelling women age 65 years and older who were moderately to severelyphysically disabled, but not severely cognitively impaired, at baseline screening. The goal of the WHAS is to determine the causes and course of physical disability. The study populationwas drawn from the 32,538 women 65 years and older who were enrolled in Medicare as of September 1992 and residing in a defined geographic area encompassing 12 contiguous zipcodes in Baltimore, Maryland.

An age-stratified random sample (n=6,521) was drawn and those selected were notifiedby mail and then visited in-person to determine eligibility to participate in the study. Thescreening interview was designed to identify the one-third most physically disabled olderwomen living in the community who were not severely cognitively impaired. The screeningmethodology was based on previous research which identified four domains of tasks ofphysical functioning in which self-report of difficulty in certain tasks clustered together, suchthat difficulty in one task was associated with difficulty in the other tasks in that group,suggesting common underlying etiologies for difficulty in each group [7]. The four domains consist of groups of related tasks representing (1) mobility and exercise tolerance, (2) upperextremity function, (3) higher functioning tasks (a subset of instrumental activities of dailyliving not including heavy housework), and (4) basic self-care (a subset of non-mobilitydependent ADLs). Using these domains of functional disability, evaluation of 1984 NationalHealth Interview Survey data from the Supplement on Aging indicated that women whoreported difficulty in two or more domains represented the most disabled one-third of womenresiding in the community [8,9]. Study eligibility was thus defined based on self-report of difficulty in one or more tasks in two or more domains of functional disability, and on a Mini-Mental State Examination (MMSE) score [10] of 18 or higher. Of the 5,316 contacted, 4,137 women agreed to be screened and 3,841 completed the interview themselves. 1,409 were study eligible, of whom 1,002 completed the baseline interview administered and thecomprehensive home-based nurse-administered examination. Other information obtainedincluded demographic characteristics, self-reported health status, and history of physician-diagnosed chronic conditions.

II - FINDINGS ON THE CHARACTERISTICS OF DISABLEMENT

The disability patterns observed in the screened population, representative of womenage 65 years and older, are illustrated in Table 1. Each participant was asked whether, byherself and without assistance from another person or special equipment, she had any difficultywith each of 15 tasks. Tasks were assigned to each of 4 specific domains of function, based on prior research [5], (see footnote, Table 1 for tasks). Table 1, part A, shows the percentage of women screened who reported difficulty in each of the four domains. The highest rate of self-°reported difficulty was in the mobility domain, where over 49 percent of screened womenreported difficulty in one or more tasks. Approximately 22 percent reported difficulty in theself-care domain and 22 percent in the higher functioning tasks of household management. Rates for difficulty for all individual self-care items were slightly higher in this representativepopulation in Baltimore, Maryland than found in the general U.S. population of women age 65years and older [11].

Table 1 part B shows the distribution of the number of domains in which participantshad difficulty with one or more items. Women who had no difficulty in any domain ordifficulty in only one domain constituted 43.7 percent and 20.1 percent of the screenedpopulation, respectively, and were ineligible for the main study. Those with difficulty in two or more domains of physical functioning made up 36.2 percent of those screened, slightly morethan the one-third most disabled in the community. Most of the women with two domains ofdifficulty reported having mobility and upper extremity problems, while the majority ofwomen with difficulty in three domains reported problems with these two domains as wellasproblems with either higher functioning or self-care. The most severely disabled women,those reporting difficulty in all four domains, constituted about 13 percent of the screenedpopulation, but this percentage rose steeply with increasing age, to 30 percent of those age 85years and older.

Table 1

Disability Patterns of Representative Population of Women 65 Years and Older for Four Domains of Functioning

DISABILITY STATUS	TOTAL (N=3841)	AGE		
		65-74 (N=1777)	75-84 (N=1170)	85+ (N=894)
A. Difficulty in domains (%)				
Mobility tasks*	49.6	41.5	54.9	71.7
Upper extremity tasks +	34.5	29.6	37.0	51.1
Higher functioning tasks **	22.0	14.2	25.6	48.6
Self-care tasks ++	21.8	15.8	24.0	45.0
B. Disability by number of domains (%)				
Study Ineligible:				
No domains	43.7	51.7	38.2	22.3
One domain	20.1	19.5	22.3	15.2
Study Eligible:				
Two domains	13.6	13.0	13.9	16.4
Three domains	9.9	7.7	11.3	16.3
Four domains	12.7	8.1	14.4	29.9

(Source: WHAS, screening interview, 1992-1995)
* mobility tasks-walking 1/4 mile; walking up 10 steps w/out resting; getting in and out of bed or chairs; heavy housework.
+ upper extremity tasks-raising arms up over head; using fingers to grasp or handle; lifting/carrying 10 pounds.
**higher functioning tasks-using the telephone; light housework; meal preparation; shopping.
++ self-care tasks-bathing or showering; dressing; eating; using the toilet.

Compared to the U.S. female population in 1990, a slightly lower percentage of thescreened population was age 65 to 74 years (53% versus 55%), and a slightly lower proportionwas 85 years and older (10% versus 12%) [12]. Black women made up one quarter of the population screened for the WHAS. Overall, 42 percent of the screened population in theWHAS had 12 or more years of education, compared to 56 percent for women age 65 yearsand older in the United States [13].

III - CHARACTERISTICS OF MODERATELY TO SEVERELY DISABLED OLDER WOMEN

The women recruited to participate in the WHAS represent the approximately one-thirdmost disabled older women living in the community. Table 2 displays the demographiccharacteristics of this study population, including age, race, education, income and maritalstatus. Because the original sampling was age-stratified to include a higher number of very oldparticipants, data in this and subsequent tables are weighted representing the total populationage 65 and older. Notably, 28 percent of this disabled population were Black (slightly higher than the proportion in the reference, screened population) and 71 percent White, and 17 percent had annual incomes of less than $6,000 per year. Only 25 percent were married at thetime of the baseline evaluation.

Table 2

Demographic Characteristics and Cognitive Functioning of Participants in Baseline Assessment

Demographics, Disability, and Cognitive Functioning	Total (N = 1002)–
Age (%)	
65-74	44.2
75-84	40.7
85 +	15.1
Race (%)	
Black	28.3
White	71.1
Other	0.6
Years of Education (%)	
0-8	40.5
9-11	23.1
12	18.3
more than 12	18.1
Income (%)	
Less than $6,000	17.4
$6,000-$9,999	26.5
$10,000-$14,999	13.2
$15,000-$24,999	15.5
$25,000-$34,999	6.9
$35,000 or more	7.9
Unknown/refused	12.6
Marital Status (%)	
Married	24.5
Widowed	57.3
Separated	3.1
Divorced	7.7
Never married	7.5
Mini-Mental State Examination Score (mean), Range : 18-30	26.7

(Source: WHAS, screening and baseline interviews, 1991-1995)
1 All variables except income have less than 1% missing data. Results are based on non-missing data.
2 Descriptive statistics are based on weighted data.
3 Categories for each item may not add up to 100% due to rounding.

Even within this substantially disabled group there was great diversity in the type andamount of disability. As shown in Table 3, 17 percent of this group reported receiving help with ADL, while 35 percent had no difficulty with ADLs - even though moderately disabled. The oldest old, age 85 years and over, had the highest proportion with any ADL difficulty (75%) and the highest proportion who received help with ADLs (22%). In contrast, 61percent of the WHAS participants age 65 to 74 years old reported having any ADL difficultyand 15 percent received help with ADLs, while 39 percent of this age group had moderate disability.

Table 3

Disability Level of Participants in Baseline Assessment

Disability leval (%)	TOTAL (N=1002)	Age Group		
		65-74 (N=388)	75-84 (N=311)	85+ (N=303)
Moderate	35.4	39.4	34.9	25.0
ADL Difficulty: receives no help	47.5	45.9	47.4	52.8
ADL Difficulty : receives help	17.1	14.8	17.7	22.3

Source: WHAS, screening and baseline interviews, 1992-1995)

Figure 1 illustrates combinations of disability present among study participants. Nearly40 percent reported difficulty in two domains, 28 percent in three domains, and the remainingone-third in four domains of functioning. The frequency of disability in four domainsincreased with age. Slightly over 30 percent of women age 65 to 74 years reported difficultyin four domains, while nearly 50 percent of those age 85 years and older were disabled in fourdomains.

Table 4 describes the frequency of difficulty in specific tasks in this disabled segment ofcommunity-dwelling older women. Nearly three-quarters (74%) of study participants reporteddifficulty walking one-quarter mile; the proportions increased with age. In a substantially lessdemanding mobility task, walking across a small room, 25 percent reported difficulty,including 44 percent of women age 85 years and older. Lower proportions reported difficulty in less physically demanding tasks, with 45 percent reporting difficulty bathing or showering,41 percent difficulty with shopping and 19 percent difficulty with meal preparation. Thus,even within specific tasks there was a wide range of severity of disablement in this mostdisabled one-third of older women in the community.

Figure 1
Number of Domains of Disability for Total Population
and by Age Group

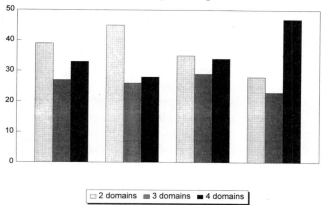

2 domains ▦ 3 domains ■ 4 domains

Table 4
Frequency of Task Difficulties in Moderately to Severely Ã Disabled
Women Living in the Community

Task or Activity	Overall (N=1002)	% Reporting Difficulty		
		Age Group		
		65-74 (N=388)	75-84 (N=311)	85+ (N=303)
Walking 1/4 mile (2-3 blocks)	74.4	69.7	76.5	82.4
Walking up 10 steps without resting	57.9	49.3	53.3	55.3
Walking across a small room	25.5	19.4	25.2	44.1
Lifting/carrying 10 lbs, e.g.,				
a bag of groceries	65.7	67.0	66.4	59.8
Turning a key in a lock	11.5	9.2	13.0	13.9
Shopping for personal items	40.9	33.6	39.7	65.0
Preparing own meals	19.0	15.8	20.3	24.9
Managing own money	14.8	10.0	15.4	27.0
Using the telephone	10.1	6.8	11.0	17.2
Taking medications	3.9	1.9	4.3	8.7
Bathing or showering	44.8	39.4	46.9	55.1
Dressing	21.4	19.1	23.0	23.7
Using the toilet	20.4	17.2	21.4	27.2
Eating	9.1	8.4	10.0	8.6

(Source: WHAS, screening and baseline interviews, 1992-1995)

A substantial proportion of the population used assistive devices, including canes(27%), walkers (11%) and wheelchairs (11%) (Table 5). Three percent of these community-dwelling women reported not being able to walk at all. Notably, strategies for ambulationvaried depending on whether they were inside or outside the home. Outside the home, ahigher proportion reported using a cane or holding onto another person to ambulate, comparedto inside. Inside the home, participants were most likely to report reaching out for and holdingonto furniture and walls (38%) or using a cane (19%).

It is notable that a substantial proportion of the population reported personal adaptationsto improve ambulation, such as holding onto walls, rather than use of assistive devices. Studyparticipants also reported employing compensatory strategies in their mode of performance ofnumerous other tasks, whether or not they had difficulty with a task. For example, amongthose with difficulty shopping, 80 percent reported changing the method that they used to shop [14]. This compensatory strategy is likely a response to functional decline that may preserve task performance. Identifying these strategies may be useful in understanding howindividuals minimize disability and maintain independence.

Table 5
Use of Walking Aids and Supports`

	Overall (%)	Outside Home (%)	In Home (%)	In the Dark (%)
When Walk :				
Use a cane	37.0	34.3	19.3	--
Use a walker	11.2	6.7	9.2	--
Reach out for and hold onto walls	41.0	21.0	38.4	40.3
Hold onto another person	32.3	28.5	6.2	7.0
Cannot walk	3.1	--	--	--
Use a wheel chair	11.1	9.0	5.4	--

Source: WHAS, screening and baseline interviews, 1992-1995)

Use of human assistance is another important form of compensatory strategy used in thepresence of task difficulty. There was a wide range of the frequency of receiving help,depending on the task. For example, overall, 71 percent of these disabled women reported receiving help with heavy housework, 37 percent help with managing money, 21 percent withmeal preparation, 16 percent with bathing, 11 percent with dressing,

7 percent with takingmedications, 5 percent with using the telephone and 3 percent with using the toilet. Table 6 shows the frequency of receiving help for selected higher functioning tasks, or InstrumentalActivities of Daily Living (IADLs), by self-reported presence of task difficulty andperformance capability. For all tasks, a proportion of women who reported no difficultyreported receiving help, but at a lesser rate than those with difficulty. For example, nearly allwomen reporting that they could not shop reported receiving help, 72 percent who haddifficulty got help and 27 percent with no difficulty had help shopping. It is likely that forsome individuals, receipt of help may mask difficulty with a task, while for others it maycontribute to the recognition of task difficulty.

Table 6
Frequency of Receiving Help for Higher Function Tasks

	No difficulty (%)	Difficulty (%)	Unable to Do (%)	Doesn't Do (%)
Shopping for personal items	55.6	14.1	26.8	3.5
- Receives help	26.8	71.5	95.9	83.3
Managing own money*	78.9	7.8	7.0	6.4
- Receives help	14.0	72.0	61.2	39.8
Using telephone	89.4	8.2	1.9	0.5
- Receives help	2.2	28.7	56.9	--
Taking mediations	95.4	2.6	1.3	0.7
- Receives help	3.7	84.8	97.8	14.7

(Source: WHAS, screening and baseline interviews, 1992-1995)
* paying bills or keeping a bank account

Another adaptation examined, the usage of rooms in a person's house, is shown in Table 7. Twelve percent of these moderately to severely disabled older women reportedhaving stopped using, on average, one-third to one-half of the rooms in their house because ofa health or physical condition. Both the proportion who stopped using rooms and thepercentage of rooms no longer used increased substantially with age.

Table 7

Decreased Usage of Rooms

	Total (N=1002)	Age			Disability Level		
		65-74 (N=388)	75-84 (N=311)	≥ 85 (N=303)	Moderate (N=343)	ADL Difficulty	
						Receives No help (N=478)	Receives Help (N=?)
Have stopped using rooms in house because of health or physical condition,							
% Yes :	12.1	11.9	11.5	14.6	3.4	10.5	34.7
If yes, % of rooms (mean) :	40.0	32.6	42.8	47.9	29.7	36.2	43.8

(Source: WHAS, screening and baseline interviews, 1992-1995)

The living circumstances and the physical and social environment of older adults cangreatly influence their quality of life and functional independence in the community. Thefollowing describes the living circumstances and some of the activities pursued by the disabledolder women in the WHAS.

Despite substantial disability, the WHAS participants most commonly lived alone (45percent), while 20 percent lived with their spouse and just over 30 percent lived with others who were not a spouse. Most of the married women lived with only their spouse (20% of thesample) (Table 8). One quarter of married women (4.9 percent overall) lived with others aswell as their spouse. The households were typically small. Adult children were the mostcommon living companions, followed by spouse, grandchildren, and other relatives includingsiblings. The presence of non-relatives in the household was rare. Household compositionvaried greatly by participant age and functional status. For example, just over one third ofthose age 65 to 74 years lived alone, compared to more than half of those age 75 to 84 years,and 61 percent of the oldest over 85 group. The extended family household (i.e., living withgrandchildren) was most common among those age 65 to 74 years (16.4 percent) and relativelyrare for those age 85 years and older (5.3 percent). Women who received help in activities ofdaily living were the least likely to live alone and most likely to live with nonspouse others.

Table 8

Living Arrangements: Moderately to Severely Disabled Women ≥ 65
Living in the Community

	Disability Level		
	Moderate	ADL Difficulty	
	(N=343)	Receives No Help (N=478)	Receives Help (N=181)
Household Composition	%	%	%
Alone	44.6	54.3	26.4
Spouse Only	19.9	15.0	19.0
Spouse and others	4.9	5.3	8.5
Others only	30.6	25.4	46.1

(Source: WHAS, screening and baseline interviews, 1992-1995)

It is noteworthy that functional limitations do not necessarily prohibit older womenfrom contributing to the household. Almost four-fifths of the participants had primaryresponsibility for preparing meals in their households. Although this rate decreased withincreasing age largely because of health problems, 65 percent of women age 85 years and olderstill prepared meals for themselves and often others. Among women age 65 to 74 years, while58 percent lived alone or with only their spouse, 82 percent had the main responsibility formeal preparation.

Frequency of engaging in five physically demanding activities most commonlyperformed by older women was also assessed: walking, household chores, outdoor chores,dancing and regular exercise programs. Overall, household chores was the most frequentlyperformed activity followed by walking for exercise. However, in the oldest age group, walking was more frequent. One-quarter of these disabled women reported 3 or more hours ofexercise per week, and one-third had walked for exercise in the past week. Walking was thepredominant activity reported by the most severely disabled women. The levels ofparticipation in walking and in any physical activity were surprisingly similar to thoseobserved in a general population of older persons [15]. Overall, this cohort of older disabled women reported higher levels of participation in physical activity and exercise than might beexpected given the high prevalence of difficulty in mobility-related tasks (Table 4). Dancingand bowling were uncommon, reported by less than 6 percent and 2 percent, respectively. With the exception of walking, the proportion who participated in each activity decreased withincreasing age, particularly for household and outdoor chores. The percent of women who didany physical activity decreased with increasing age.

Participation in physical activity alsodeclined with increasing severity of disability.

Social contact and activity were assessed in several ways. First, life space, that is, thefrequency with which participants leave their home in a typical week, was indicated as thefrequency of leaving the home and whether they left the neighborhood. Seventeen percent lefttheir home less than once a week on the average, while another 17 percent left their home 1-3times per week. The majority of the oldest women (age 85+) did not leave their neighborhoodin a typical week and this age group had the highest proportion (29%) who did not leave theirhome. Similar trends were observed for disability, with the most severely disabled having thehighest rates of not leaving the home.

Social contact also tended to diminish with increasing disablement. For example, 23percent of these disabled women reported less than one face to face contact per week, with a range from 18 percent of those with moderate disability to 31 percent of those who were ADLdependent. The oldest women had the lowest frequency of telephone and face-to-face contactwith persons residing outside their home. Notably, two-thirds of these moderately to severelydisabled older women reported never attending cultural events, like concerts or movies andless than 50 percent regularly attended church. Some of this social isolation could be a resultof the severity of disability, but other factors such as income and transportation access mightbe important. For example, only 25 percent currently drive.

These data portray great diversity in the experience of disablement, even within thismost disabled one-third of older women in the community. Many disabled older adults arequite active and employ a variety of strategies to cope with functional limitation and maintainindependence. In addition, these data suggest opportunities for enhancing both social andphysical activity, if desired, in a substantial segment that appear to be isolated. The experienceof disablement has many adverse components to it but includes a wide range.

REFERENCES

1. Cohen RA, Van Nostrand JF. (1995). Trends in the health of older Americans: United States, 1994. Vital Health Statistics 3(30).
2. LaPlante MP. (1993). Prevalence of mobility and self-care disability - United States, 1990. MMWR 42:760-768.
3. Weiner JM, Hanley RJ, Clark R, Van Nostrand JR. (1990). Measuring the activities of daily living: Comparisons across national surveys. J Gerontol Soc Sci 45:S229-S237.
4. Hing E, Sekscenski E, Strahan G. (1989). The national nursing home survey: 1985 summary the United States. Vital Health Statistics 13(97).
5. Fried LP, Bush TL. (1988). Morbidity as a focus of preventive health care in the elderly. Epidemiol

Rev 10:48-64.

6. Soldo BJ, Manton KG. (1985). Health status and service needs of the oldest old: Current patterns and future trends. Milbank Mem Fund Q 63:286-319.

7. Fried LP, Ettinger WH, Hermanson B, Newman AB, Gardin J for the CHS Collaborative Research Group. (1994). Physical disability in older adults: A physiological approach. J Clin Epidemiol 47:747-760.

8. Kasper JD, Shapiro S, Guralnik JM, õBandeen-Roche K, Fried LP. Use of domains of physical functioning to identify and recruit a study cohort of moderately and severelydisabled older women in the community: the Women"s Health and Aging Study. Submitted.

9. Women's Health and Aging Study Manual of Operations. (1993).

10. Folstein MF, Folstein SE, McHugh PR. (1975). "Mini-Mental State": A practical for grading the cognitive state of patients for the clinician. J Psychiatr Res 12:189-198.

11. Dawson D, Hendershot G, Fulton J. Aging in the eighties: Functional limitations of individuals age 65 years and over. (1987). Advance Data No. 133. DHHS Pub. N (PHS) 87-1250. Hyattsville, MD: National Center for Health Statistics.

12. US Bureau of the Census. (1992). Sixty Five Plus in America. Current Population Reports, Special Studies, P23-178, Washington, D.C.: US Government Printing Office.

13. Aging America. Trends and Projections. (1991). DHHS Pub. No. (FCoA) 91-28001. Washington, D.C.: US Department of Health and Human Services.

14. Williamson JD, Fried LP. (1995). Adaptation to disability. The Women's Health and Aging Study: Health and Social Characteristics of Older Women with Disability. NIHPublication No. 95-4009.

15. Seigel PZ, Brackbill RM, Heath GW. (1995). The epidemiology of walking for exercise: Implications for promoting activity among sedentary groups. Am J Public Health 85:706-709.

THE MENOPAUSE CLINICAL ASPECTS AND CURRENT TRENDS IN THERAPY

H. KAMEL, F. E. KAISER

Division of Geriatric Medicine. St. Louis Universitv School of Medicine, and the Geriatric Research Education and Clinical Center, St. Louis VA Medical Center, St. Louis, Missouri.

Menopause represents a major, critical turning point in a woman's lifespan. It marks a time of dramatic hormonal and often social change for women. Risk factors and health needs are both likely to change as woman pass through menopause [32]. Menopause has been shown to have a potential role in the etiology of some major age related diseases in women, such as cancer, cardiovascular disease, osteoporosis, and depression [32,33]. The continuing increase of female life expectancy has resulted in a marked increase of women who live years beyond menopause. Women can nowadays expect to live one third of their lives in a potential hormonally deficient state. Using age 50 as a proxy for menopause, about 25 million women undergo menopause each year. By 2030, the world population of postmenopausal women, is projected to increase to 1.2 billion, with 47 million new "entrants" each year [32].

For many years, there was little scientific research on menopause. Studying a normal physiologic event did not generate much interest among scientists. However, since the early 1970s, the interest in menopause research has increased. Motivation for this interest arose from the fact that in advanced societies, the overwhelming majority of women will experience menopause and can expect to live approximately 30 years beyond it [33]. This article represents an overview of the health changes that women face as they traverse menopause and the years beyond. Indications, contraindications, and risks and benefits of hormone replacement therapy are reviewed in depth. Alternative therapies are discussed and the role of preventive health measures are stressed.

I - MENOPAUSE: DEFINITION

The World Health Organization has suggested the definitions in Table 1 to label the events of the natural menopause [34]. Menopause is that point in time when permanent cessation of menstruation occurs following the loss of ovarian activity [1]. The prefix meno is derived from the Greek men meaning month and has been used to refer to the menstrual cycle. Pause signifies the cessation of the process. The transition from regular ovulatory cycles to the menopausal state is usually not an instantaneous event. Rather, it is a series of hormonal and clinical alterations that reflect declining ovarian function. The period of time when a woman passes from the reproductive stage of life to the postmenopausal years is referred to as perimenopause (or climacteric). It includes the period prior to menopause when endocrinologic, clinical, and biologic changes associated with menopause are occurring, as well as the first year following menopause [1,34]. Postmenopause, on the other hand, is defined as the year of menopausal amenorrhea and the time thereafter [34].

Table 1
Definition of terms associated with menopause [34]

Menopause	Permanent cessation of menstruation following loss of follicular activity. At least twelve [12] months of amenorrhea at the time of mid-life.
Perimenopause subsequent	Period (2-8 years or more) prior to menopause, and 1 year of amenorrhea following menopause.
Climacteric	Equivalent to the "perimenopause".
Postmen o pause	Time after menopause, including the year of amenorrhea.

Although various menopausal median age ranges have been recorded in different countries, based upon cross-sectional studies, the median age has been estimated to be somewhat between 50 and 52 years [1,2,35]. In the longitudinal Massachusetts Women's Health Study, which provides us with data from 2,570 women, the median age for menopause was 51.3 years, and the age range was 48 to 55 years [33]. In this latter study, only current smoking was identified as a cause of earlier menopause, a shift of approximately 1.5 years. Factors that did not affect the age of menopause included the use of oral contraception, socioeconomic status, and marital status. In 1934, Treolar initiated a follow-up study of students enrolled at the University of Minnesota; in 393 of these women who later experienced spontaneous menopause, the mean age of menopause was 55.7 years, and the median age was 51.4 years [4,5]. The average age for beginning the perimenopausal transition was 45.1 years, and the age range that included 95% of the women was 39-51 years. The mean duration of the perimenopausal transition was 5.0 years. Unlike the decline in age of menarche that occurred with an improvement in health and living conditions, most historical investigation indicates that the age of menopause has changed little since early Greek times [39,40]. Even in ancient writings, an age of 50 years is usually cited as the age of menopause [1], for those who did reach that age.

Although there are retrospect*e data to support a clinical impression which suggests that mothers and daughters tend to experience menopause at the same age [56], this remains to be proven by longitudinal data. There is sufficient evidence to believe that undernourished women and vegetarians experience an earlier menopause [3,36]. There is no correlation between age of menarche and the age of menopause [1,36]. Due to the contribution of body fat to estrogen production, thinner women experience a slightly earlier menopause [37]. In most studies, parity and height have no influence on the age of menopause; however, one cross-sectional study found later menopause to be associated with increased parity [1,3,36,37]. There are a limited number of cross-sectional reports indicating that African-American women may have an earlier age at menopause [37,41]. Data from most studies, however, showed race had no influence on age of menopause [1,3,36,37]. An earlier menopause is associated with living at high altitudes and, as mentioned previously, with cigarette smoking [1]. There is a dose-response relationship with the number of cigarettes smoked and the duration of smoking [38].

II - MENOPAUSE: ENDOCRINOLOGY

2.1. The Normal Menstrual Cycle

The normal menstrual cycle is the result of a complex interaction between the hypothalamus, pituitary, and ovary. It is further modulated by higher cortical centers, the thyroid gland, the adrenals, and peripheral hormonal production [6]. The ovulatory cycle starts with the recruitment of many follicles. One of these becomes the dominant one and is the source of ovulation while all the other follicles undergo atresia. The ovarian follicle essentially consists of two components: an outer thecal layer and an inner granulosa cell layer. The former is assumed to produce androgens, which serve as precursors for the formation of estrogens by the granulosa cells, through aromatization. If one considers that from puberty to menopause, with a total cohort of 200,000 follicles, only about 500 will yield a mature oocyte, it becomes obvious that atresia is the dominant and continuous process in ovarian physiology. This is a key element leading to menopause [6]. The hormonal levels seen during the normal menstrual cycle have been well characterized . Estradiol is the dominant estrogen, reaching a peak level between 200 and 400 pg/ml at the time of ovulation. Circulating levels of FSH and LH are characterized by a mid-cycle surge, at which time they are near 50 and 100 mIU/ml, respectively. This is a major distinction from all other times in life, including menopause, when FSH levels dominate [6].

2.2. The Perimenopause

The transition from regular ovulatory cycles to cessation of menstruation (perimenopause) is characterized by variation in cycle length and bleeding pattern. Women who experience menopause at a young age may usually have a short transition phase. Menopause of later onset is associated with both long and short intermenstrual bleeding episodes and an overall increased mean cycle length [6,7]. Researchers have shown that during the transitional phase of perimenopause, there is extreme variability in sex steroid release [8]. In particular, alterations of circulating estradiol production varied from cycle to cycle, probably representing varying degrees of follicular maturation and function. Shideler et al, in a longitudinal study using daily measurements of urinary estrogen showed that the magnitude of estrogen released during the perimenopausal period differed widely [9]. Commensurate with this erratic secretion is the duration and amount of vaginal bleeding. It has been shown that even before menopause, the perimenopausal ovary requires greater amounts of FSH to stimulate estrogen production and, perhaps, ovulation [42,43]. Contrary to older belief [based on the report by Sherman et al [42]], estradiol levels do not gradually wane in the years before menopause, but remain in the normal range until follicular growth and development cease [1,49]. In contrast to estrogens and progestins, androgen levels remain stable during this transitional period. Studies that have examined androstenedione, testosterone, dehydroepiandrostenedione (DHEA), and DHEA-sulfate (DHEAS) have not demonstrated any change in circulating concentrations during the time prior to permanent amenorrhea [6,10].

The most sensitive measure of declining ovarian function in perimenopause is that of serum gonadotropins, in particular, FSH. While both LH and FSH are elevated in postmenopausal women, it is hypothesized that the rise of FSH signals the onset of menopausal transformation [11]. There is a dramatic rise of FSH during menopause, then a slow decline over the ensuing decades [43,44]. The precise mechanisms underlying this rise in FSH are unclear. Decreasing estrogen feedback on the pituitary and hypothalamus cannot account totally for this event, since the initial increment of serum FSH is not associated with significant decreases of circulating estradiol. In fact, LH levels may also be normal in the face of elevated FSH, which raises the issue of independent regulatory mechanisms for FSH and LH. Sherman and Korenman [8] in 1975 first proposed the existence of an ovarian hormone, "an inhibin" which would exert negative feedback control over FSH secretion. More recently inhibin has been isolated from follicular fluid. A radioimmunoassay has been developed and daily concentrations throughout the normal menstrual cycle documented [12,45,46]. Inhibin is a glycoprotein hormone composed of an alpha and a beta subunit. It is secreted by the human granulosa cell in response to FSH during follicular phase [47], and by the corpus luteum during the luteal phase in response to LH [47,48]. It is now felt that inhibin plays an important role in the regulation of the menstrual cycle. There is an age-related decrease in inhibin levels in women with regular menstrual cycle. The decline in inhibin which allows the rise in FSH reflects lesser follicular competence [50,51]. This decrease in inhibin begins around age 35, but accelerates after age 40 . It is well-recognized that the relative inability of estrogen to suppress FSH after menopause is secondary to the loss of inhibin. This indicates that inhibin has a major role in controlling FSH secretion through negative feedback [1,6]

2.3. Menopause

2.3.1. Sex Hormones

Once menopause has been established, the ovaries are essentially devoid of functional follicles. The gross appearance of the ovary becomes fibrotic and shrunken. Microscopically, two major cell populations appear: corticostromal and hilar cells. Both cell compartments contribute to the androgen production from the menopausal ovary [6,13,14]. These ultimate changes in ovarian morphology reflect follicular exhaustion and loss of ovarian estrogen production. With the onset of menopausal amenorrhea, there is a rapid fall in ovarian estrogen production (Table 2). The decline of serum estradiol occurs over a 1-year interval, and once the atretic process has been completed, serum estradiol concentration in postmenopausal women may eventually become similar to those of premenopausal individuals who have undergone oophorectomy [6,16]. The metabolic clearance rates of estradiol, estrone, androstenedione, and testosterone levels do not change with the onset of menopause [16].

The source of serum estradiol in postmenopausal period has not been clearly established. The ovary does not appear to contribute significantly, as estradiol levels are similar in postmenopausal women before and after oophorectomy [6,7,18]. Thus, the most likely source of estradiol in the postmenopausal period is the adrenal gland. Direct secretion of estradiol by the adrenal gland is not a major factor, as only minimal step-ups have been found in the adrenal vein. Peripheral conversion of testosterone to estradiol is possible, although the low conversion rate makes it insignificant. Extraglandular conversion of estrone to estradiol seems to be the most feasible explanation, as a close correlation exists between estradiol and estrone in the circulation of postmenopausal women [19]. Estrone is the predominant estrogen of menopause. Estrone is estimated to have only about 25% of the bioactivity of estradiol. Most of the circulating estrone results from peripheral conversion of androstenedione. Sites of estrone production in the body are the adrenal glands, ovaries, fat, muscle, liver, kidney, and brain [20].

Androstenedione is the major circulating androgen in menopause, although its absolute levels are about one half that seen prior to menopause [52]. Most of this postmenopausal androstenedione is derived from the adrenal, with only a small amount secreted from the ovary [1]. In comparison to androstenedione, testosterone levels are minimally reduced in menopause [15]. In effect, ovarian testosterone production in the postmenopausal woman is greater than that derived from the premenopausal individual. Much of this increase is attributed to increased stimulation of ovarian stroma by elevated LH levels. Ovarian production is confirmed by the large increase in testosterone found in the ovarian vein of postmenopausal women compared to premenopausal women [21]. The total amount of testosterone produced after menopause, however, is decreased because the amount of the primary source, peripheral conversion of androstenedione, is reduced

[22]. The menopausal decline in the circulating levels of testosterone and androstenedione is not great, approximately 15%.

Serum concentrations of DHEA and DHEAS begin to decline slowly after menopause. It is not known whether these reductions reflect aging or the postmenopausal state. Evidence to indicate a postmenopausal effect is provided by the observation that DHEA and DHEAS production in postmenopausal women increased following the administration of conjugated estrogens [23]. It has been estimated that up to 25% of DHEA may be derived from the ovary based on circulating levels after ovariectomy. Provocative testing with ACTH and dexamethasone, on the other hand, strongly supports an adrenal origin for these androgens [6]. There has recently been interest in DHEA as a therapeutic agent. The current data indicates that such a preparation will raise circulating levels of DHEA, DHEAS, androstenedione, testosterone, and dihydrotestosterone [24]. It appears to have no effect on estrone, estradiol, or sex hormone binding globulin (SHBG) levels.

The rise of gonadotropins associated with menopause actually begins before cessation of ovarian activity and menstrual bleeding. With the loss of ovarian estrogen production, the negative feedback effect of estradiol on gonadotropin release is removed and an accelerated increases of both FSH and LH ensues. Elevation of gonadotropin levels continues following the last menstrual period before stabilizing at about 12 months, for FSH and 6 months for LH. In some instances, several years may pass beyond menopause before gonadotropin level become stable. Characteristically, the rise of FSH always exceeds that of LH. There is a growing body of indirect evidence to suggest that FSH and LH are subject to different and perhaps independent control.

Inhibin, activin, and related peptides are factors that may impact gonadotropin release either directly or via steroid feedback. Careful examination of gonadotropin secretion indicates that pulse frequencies of FSH and LH do not change during menopause which suggest intact functional capacity of GnRH (Gonadotropin Releasing Hormone) secreting neurons [6,25].

Surgical oophorectomy before menopause dramatically alters hormonal dynamics. Instead of a progressive transition spanning 5 to 10 years, the body responds to the acute deprivation of ovarian estrogens, progesterone, and possibly androgens. Serum gonadotropins rise progressively following oophorectomy, and usually reach the classic menopausal levels within 1 month following surgery [6,26]. Huges et al demonstrated a 50% fall in the levels of testosterone and androstenedione, and no change in the level of estradiol and DHEAS after surgical oophorectomy [18].

Table 2
Blood Production Rates of Steroids [54]

	Reproductive age	Postmenopausal	Oophrectomized
Androstenedione	2-3 mg/day	0.5-1.0mg/day	0.4-0.8 mg/day
Dehydroepiandrosterone	6 - 8	1.5 - 4.0	1.5 - 4.0
Dehydroepiandrosterone			
sulfate	8 - 16	4 - 9	4 - 9
Testosterone	0.2- 0.25	0.05 - 0.1	0.02 - 0.07
Estrogen	0.350	0 045	0.045

2.3.2. Other Hormones

It is hard to distinguish between changes secondary to menopause itself and the natural process of aging. Prolactin levels have been reported by some to decrease [27], whereas other investigators have found no change [28]. Prolactin levels tend to rise with estrogen replacement therapy, which might indicate that changes in prolactin levels observed in postmenopausal women correlate with the menopausal state rather than aging [6].

By contrast, alterations in thyroid physiology are probably the reflection of aging [29]. Thyroxin production decreases from about 80 micrograms/day to 60 micrograms/day, with wide variations between individuals. The peripheral utilization of thyroid hormone proportionately decreases to achieve a new state of homeostasis. Interpretation of thyroid function tests must take these changes into account.

The levels of insulin-like growth factor I (IGF-I) decrease progressively with age, starting their decline in early adulthood [30]. By contrast, insulin-like growth factor II (IGF-II) levels remain stable. Growth hormone (GH) production and metabolic clearance do not change with age, particularly in women [6,31]. This decline is particularly evident during the sleeping hours and is felt to be linked to estrogen deprivation. Oral estrogen replacement therapy produces a rise in circulating GH but a paradoxical decrease in IGF-I. This may be explained by direct hepatic effect of oral estrogens. Further work is needed in this area to elucidate the mechanism(s) involved [6, 31].

III - MENOPAUSE: CLIMACTERIC SYNDROMES

Psychosocial and cultural factors have a considerable impact upon women's perception of changes that may occur during the menopausal transition [56]. Menopause can be conceptualized as including possible changes at several levels - hormonal, menstrual, vasomotor symptoms and psychological reactions to being menopausal - each of which can lead to marked variation between women in their experience of menopause [57]. It is assumed that menopause is inevitably accompanied (to a greater or a lesser extent) by hot flashes, sweats, prolonged menstrual irregularities, vaginal dryness and a host of other "symptoms" including depression, irritability, weight gain, insomnia and dizziness (58). Earlier analysis of primarily cross-sectional data in Caucasian population, however, have provided evidence that these signs and symptoms of menopause are far from ubiquitous [59, 60, 61]. These same studies have also indicated that, with the exception of hot flushes and accompanying sweats, other supposed menopausal symptoms are not directly related to this physiological change [58]. Utian [62] has argued that there are unique characteristics associated with the estrogen deficiency of menopause. These include hot flashes and sweats and changes in epithelial tissues, including the skin and vagina. These events are described below.

3.1. Hot flashes and flushes

Hot flashes or flushes are the most widely appreciated symptom of the climacteric. The hot flash is a sudden, transient sensation ranging from warmth to intense heat that spreads over the body, occurring particularly on the chest, face, and head. It is usually accompanied by flushing and perspiration and is often followed by a chill. Some women also have associated palpitation and anxiety. The duration usually 30 seconds to several minutes, and the frequency and severity are variable among women [43,63]. Hot flushes can be objectively recorded as changes in skin temperature, resistance, and core temperature [64,65]. Recent data have suggested that hot flashes occur in up to 75% of menopausal women [66]. Women who have undergone surgical menopause tend to be more likely to have hot flashes than those with natural menopause. Unlike other climacteric syndromes, hot flashes decrease as time from menopause increases [3]. Prevalence is highest in the first 2 postmenopausal years, and the episodes usually lessen with time. However, hot flashes may precede menopause by some years and may continue for 10, 20, or even 40 years or longer after menopause [67]. Most women will remain symptomatic for greater than a year, and estimates of the fraction who experience flashes for longer than 5 years range from 29ù - 50% [68, 69].

The etiology of hot flushes remains controversial. Estrogen in addition, to its effects on the reproductive tissue influences the thermoregulatory, neural, and vascular functioning. Thus, estrogen probably has peripheral as well as central effects important in the physiology of the hot flushes. Although hot flashes has been attributed to low estrogen levels, its etiology seems to involve more than just this [43]. Initially, due to the temporal correlation of LH surge with the hot flush, LH pulses were thought to be the cause of hot flashes [70,1]. However, there is substantial evidence that LH pulses themselves are not the cause of hot flushes. Women who have surgically induced pituitary insufficiency, and thus low levels of non-pulsatile LH release, do experience hot flushes [72], and premenopausal women who are treated with GnRH agonists develop hot flushes despite the suppression of pulsatile LH release by GnRH [73]. Because pulses of LH were not directly responsible for initiating hot flushes but were associated with them, it was thought that perhaps flushes are initiated at the hypothalamic level and that they involve the releasing factor for LH, GnRH [74]. Women who have an inability to make GnRH do not have hot flashes; nor do women given GnRH by bolus or pulsatile administration. Women made amenorrheic and hypoestrogenic with GnRH agonists do have such flushes [70].

Brain catecholamines and opiates have been currently proposed as the possible mediators of hot flashes [75]. Norepinephrine is related both to GnRH release and thermoregulation [76]. Alphaadrenergic blockade can diminish hot flushes [77]. The infusion of naloxone, an opioid antagonist, produces a rise in LH in premenopausal women but not postmenopausal women [78]. In postmenopausal females, high LH levels are suppressed with estrogen administration, and subsequent administration of naloxone reverses this suppression [78]. Based on these data, a working hypothesis for the etiology of hot flushes is that the loss of ovarian function and the accompanying reduction in hypothalamic opioid tone results in thermoregulatory instability [63].

Hot flashes can and do disrupt a woman's sense of well-being and can cause problems in her social and professional life. One of the primary problems with hot flashes is the disruption of sleep; often the woman not only awakens, but is drenched [79]. Many women adapt, by modifying their diet and behavior by reducing room temperature and wearing light, layered clothing. However, for more than 25%, these flushes are enough for them to seek medical attention for relief.

Randomized, placebo controlled trials have established that hormonal and non-hormonal therapies are effective for hot flushes. Estrogen reduces both perceived and objectively measured hot flashes

[80,81,82,83,121]. There is a dose-response relationship of the degree of hot flush suppression to the amount of estrogen administered (81). When treating hot flushes, therefore, it is rational to titrate the dose of estrogen to symptom control. Since hot flush frequency decreases with time, women who initially require higher doses of estrogen may tolerate subsequent dose reduction.

Alternatives to estrogen include progestins, clonidine, and methyldopa. The progestogens medroxyprogesterone acetate (Provera and Depo-Provera) and megestrol (Megace), when given in high-enough doses, are approximately 70% effective in relieving hot flashes, but have not been shown to be cardioprotective or to prevent osteoporosis [84,85,115]. Clonidine hydrochloride, an alpha-adrenergic agonist, with some alpha-adrenergic antagonist effects may act as a peripheral vascular stabilizer to reduce menopausal flushing. Dosages of 25 to 75 mcg twice a day orally, or the 100 mcg (0.1 mg) transdermal patch once a week, are recommended. Clonidine should not be used in patients with cardiovascular disease, coronary insufficiency, recent myocardial infarction, or Raynaud's syndrome. Side effects include hypotension, bradycardia, lethargy, irritability, weakness, somnolence, diminished or absent reflexes, miosis, vomiting, and hyperventilation [7,86,115]. Methyldopa, 250 mg po tid, has also been shown to reduce hot flushes by 30%. However, the side effect profile with methyldopa is also substantial, with 60% of subjects complaining of dizziness, nausea, and fatigue [63,87].

Bellergal is another agent used to treat hot flashes. Bellergal is a combination of ergotamine, belladonna alkaloids, and phenobarbital. Because of its autonomic effects, in the 1960s and 1970s, it was used to treat menopausal symptoms of hot flashes, sweats, restlessness, and insomnia. The combination of 300 mcg ergotamine tartrate, 100 mcg belladonna alkaloids, and 20 mg phenobarbital, one tablet in the morning and at noon, and two at bedtime, is available in Canada. Bellergal-S (Spacetab) is available in the United States; it contains twice the amounts listed above for each ingredient and can be used once a day or twice a day [115]. Contraindications include peripheral vascular disease, coronary artery disease, hypertension, and impaired hepatic or renal function. Blurred vision, palpitations, dry mouth, decreased sweating, decreased gastrointestinal mobility, urinary retention, tachycardia, flushing, and drowsiness may occur rarely, and this medication may be habit forming due to the phenobarbital content [115]. Other forms of treatment including Vitamin E, acupuncture, and exercise have little benefit on flashes [43,116]. Diets with high phytoestrogens such as tofu may provide some relief.

3.2. Changes

The skin is a target tissue for steroid hormones. Estrogen binds to receptors in the skin where it stimulates protein production (protoglycans, collagen, elastin), and influences water content and hyaluronic acid (major skin components). In postmenopausal women, the skin becomes thinner (due to loss of collagen fibers), dryer (due to water loss), less elastic, and more wrinkled (due to loss of elastic fibers). These changes are more evident in the face, the skin area richest in estrogen receptors and the one most exposed to the environment, particularly the sun [88]. In some experimental studies estrogens have been shown to increase the activity of fibroblasts and water, hyaluronic acid and collagen dermal contents [89,90,91]. Some studies have demonstrated that estrogen treatment increases skin thickness, mitotic activity of keratinocytes, and dermal collagen content in postmenopausal women. Vaillant et al demonstrated by non-invasive measurements of physical parameters of the skin an increase in skin thickness in women treated by hormone replacement versus women not treated by hormone replacement [117]. In another study by Pierard et al estrogen has been shown to limit age-related increase in cutaneous extensibility and thus slowing the progress of intrinsic cutaneous aging [118].

The Lower urinary tract is another site affected with the lowered estrogen levels seen after menopause. Estrogen receptors have been isolated from the urethra and, to a lesser extent form the trigone of the bladder [92,93]. In postmenopausal women, the urethra becomes thinner due to regression of its squamous epithelial layer [94]. There is also atrophy of the periurethral tissue leading to a decrease in the pressure generated by the urethra and surrounding tissue which is important in maintaining continence [95]. Lowered bladder sensory threshold to void has also been reported in postmenopausal women [96]. The symptomatic consequences of the postmenopausal anatomic-physiologic changes in the lower urinary tract include dysuria, urgency, frequency, suprapubic discomfort, stress incontinence, and urge incontinence [97,98,99]. All these problems can be significantly improved by estrogen. There are now important data documenting that the frequency of urinary tract infections may be decreased by estrogen use in postmenopausal women, and there are data suggesting that certain patients with genuine stress urinary incontinence may improve when given estrogen [100,101]. This is certainly true for urge incontinence in such patients [43]. Non hormonal means of managing these symptoms include: biofeedback therapy, and Kegel exercises. Kegel exercises are exercises developed by Arnold Kegel in 1949, and are designated to strengthen the pubococcygeus muscle (the part of the levator and muscular sling that surrounds the vagina and provides support for the urethra, vagina, and rectum) [115].

The Lower genital tract is another site affected by the hypoestrogenemic state in postmenopausal women. The vulva becomes atrophic and loses most of its collagen, adipose tissue, and water-retaining ability and becomes flattened and thin [102]. Vaginal shortening and narrowing occurs as the vaginal walls become thin, and lose elasticity. The vagina in this setting produces fewer secretions and loses most of its lubricating ability in response to sexual stimulation. All of these changes tend to decrease comfort and interest in coitus. Much of the clinical literature suggests that estrogen administration alleviates symptomatology associated with atrophic vagina and dyspareunia [34,105]. Several lubricants are also available to counteract dyspareunia from vaginal dryness but do not reverse the thin mucosa seen in estrogen depleted women [115].

3.3. Psychologic Symptoms

During fetal life, estrogen exerts organizational effects on brain development that are thought to be permanent. In adulthood, estrogen has activational effects on brain function via its transitory regulation of brain plasticity and the concentration of specific neurotransmitters [106]. Particularly susceptible to the actions of estrogen are the limbic structures (e.g., amygdala and hippocampus) responsible for maturation and maintenance of sexual behavior and reproductive function as well as memory and adaptive responses.

Estrogens bind to receptors abundant in limbic structures and influence the biochemistry of the brain by altering the concentrations and availability of neurotransmitter amines, including serotonin. First, estrogen increases the rate of degradation of monoamine oxidase, the enzyme that catabolizes serotonin [107]. Second, estrogen regulates the amount of free tryptophan that reaches the brain. Tryptophan, a naturally occurring amino acid, is the precursor of serotonin. It has been demonstrated that estrogen displaces tryptophan from its binding sites to plasma albumin both in vivo and in vitro [108]. This allows more free tryptophan to be available to the brain, where it can be metabolized to serotonin. Finally, estrogen enhances the transport of serotonin [109]. These three mechanisms of estrogenic action on brain biochemistry explain how estrogen may affect mood, particularly in view of the overwhelming evidence that depression is, in large part, a disease of serotonin deficit. It is reasonable to hypothesize, therefore, that the decrease in estrogen around the time of menopause may affect mood in some proportion of women [106].

A number of investigators have attempted to link menopause with various psychological diseases, particularly depression. Many have been unsuccessful. However, more recent data have appeared involving a link between menopause and changes in mood, memory, and sexual function [110]. It must be acknowledged that sociocultural factors, individual characteristics, and the environment all interact to influence the menopausal experience [43]. A large proportion of women enter menopause viewing it as a new life period heralding its own advantages (e.g., freedom from child-bearing and rearing) and disadvantages (e.g., aging, and altering body habitus). Others find it a period of considerable stress, viewing it as signaling the termination of physiologic and psychologic youth. They suffer, with varying degrees of severity: loss of selfimage, apprehension and anxiety, amnesia, and difficulty in concentrating and in making decisions [88].

A number of epidemiologic studies have failed to document an increase in depressive symptoms around the time of menopause, with the single exception of a study from Massachusetts, which did suggest a link with surgical menopause [43,111]. Data from more current studies of depression, taken from work in menopause clinics, suggest a different story. The linkage was positive, particularly for perimenopause, between mood and hormonal status. There are recent data suggesting that replacement of estrogen and androgen may be beneficial for such depression [43,111]. Double-blind studies have found improvements in self-reported irritability, anxiety, and dysphoria in women treated with estrogen alone or combined with progestin [80,120]. Two studies attempted to separate the primary psychologic effects of hormones from those improvements that might be attributed to relief of hot flushes. Campbell and Whitehead [80] administered 1.25 mg of conjugated estrogen to 64 subjects daily for 2 months in a crossover design study. Symptoms that improved included hot flushes, poor memory, anxiety, optimism, and worry about age. A subgroup analysis of women who did not suffer from hot flushes found that poor memory, anxiety, and worry about age improved in this group, arguing that the effect of hormone therapy on mood is independent of improvement in hot flushes [63]. In the second study, Ditkoffet al [120], reported the effects of treatment with conjugated estrogen in 36 nondepressed surgically menopausal women who did not suffer from hot flushes. Significant improvement in depression scores were evidenced after estrogen therapy. Non-hormonal alternatives include antidepressants, and attention to deleting caffeine, and alcohol from diet [103]. Relaxation or behavioral therapy have been advocated, but the long term benefits have not been evaluated [104,115].

Data on estrogen and cognitive function are even more intriguing. Although many studies have been inconsistent, newer data strongly suggest that in appropriately treated menopausal women, estrogen does play an important role in maintenance of short-term memory. The capacity for long-range memory does not seem affected [43]. Preliminary data also suggest that estrogen may retard the likelihood or the severity of Alzheimer's disease [112]. More data is needed in this field.

Menopause is associated with anatomical, physiological and psychological changes that often influences sexuality in the aging female. The decreased estrogen levels have a multitude of effects on sexual function, including decreased support of female pelvis, loss of ability to adequately lubricate the urogenital tissue, and changes in body configuration. This situation is aggravated by the alterations in the skin, breasts, muscles and skeleton caused by estrogen loss. For many women, these changes translate into a poorer self-image, diminution of self esteem and, may incur, a loss of sexual desire. This is especially true of women with dyspareunia secondary to loss of vagina lubrication. Social expectations may have a negative impact on sexuality, as many cultures still believe that older women become sexually "retired" [113,114,119]. Furthermore, decreased libido is reported with increasing age [63]. Data from the literature suggest that estrogen administration alleviates symptomatology associated with atrophic vagina and dyspareunia [105]. However estrogen alone lacks the ability to stimulate libido. Currently there are studies being done using oral androgens to stimulate libido (43). However, more work is needed to define and clarify the roles, indications, and side effects of these hormones.

IV - MENOPAUSE: LONGER TERM SYNDROMES DUE TO DEFICIENCY

4.1. Osteoporosis

Osteoporosis is an "age-related disorder characterized by decreased bone mass and increased susceptibility to fracture in the absence of other recognizable causes of bone loss" (National Institutes of Health Consensus Panel). Osteoporosis has been considered the classic estrogen deficiency disease and labeled by Utian [62] as a menopausal related disease. Until recently, a diagnosis of osteoporosis was by necessity clinical, requiring a history of one or more low-trauma fractures

[122,123]. However, the introduction of accurate noninvasive bone mass measurements afforded the opportunity to make an early diagnosis of osteoporosis. Bone mineral density (BMD) of patients with osteoporotic fractures was generally found to be lower than that of agematched nonfractured controls. The Word Health Organization recently based the diagnosis of osteoporosis on the presence of a spinal bone density more than 2.5 standard deviation below the mean for young adults [124,125]. Using this value, approximately 30% of postmenopausal women would be designated as having osteoporosis, with an even higher number having osteopenia (bone density greater than 1 standard deviation below young adults).

The underlying etiologies and distinction between the two types of primary osteoporosis, type I (or postmenopausal osteoporosis), and type II (or senile osteoporosis), are complex. Type I osteoporosis affects mainly trabecular bone resulting in fractures in vertebral bodies and the distal forearm. It occurs with greater prevalence in women 6:1 (women to men ratio) and is related to accelerated bone loss in women during the first two decades after menopause [126,127,128,129]. Type II osteoporosis, on the other hand, affects both trabecular and cortical bone and is associated with fractures ofthe femoral neck, proximal humerus, proximal tibia, and pelvis [130]. The primary pathogenesis is related to impaired production of 1,25-dihydroxy vitamin D [131].

Estrogen deficiency plays a very important role in the pathogenesis of postmenopausal osteoporosis [132]. Estrogen inhibits bone resorption and positively affects calcium balance, either directly, by acting on osteoclasts through estrogen receptors, or indirectly, by suppressing, the production of bone-resorbing cytokines [133,134,135,136]. The loss of bone after menopause follows an exponential pattern [137,138,139,140]. Most bone is lost during the first 3 to 6 years after menopause [141,142,143,144], but some loss related to low estrogen levels may continue for up to 20 years [145]. While many studies have found evidence of some bone loss in perimenopause [146,147,148,149,150,151], others observed no significant changes preceding menopause [152,153,154].

There are an increasing number of studies relating menopause to biochemical markers of bone turnover [155]. One study of 178 women, aged 29-78 years, found that the estrogen decline after menopause occurred simultaneously with changes in bone turnover [153]. Many researchers have observed alteration in serum osteocalcin (a biochemical marker of bone formation) levels during menopause [156,157,158,159,160,161]. However, some studies have found different menopause phase-specific patterns for osteocalcin levels, such as a continuous increase from premenopause to postmenopause [160], or a decline before menopause, a rise at menopause, and a fall in the seventh and eight decades of life [159].

Markers of bone resorption have also been found to be associated with bone changes in menopause [34]. A study of 68 women, aged 50-76 years, who had experienced natural menopause, found deoxypyridinoline decreased with age and slightly with menopausal age [162]. There is a consistently reported rise in hydroxyproline, another indicator of total bone resorption, accompanying menopause [34,153,157,160]. Moreover, urinary calcium excretion has been found to increase at menopause [153,159,160,161,163], and after menopause [121,163]. The increased calcium excretion found in menopause has been shown to be negatively associated with bone density and bone mineral content [34,163,164].

Drugs used to treat osteoporosis may be grouped into those that decrease bone resorption and those that increase bone formation. Drugs that inhibit bone resorption do not generally affect bone mass [165]. They are most effective when bone turnover is increased, and their effect is greater on cancellous bone than on cortical bone, in which the rate of turnover is lower [165]. The agents, from this group, currently approved in the United States include estrogen, calcitonin (both nasal spray and parentally administered) calcium, vitamin D, and alendronate [166,167]. Drugs that increase bone formation, on the other hand, increase bone mass. At this time, these agent remain relatively experimental. The side effects of the regimens used to date appear to prevent their widespread use [168]. One drug in this group, slow-release sodium fluoride, has been available in Europe for this indication for many years, and has been recently been recommended for approval in the U. S. by an advisory committee of the U. S. Food and Drug Administration (FDA).

Estrogen administered soon after menopause, prevents the early phase of bone loss [142,143], and decreases the incidence of subsequent osteoporosis-related fractures by about 50 percent [165,169,170]. Some investigators postulate that the use of estrogen in patients with established osteoporosis may still be effective, increasing mean vertebral bone mass by 5 percent and reducing the vertebral fracture rate by half [171,172]. Estrogen most commonly administered as Estradiol at a dose of 0.625 mg/day given orally for the first 25 days of each month (lower doses are usually ineffective). Estradiol administered in a percutaneous patch or gel for transdermal absorption, is also effective in preventing bone loss [173,174]. The use of estrogen during only the early postmenopausal period appears to be inadequate [175]. A study of older women from the Farmingham observational group showed that the previous use of estrogen was not protective against fractures of the hip that occurred ten to twenty years after the termination of treatment [176]. Only use of estrogen for more than seven years was found to be protective. Lindsay et al [178] demonstrated that cessation of estrogen therapy begun at menopause leads to an accelerated bone loss that is comparable to that observed after menopause. Thus, for maximal protection against osteoporosis, estrogen replacement therapy should be administered for at least 20 years, and perhaps, indefinitely [179,180]. Tamoxifen, tibilone, and raloxifene are examples of several tissue specific partial estrogen agonists presently being investigated as alternatives to natural estrogens for prevention of osteoporosis. More detailed discussion of these agents as well as the advantages and disadvantages of estrogen replacement therapy can be found in the hormone replacement section of this review.

Calcium in addition to being a substrate for bone mineralization, has an antiresorptive effect on bone by suppressing parathyroid hormone secretion. In postmenopausal women, the effects of supplemental calcium varies by skeletal region, with cortical sites being generally more responsive than trabecular sites [181]. Studies in women within the first 5 years of menopause [182,183,184] show that calcium supplementation has a consistent positive response on BMD in sites rich in cortical bone such as the proximal femur, and that this is expected to result in reduced long bone fractures. At the more trabecular spine sites, calcium induces an initial increase in bone density through closure of remodeling space but there are little data that it provides cumulative benefit after the first year of treatment. This transient effect appears significant, however, in view of the recent finding of Recker et al, that supplemental calcium reduced spine fracture rates [185]. On the basis of these and other findings, a National Institutes of Health Consensus Development Conference panel in June 1994 considered a calcium intake of 1500 mg per day to be optimal for postmenopausal women not taking estrogen and 1000 mg per day optimal for women on hormone replacement therapy [186]. Both ofthese figures are higher than 800 mg per day, the current Recommended Dietary Allowance for adult women [181,187].

Vitamin D is one of the primary regulators of calcium homeostasis in the body and is critically important for the normal mineralization of bone [188]. It stimulates calcium and phosphate absorption from the small intestine and mobilizes calcium from bone [115]. Subclinical vitamin D deficiency and associated secondary hyperparathyroidism are common in elderly women, particularly those confined to nursing homes. In these women, a dose of 800 IU of vitamin D3 (Cholecalciferol) daily (the equivalent of 2 multivitamin tablets) combined with calcium supplements (1 to 1.5 g elemental calcium daily) is effective in maintaining bone mass and decreasing the incidence of hip fracture [189,190]. Vitamin D3 (Cholecalciferol) is the parent vitamin D compound and is the most widely prescribed by physicians. It is cheap and safe. Calcitriol (1,25(oh)2D) is the active vitamin D metabolite. Calcitriol, in addition, to its action on the intestine to stimulate calcium absorption, may also stimulate osteoblast activity [191,192]. Treatment with calcitriol has been shown to reduce bone loss [193], and in some studies, increases bone mass [191,192]. In contrast to the parent vitamin D, the margin between ineffective doses of calcitriol, and those that induce hypercalcemia or hypercalciuria, is relatively narrow. Calcitriol analogues that have greater margins of safety in laboratory animals have been developed [194,195]. One of these analogues, alfacacidol, have been recently studied in a prospective, randomized study involving 66 osteoporotic postmenopausal women, and has been shown to prevent further bone loss with minimal side effects [196]. Further clinical trials of these agents in women with osteoporosis are in progress.

Biphosphonates are carbon-substituted analogues of pyrophosphate, an endogenous physiologic inhibitor of bone mineralization. They were initially developed as inhibitors of growth and dissolution of calcium crystals but were subsequently found to inhibit osteoclast-mediated bone resorption [197]. Because of this action, bisphosphonates were used to treat conditions characterized by excessive osteoclastic bone resorption such as Paget's disease of bone and malignancy-associated hypercalcemia, for which they are now the treatment of choice [197]. Increasing understanding of the pharmacological properties of bisphosphonates led to their application to the treatment of other skeletal disorders such as osteoporosis. In a multinational trial by Liberman et al [198] a total of 994 women with postmenopausal osteoporosis (defined by bone density of 2.5 standard deviations below the mean for young women) received either placebo or various regimens of alenderonate: 5 or 10 mg a day for three years, or 20 mg a day for two years followed by 5 mg a day for a third year. All subjects also received elemental calcium. Overall, treatment with alendronate was associated with a 48 percent reduction in the proportion of women with new vertebral fractures (3.2 percent, vs. 6.2 percent in the placebo group; p=0.03), a decreased progression of vertebral deformities (33 percent, vs. 41 percent in the placebo group, p=0.028), and a reduced loss of height (p=0.005) and was well tolerated. Alendronate is currently the only bisphosphonate approved for treatment of osteoporosis in the United States [166].

Calcitonin can be used to treat osteoporosis, although patients who have osteoporosis do not have a deficiency of this hormone [199].

Calcitonin has been shown to have analgesic properties, and is currently used by many clinicians for the short-term amelioration of pain associated with fractures due to osteoporosis [200]. It has also been shown to bind to specific receptors on the osteoclasts inhibiting its resorptive activity [133]. Calcitonin has been shown to be a safe alternative for the treatment of osteoporosis in women who can not take estrogen [201]. Women who have high-turnover osteoporosis or who have pain because of a recent vertebral fracture are likely to benefit most from its use [133].

Salmon calcitonin is much more potent than human calcitonin, but its use may lead to resistance associated with increased titers of antibodies that neutralize calcitonin. Until recently salmon calcitonin was available only by subcutaneous or intramuscular injections. Intranasal salmon calcitonin has been shown by several investigators to be as effective and safe for the prevention of bone loss in postmenopausal women with reduced bone mass [202,203]. It also posses similar analgesic effects to those of the other forms. Salmon calcitonin administered by nasal spray (200 IU per day) has been recently approved by the FDA for prevention and treatment of osteoporosis in the United States [166].

Sodium Fluoride is the only agent available now that can stimulate osteoblastic proliferation and function and increase bone formation. When sodium fluoride is used to treat osteoporosis, there is a continuous increase in bone mass of the spine [204,205]. In some series this increase in bone mass is accompanied by decreased incidence of spinal fractures [206,207], but the therapy may result in an increased risk of fractures of the hip as well as other nonvertebral fractures [208,209]. Even in a series in which a satisfactory effect of sodium fluoride is observed, some patients do not respond at all. Some patients develop side effects, including knee, and ankle pains attributed to microfractures; others cannot tolerate the drug because of nausea. An oral slow-release form is better tolerated with fewer gastrointestinal and rheumatic complications [166].

Pak et al [207] recently reported that patients with postmenopausal osteoporosis treated with slow-release sodium fluoride had a lower rate of vertebral fractures and a higher fracture free rate (defined as the absence of fractures during the trial) compared with a group of controls who had received calcium. A substantial increase in bone mass of the lumbar vertebrae of 4 to 5 percent per year for four years, an average increase in bone density of femoral neck of 2 to 4 percent per year, and no change in bone density of the radial shaft were observed in patients who had received fluoride. The frequency with which side effects and appendicular fractures occurred was similar in the two groups. At the present time, the use of fluoride in the United States is considered relatively experimental, although this might change in the near future. Various formulations of fluoride have been available in Europe for this indication for many years [166] .

4.2. Cardiovascular disease

Extensive epidemiologic and postmortem studies have identified a link between menopause and cardiovascular disease. Early studies in Framingham, Massachusetts, and Sweden suggested a menopausal effect on the risk of heart disease [211]. The Framingham study found a greater than twofold age-adjusted increase in the risk for coronary heart disease among postmenopausal compared with premenopausal women [212]. It also showed that sex-specific differences in the manifestations of coronary heart disease occur. Women have a delayed onset of coronary disease by 10 years relative to men, whereas myocardial infarction and sudden death are delayed by 20 years. The first symptom of coronary heart disease in women is likely to be angina pectoris, whereas men more often present with acute myocardial infarction. However, after the onset of angina, men are more likely to have a coronary event than are women. Sudden death is more common among men in all age groups. Case fatality rates are higher for women than for men in most age strata [210,212]. Schouw et al, in an attempt to explore the relation between the age of menopause and subsequent cardiovascular mortality, studied a cohort of 12,115 postmenopausal women aged 50-65 years at enrollment in a breast cancer screening project in 1974-77; the women were followed up for a median of 16 years [224]. The results clearly showed an increased risk of cardiovascular mortality for women who have early menopause indicating that longer exposure to endogenous estrogen protects against cardiovascular events.

Knowledge of mechanisms to explain menopause as a risk factor for heart disease have evolved primarily through studies of the administration of exogenous estrogen. Suggested mechanisms include the inhibition of atheromatous plaque formation (through action on the intima, platelet, and arterial musculature), improvement of vascular flow, and improvement of the lipoprotein and lipid profile [211].

The effects of estrogen on lipoprotein lipid metabolism are summarized in table 3. Using isotopelabeled cholesterol, it has been shown that women receiving estrogen catabolize LDL cholesterol and produce HDL cholesterol to a significantly greater degree than women receiving placebo [214]. The use of unopposed conjugated equine estrogens at a dosage of 0.625 mg/day decreased LDL cholesterol by 12-19% and increased HDL cholesterol by 9-13% [215]. In the Lipid Research Center long-term study of women, it has been reported that changes in cholesterol metabolism induced in women receiving estrogens accounted for approximately 25% of the cardiovascular benefit [213,216].

Table 3

Effects of Estrogen on Lipoprotein Lipid Metabolism [213]

---

*   Increased rate of removal of chylomicron remnants by the liver
*   Increased VLDL secretion from the liver Increased hepatic uptake of VLDL remnants
*   Increased Uptake of LDL by the up-regulated LDL receptor with consequently lower plasma LDL cholesterol concentrations
*   An increase in synthesis of apoprotein A-1 and therefore a concomitant increase in HDL cholesterol in the plasma
*   Increased bile acid secretion to remove cholesterol from the body

VLDL= very low-density lipoprotein cholesterol; LDL= low-density lipoprotein cholesterol; HDL= high-density lipoprotein cholesterol.

In addition to metabolic effects, estrogens have direct effects on the arterial wall [217]. These effects are summarized in Table 4. Estrogens are antioxidants [218,219] and appear to protect the endothelial cell from injury due to stress. This is potentially important because of the large number of atherogenic properties of oxidized LDL (Table 5). Recent tissue culture experiments have indicated that estrogens inhibit endothelial cell expression of adhesion molecules; this action may inhibit the platelet aggregation and adhesion seen in the early stages of atherosclerosis. Other anti-atherogenic actions of estrogens include reduction of arterial cholesterol ester influx and hydrolysis, reduction of lipoprotein-induced arterial smooth-muscle proliferation, and inhibition of foam cell formation. These anti-atherosclerotic effects probably explain the 56% reduction in the risk of angiographically demonstrated coronary heart disease in estrogen users compared with non-users [213,220]. Estrogen has also been shown to induce arteriolar relaxation in vessels without endothelium [214], and estrogen receptors have been demonstrated in smooth muscle cells form human coronary arteries postmortem [221].

Table 4
Potentially Atherogenic Properties of Oxidized Low-Density Lipoprotein
[222]

* Cytotoxic to endothelial cells and smoothmuscle cells
* Causes cholesterol accumulation in macrophages
* Chemotactic for monocytes
* Inhibits macrophage migration
* Increases adhesiveness of monocytes and endothelial cells
* Alters production of growth factors and inflammatory mediators
* Inhibits endothelium-derived vasodilator activity
* Alters prostaglandin production
* Promotes platelet aggregation

Table 5
Direct Effects of Estrogen's on the Arterial Wall [223]

* Reduced LDL accumulation, arterial cholesterol influx, and hydrolysis
* Inhibition of platelet aggregation
* Reduced lipoprotein-induced arterial smooth-muscle proliferation
* Inhibition of myointimal proliferation associated with mechanical injury or induced by stress
* Decreased collagen and elastin production
* Increased arterial smooth-muscle prostacyclin production
* Inhibition of foam cell formation

LDL = low-density lipoprotein cholesterol

The effect of hormone replacement therapy on coronary heart disease in postmenopausal women has been the subject of extensive research. More than 30 observational studies and one small randomized, controlled clinical trial have provided evidence that estrogen replacement reduces cardiovascular risk by approximately 50% [210]. Four studies [225,226,227,228] that used coronary arteriography to document the presence of coronary atherosclerosis have provided some of the most compelling evidence that estrogen replacement reduces cardiovascular risk in postmenopausal women. One of these studies, [Sullivan et al [225]] studied 2,188 women over the age of 55 or with a history of bilateral oophorectomy who presented for angiography between 1972 and 1984. Data were obtained at admission regarding known risk factors for coronary disease and current estrogen use. There were 1444 women with substantial coronary disease, compared with 744 who had normal coronary arteries. Only 2.7% of those with coronary disease used estrogen, in contrast to 7.7% of the controls, a difference that was statistically significant. Logistic regression analysis disclosed that the most important independent risk factors for the presence of coronary disease were age, high cholesterol level, smoking, diabetes mellitus, and hypertension. The only factor significantly associated with the absence of coronary disease was estrogen.replacement therapy [210]. These observations have been confirmed by the other three additional angiographic studies (Table 6).

Table 6
Angiographic Studies of the Relation of Estrogen
Replacement Therapy and Coronary Artery Disease (210)

Investigator	N	Relative risk	P
Sullivan et al (225), 1988	2188	0.40	.002
Gruchow et al (226),1988	933	0.59	<.01
McFarland et al (227),1989	345	0.50	<.01
Hong et al (228(, 1992	90	0.13	<.001

The effect of estrogen replacement therapy on survival in women with angiographically documented coronary disease was studied by Sullivan et al [229]. He found that the greatest improvement in total mortality took place in those women with substantial coronary stenosis; less benefit was observed in those without disease. Angiographic studies have also confirmed the importance of high-density lipoprotein cholesterol in mediating the beneficial effect of estrogen on endothelial function. Bush et al [230] studied 2270 women for an average of 5 years. There were 44 deaths in 1677 non-users, compared with six deaths in 593 users. Estrogen users had a higher mean HDL cholesterol level compared to non-users. When HDL cholesterol was added to the regression model, the protective effect of estrogen was attenuated by greater than 40%, suggesting that HDL cholesterol was partially responsible for the protective effect. Although the addition of progestins to estrogen attenuates some of estrogen's effect on high-density lipoprotein cholesterol, limited observational data have suggested that the cardioprotective effect is not reduced [231,232].

V - MENOPAUSE: HORMONE REPLACEMENT THERAPY

Estrogen replacement therapy in menopause can be aimed at treating the symptomatic consequences, such as urogenital atrophy or at the prevention of the long-term sequelae, such as osteoporosis. Menopause-related conditions for which estrogen therapy is used clinically are summarized in table 7.

Table 7

Common clinical Uses For Non-Contraceptive Estrogens [63]

Hot Flushes	Dysphoric mood
Atrophic urethritis	Dyspareunia
Stress incontinence	Decreased sexual motivation
Sensory-urge incontinence	Osteoporosis prevention
Atrophic vaginitis	Cardiovascular disease prevention

The choice of hormone regimen or a non-hormonal therapy must be based on each individual patient's treatment goals and medical history. Medical evaluation should include a complete history, with attention to contraindications and precautions to hormone therapy table 8, general physical exam, gynecologic exam, pap smear, and mammogram. Re-evaluation is recommended in three months to assess therapeutic effectiveness and any side effects, annual follow up is adequate if no problem intervene. Patients should be counseled as to what type of bleeding pattern might represent a problem so that this can be promptly evaluated [63].

Table 8

Absolute And Relative Contraindications
To The Use Of NON-Contraceptive Estrogens [63]

Absolute
   Undiagnosed vaginal bleeding
   Known/Suspected breast cancer
   Known/Suspected endometrial cancer
   Active venous thrombosis
   Malignant melanoma

Relative

   Uterine leiomyoma
   Endometriosis
   History of cholelithiasis
   History of migraine
   Hypertriglyceridernia
   History of pregnancy related thrombosis
   History of oral contraceptive-related thrombosis
   Liver disease

Estrogen should be administered at the lowest dosage compatible with symptom relief or disease prevention. This will minimize estrogen-related symptomatic side effects, such as breast tenderness, and may diminish potential toxicity. Estrogen is most commonly administered as estradiol at a dose of 0.625 mg/day given orally for the first 25 days or daily each month (lower doses are usually ineffective in preventing long term complications) [130]. Estradiol can also be administered in a percutaneous patch or gel for transdermal absorption. Several studies have shown transdermal estradiol to be as effective as orally administered estradiol in preventing postmenopausal bone loss [173,174,233]. Transdermal estradiol, however, lacks the favorable effects of orally administered estradiol on HDL levels. This is attributed to the fact that the transdermal route avoid the "first pass" effect on the liver and/or intestine [234,235]. However, transdermal estrogen may be better tolerated in women with migraines, hypertriglyceridemia or gall bladder disease.

Although estrogen has favorable effects on bone mass, and the cardiovascular system in postmenopausal women, estrogen replacement therapy is not without complications. It increases the risk of endometrial cancer [236], an effect that can be eliminated by concurrent administration of a progestin [237,238]. In women following hysterectomy, progestogens are not necessary, but in women with a uterus, a progestogen (e.g., medroxyprogesterone 5 mg/day) may be added for the first or last 12- 14 days of estrogen administration. Estrogen and a low dose progestogen (e.g., medroxyprogesterone 2.5 mg/day) may also be administered continuously [130]. None of the progestin regimens modifies the protective effect of estrogen on bone mass, and progestogens have positive effects on bone [132]. Most ofthe cardiovascular benefits associated with estrogen are preserved when progestin is given cyclically, but the continuous use of progestin diminishes some of the cardiovascular benefits of estrogen [133]. Whether estrogen therapy increases the incidence of breast cancer has not been settled. Menopause protects women against breast cancer, and some evidence suggests that the administration of estrogen for 15 years or more slightly increases the risk of such cancer, especially when it is combined with progestin [239,240]. Some researchers have suggested that estrogen therapy should not be initiated until the patient is sixty-five years old because prolonged use increases the risk of breast cancer [177]. This approach, however, is unlikely to gain wide acceptance, especially since lack of estrogen is associated with accelerated bone loss.

It is important to monitor the endometrium of patients on hormone replacement therapy. Endometrial biopsies can be performed easily in the outpatient setting with new, flexible sampling devices. Biopsies have been recommended pretreatment and annually in women with a uterus who do not wish to take or are intolerant to progestins [241]. However, this is unacceptable to many women as a baseline screen. Surveillance biopsies are recommended if breakthrough bleeding occurs up to 2-3 days post progesterone. In the 12-day regimen, bleeding is expected to commence after the 9th day of progestin use [242]. When 2.5 mg of medroxyprogesterone is used continuously, the need for the surveillance biopsies in the initial year can be difficult to assess because the first year of therapy is characterized by routine erratic spotting and bleeding. Since bleeding is usually light to moderate in amount and short in duration, a biopsy is recommended if bleeding is heavy or prolonged [63,243,244]. Recent advances in transvaginal endometrial ultrasound may ultimately make it possible to perform endometrial surveillance non-invasively [245,246]. In initial studies, an endometrial thickness of less than 5 mm has been associated with the absence of hyperplasia. Further studies of this test are necessary, before it can be accepted for clinical use [63].

5.1. Partial Estrogen agonists

Several tissue specific partial estrogen agonists are presently being investigated as alternatives to natural estrogens for hormone replacement therapy. The most frequently mentioned of these partial agonists are tamoxifen, tibilone, and raloxifene.

Tamoxifen is a synthetic antiestrogen currently approved in the United States as an adjuvant therapy in the treatment of breast cancer in postmenopausal women [179]. Studies of postmenopausal women treated with tamoxifen demonstrated a partial protective effect on the skeleton [247,248,249]. Love et al [247], in a two-year randomized, double-blinded, placebocontrolled trial, studied the effects of tamoxifen on bone mineral density (BMD) in 140 postmenopausal women with breast cancer. In women given tamoxifen, the mean BMD of the lumbar spine increased by 0.61 percent per year, whereas in those given placebo it decreased by 1.00 percent per year (pco.ool) Radial BMD decreased to the same extent in both groups. Furthermore, tamoxifen was found to increase high-density lipoprotein cholesterol, sex hormone binding globulin, and testosterone binding globulin while simultaneously decreasing low-density lipoprotein cholesterol and in breast cancer patients [250,251,252,253], suggesting that it has estrogen-like effect on the liver [179]. Major side effects from tamoxifen include hepatic toxicity, and venous thrombophlebitis [179,254].

Tibilone is synthetic steroid with mixed properties of estrogen, progestin, and androgen. Because of its estrogenic properties, it relieves menopausal symptoms and decreases bone resorption activity. However, because of its progestogenic and androgenic properties, it has a reduced effect on stimulating endometrial proliferation. Thus uterine bleeding occurs less frequently, and the occurrence of endometrial cancer presumably will be very low [255,256,257,258]. Tibilone, in general, appears to be similar to estrogen in its effects on bone [256,259]. Its main advantages over cyclic therapy with estrogen and progestin appears to be the lower incidence of vaginal bleeding and breast tenderness [256,257,260]. The major disadvantages of tibilone therapy compared with estrogen replacement therapy (ERT) is its less favorable effect on the serum lipid profile [261,262]. It has been demonstrated by several authors that long-term tibilone therapy is not associated with a decrease in LDL cholesterol as occurs with ERT, and it maintains or reduces the pretreatment levels of HDL cholesterol, whereas oral ERT increases it [263,264]. Like estrogen, however, it does reduce the serum concentration of lipoprotein (a), an independent risk factor for coronary artery disease [265]. All-in-all, however, tibilone would be expected to afford less protection against coronary artery disease than does ERT [255]. Tibilone is currently approved for clinical use in several European countries, but not in the United States.

Raloxifene (LY 139481 HCL) is a benzothiophene derivative that has the unique property of acting as an estrogen agonist in bone and liver, and as pure antagonist in uterine tissue [266,267]. Black et al investigated the effects of raloxifene on bone loss, serum lipids, and tissue in ovariectomized (OVX) rat model as compared to that of ethynyl estradiol, and concluded that raloxifene prevents bone loss and lowers serum cholesterol in ovariectomized (OVX) rats without producing significant estrogenic effects on uterine tissue [266]. Similar effects are also observed in humans [268,269]. Raloxifene's minimal stimulatory effect on endometrial epithelium suggests a lower cancer risk compared with chronic administration of estrogen, which makes it a promising drug for postmenopausal women that merits further investigation.

The precise mechanism for raloxifene's selective agonistic effect on bone and lipids and antagonistic effect on uterus and breast remains uncertain. Some investigators suggested that raloxifene exerts its effects through the estrogen receptor [269], while others have described other potential binding sites, indicating that non-estrogen receptor-based mechanisms cannot be ruled out [270]. Yang et al [271], using the OVX rat model, demonstrated that the effect of both estrogen and raloxifene on bone is mediated through their interaction with estrogen receptor which in turn activate the expression of the human Transforming Growth Factor-B3 (TGF-B3) gene. In a follow up study [272], the same group of investigators compared estrogen and antiestrogen regulation of the TGF-B3 gene, and found that TGF-B3 gene activation by raloxifene was mediated by a polypurine sequence, which they called the raloxifene response element, and did not require the DNA binding domain of the estrogen receptor. They concluded that estrogen receptor, in combination with different estrogen entities, regulate more than one DNA response element, namely the estrogen response element and the raloxifene response element, which might explain the wide spectrum of estrogen effect in humans, especially in nonreproductive tissue. Furthermore, the distinct effects of selective estrogen receptor modulators, at the estrogen response element and the raloxifene response element may explain the tissue-selective estrogen agonist or antagonist activity of compounds such as raloxifene.

CONCLUSIONS

The Massachusetts Women's Health Study, a large and comprehensive prospective, longitudinal study of middle-aged women, provides a powerful argument that menopause is not and should not be viewed as a negative experience by the vast majority of women [273]. Menopause should serve to remind patients and clinicians that this is a time for education. Besides the general issues of good health, preventive health care education should be focused on cardiovascular disease and osteoporosis because of their relation to the decline in estradiol levels with menopause. Interventional strategies to decrease the impact of menopause must be considered with each patient.

Postmenopausal hormone therapy deserves consideration as an important component of preventive health care for older women. Except in the presence of overt medical contraindications, the choice of undertaking treatment with estrogen replacement therapy should always be considered. One can argue that protection against cardiovascular disease is the major benefit of postmenopausal estrogen replacement therapy; however prevention of osteoporosis is another benefit of considerable magnitude. Postmenopausal hormone therapy and its alternatives should be an option offered to most women as they consider their paths for successful aging [1].

REFERENCES

1. Byyny RL, Speroff L. A clinical Guide for the Care of Older Women 2nd Ed., pp. 143-160, Williams & Wilkins, Baltimore, 1996.
2. Weg RB, Menopause: Biomedical Aspects, in The Encyclopedia of Aging (Maddox GL Ed.), pp. 622-628, Springer Publisher Company, New York, 1995.
3. Mckinley SM, Brambilla DJ, Posner JG. The normal menopause transition, Maturias 14: 103, 1992.

4. Treloar AE, Boynton RE, Borghild GB, Brown BW. Variation of the human menstrual cycle through reproductive life, Int. J Fertil 12:77, 1967.
5. Treloar AE. Menstrual cyclicity and the pre-menopause, Maturitas 3:249, 1981.
6. Chang RJ, Plouffe L, Schaffer. Physiology of the Menopause in Comprehensive management of menopause (Plouffe L, Ravnikar V, et al. Eds.), pp 3-13, Springer-Verlag, New York, 1994.
7. Korenman SG, Sherman BM, Korenman JC. Reproductive hormone function: the perimenopausal period and beyond. Clin Endocrinol Metab. 7:625, 1978.
8. Sherman BM, Korenman SG. Hormonal characteristics of the human menstrual cycle throughout reproductive life. J Clin Invest. 55:699, 1975.
9. Shideler SE, Devane GW, Kalra PS, Bernischke K, Lasley BL. Ovarian-pituitary hormone interactions during the perimenopause . Maruritas 11:331, 1989.
10. Longcope C, Franz C, Morello C, Baker R, Johnston CC. Steroid and gonadotropin levels in women during the perimenopausal years. Maturitas 8: 189, 1986.
11. Lenton EA, Sexon L, Lee S, Cooke ID. Progressive changes in LH and FSH and LH:FSH ratio in women throughout reproductive life Maturitas 10:35, 1988.
12. Burger HG. Inhibin. Reprod Med Rev. 1: 1, 1992.
13. Peluso JJ, Steger RW, Jaszczak S et al. Gonadotropin binding sites in human postmenopausal ovaries. Fertil Steril 27:788, 1976.
14. Nicosia SV. Ovarian changes during the climacteric. In: Mastroianni L, Paulsen CA, Eds. Aging, Reproduction and the Climacteric, pp. 179, New York: Plenum Press, 1986.
15. Judd HL. Hormonal dynamics associated with the menopause. Clin Obstet Gynecol 19:775, 1976.
16. Longcope C. Hormone dynamics at the menopause. Am J Obstet Gynecol 130:564, 1980
17. Judd HL, Lucas WE, Yen SSC. Serum 17-beta- estradiol and estrone levels in postmenopausal women with and without endometrial cancer. J Clin Endocrinol Metab. 43:272, 1976.
18. Huges Cl, Wall LL, Creasman WT. Reproductive hormone levels in gynecologic oncology patients undergoing surgical castration after spontaneous menopause. Gyn Oncol 40:42, 1991.
19. Longcope C, Kato T, Horton R. Conversion of blood androgens to estrogens in normal adult men and women. J Clin Invest. 48:2191, 1960.
20. Longcope C, Pratt JH, Schneider SH, Fineberg SE. Aromatization of androgen by muscle and adipose tissue in vivo. J Clin Endocrinol Metab. 46: 146, 1978.
21. Judd HL, Judd GE, Lucas WE, Yen SSC. Endocrine function of the postmenopausal ovary. Concentration of androgen and estrogen in ovarian and peripheral venous blood. J Clin Endocrinol Metab. 39: 1020, 1974.
22. Calcanog A, Sall S, Gorden GG, Southern A1. Androstenedione metabolism in patients with endometrial cancer. Am J Obstet Gynecol. 129:553, 1977.
23. Abraham GE, Maroulis GB. Effect of exogenous estrogen on serum progesterone, cortisol, and androgens in postmenopausal women. Obstet Gynecol 45:271, 1975.
24. Mortola JF, Yen SSC. The effects of oral dehydroepianderosterone on endocrine-metabolic parameters in postmenopausal women. J Clin Endocrol Metab 71:696, 1990.
25. Knobil E, Wildt L, Belchetz PE, Marshall G. Control of the rhesus monkey menstrual cycle: permissive role of hypothalamic gonadotropin releasing hormone. Science 207:1371, 1980.
26. Monroe SE, Jaffde RB, Midgley AR Jr. Regulation of human gonadotropins, XIII: changes in serum gonadotropins in menstruating women in response to ooophorectomy. J Clin Endocrino Metab. 34:420, 1972.
27. Vekemans M, Robyn C. Influence of age on serum prolactin levels in women and men. Br. Med. J. 4:738, 1975.
28. Andrson JR, Schroeder E, Lebech PE. The effect of postmenopausal women of natural human and artificial estrogens on the concentration in serum of prolactin . Acta Endocrinol. 95:433, 1980.
29. Spaulding SW. Age and the thyroid . Endocrinol Metab Clin N Am. 16: 1013, 1987
30. Hammerman MR. Insulin-like growth factors and aging. Endocrinol Metab Clin N Am16:995, 1987.
31. Ho KY, Weissberger AJ. Secretory patterns of growth hormone according to sex and age. HormRes. 33:7, 1990.
32. Hill K. The demography of menopause. Maturitas 23(2): 113-27,1996.
33. Avis AE, Mckinlay SM. The Massachusetts Women's Health Study: An Epidemiologic Investigation of the Menopause. J Am Wom Assoc. 50(2):45-49, 1995.
34. Sowers MR, La Pietra MT. Menopause: its epidemiology and potential association with chronic diseases. Epidemiol Rev 17(2):287-302, 1995.
35. McKinalay SM, Bigano NL, Mckinalay JB. Smoking and age at menopause, Ann Intern Med 103:350, 1985.
36. Torgerson DJ, Avenell A, Russel IT, Reid DM. Factors associated with onset of menopause in

women aged 45-49, Maturitas 19:83, 1994.

37. MacMahon B, Worcester J. Age at menopause U. S. 1960-62, vital Health Stat 11: 1, 1966

38. Midgette AS, Baron JA. Cigarette smoking and the risk of natural menopause, Epidemiology 1: 474, 1990.

39. Amundsen SW, Diers CJ, The age of menopause in classical Greece and Rome, Hum Biol 42:79, 1970.

40. Amundsen DW, Diers CJ. The age of menopause in medieval Europe, Hum Biol 45:605, 1973.

41. Stanford JL, Hartage P, Brinton LA, et al. Factors influencing the age at natural menopause. J Chronic Dis 40:995-1002, 1987.

42. Sherman BM, West JH, Korenman SG.The menopausal transition; analysis of LH, FSH, estradiol and progesterone concentrations during menstrual cycles of older women. J Clin Endocrinol Metab 42:629-36, 1976.

43. Hammond CB. Menopause and hormone replacement therapy: an overview. Obstetrics & Gynecology 87(2 Suppl): 1 S-15S, 1996.

44. Chakravarti S, Collins WP, Forcast JD, et al. Relation between plasma hormone profiles, symptoms, and response to estrogen treatment in women approaching the menopause. Br Med J 1: 1983-5, 1979.

45. Richardson SJ. The biological basis of the menopause. Bailliere's clinical endocrinology and metabolism 7(1):1-16, 1993.

46. McLachlan RI, Robertson DM, Healy DL, et al. Circulating immunoreactive inhibin levels during the normal human menstral cycle. Journal of Clinical Endocrinology and metabolism 65:954-961, 1987.

47. Hillier SG, Wickings EJ, Illingworth PI et al. Control of immunoactive inhibin production by human granulosa cells. Clinical Endocrinology 35:71-78, 1991.

48. Roseff SJ, Bangah ML, Kettel LM, et al. Dynamic changes in circulating inhibin levels during the luteal-folicular transition of the human menstrnal cycle. Journal of clinical endocrinology and metabolism 69:1033-1039, 1989.

49. Rannevik G, Jeppsson S, Johnell O, Bjerre B, Yaurell-Borulf Y, Svanberg L. A longitudinal study of the perimenopausal transition: altered profiles of steroid and pituitary hormones, SHBG and bone mineral density, Maturitas 21: 103,1995.

50. MacNaughton J, Banah M, McCloud P, Hee J, Burger H. Age related changes in follicle stimulating hormone, luteinizing hormone, oestradiol and immunoreactive inhibin in women of reproductive age. Cli Endocrinol 36:339, 1992.

51. Hee J, MacNaughton J, Bangah M, Burger HG. Perimenopuasal patterns of gonadotrophins, immunoreactive inhibin, oestradiol and progesterone, Maturitas 18:9, 1993.

52. Gosden RG. Follicular status at menopause. Hum Repro 2:617, 1987.

53. Meldrum DR, Davidson BJ, Tataryn IV, Judd HL. Changes in circulating steroids with aging in postmenopausal women, Obstet Gynecol 57:624, 1981.

54. Rannevik G, Jeppsson S, Johnell O, Bjerre B, Yaurell-Borulf Y, Svanberg L. A longitudinal study of the perimenopusal transition: altered profiles of steroid and pituitary hormones, SHBG and bone mineral density. Maturitas 21: 103, 1995.

55. Longcope C, Jaffe W, Griffing G. Production rates of androgens and oestrogens in post-menopausal women. Obstet Gynecol 59:680, 1982.

56. Robinson G. Cross-cultural perspectives on menopause. J Nerv Ment Dis 184(8): 453-8, 1996.

57. Cramer DW, Xu H, Harlow BL. Family history as a predictor of early menopause. Fertil Steril 64(4):740-5, 1995.

58. Hunter MS. Predictors of menopausal symptoms: psychosocial aspects. Bailliere's Clinical endocrinology and Metabolism 7(1): 33-45, 1993.

59. Avis NE, Kaufert PA, Lock M,McKinlay SM, Vass K. The evolution of menopausal symptoms. Bailliere's Clinical Endocrinology and Metabolism 7(1): 17-32, 1993.

60. Neugarten BL & Kraines RJ. Menopausal symptoms in women of various ages. Psychosomatic Medicine 27: 266-273, 1965.

61. Greene JG & Cooke DJ. Life stress and symptoms at the climacterium. British Journal of Psychiatry 136: 486-491, 1980.

62. Utian WH. The place of oestriol therapy after menopause . Acta Endocrinol Suppl (Copenh) 233:51-6, 1980.

63. Greendale GA, Judd HL. The Menopause: Health Implications and Clinical Management. JAGS 41 :426-436, 1993.

64. Meldrum DR, Shamonki IM, Fumar AM et al. Elevation in skin temperature of the finger as an objective index of postmenopausal hot flashes: Standardization of the technique. Am J Obstet

Gynecol 135:713-717, 1979.

65. Tataryn IV, Lomax P, Bajorek JG, et al. Postmenopausal hot flashes: Disorder of thermoregulation. Maturitas 2: 101-107, 1980.

66. Kronenberg F. Hot flashes. In: Lobo RA, ed . Treatment of the postmenopausal women: Basic and clinical aspects. New York: Raven Press pp. 97-117, 1994.

67. Askel S, Schomberg DW, Tyrey L, Hommond CB. Vasomotor symptoms, serum estrogen and gonadotropin levels in surgical menopause. Am J Obstet Gynecol 126: 165-9, 1976

68. Thomson B, Hart SA, Durno D. Menopausal age and symptomatology in general practice . J Biol Sci 5:71, 1973.

69. McKinley S, Jeffreys M. The menopausal syndrome. Br J Pre Soc Med 28: 108- 115, 1974.

70. Casper RJ, Yen SSC, Wilhem MM. Menopausal flushes: A neuroendocrine link with pulsatile LH secretion. Science 205 :823-5, 1979.

71. Tataryn IV, Meldrum DR, Lu KH, et al. LH, FSH, and skin temperature during menopausal hot flush. J Clin Endocrinolol Metab 49: 1952-4, 1979.

72. Meldrom DR, Erlik Y, LU JK, et al. Objectively recorded hot flushes in patients with pituitary insufficiency. J Clin Endocrinol Metab 52:684-687, 1981.

73. Casper RF, Yen SSC. Menopausal flushes: effect of pituitary gonadotropin desensitization by a potent luteinizing hormone-releasing factor agonist. J Clin Endocrinol Metab 53: 1056-1058.

74. DeFazio J, Meldrum DR, Laufer L, et al. Induction of hot flushes in premenopausal women treated with a long-acting GnRH agonist. J Clin Endocrinol Metab 56:445-8, 1977.

75. Lu JKH, Judd HL. The neuroendocrine aspects of menopausal hot flushes. In: Schonbaum E, ed. The climacteric Hot Flush. Prog Basic Clin Pharmacol. Basel: Larger, vol 6, pp 83-99, 1991.

76. Judd HL. The basis of menopausal vasomotor symptoms. In: Mastroianni L Jr, Paulsen CA, eds. Aging, Reproduction and the Climacteric. New York: Plenum Press 215, 1986.

77. Laufer LR, Erlik Y, Meldrum DR et al. effect of clonidine on hot flashes in postmenopausal women. Obstet Gynecol 60:583-586, 1982.

78. D'Amico JF, Greendale GA, LU JKH et al. Induction of hypothalamic opioid activity with trasnsdermal estradiol administration in postmenopausal women, Fertil Sterill 55:754-758, 1991.

79. Erlik Y, Tataryn IV, Meldrum DR, et al. Association of waking episodes with menopausal hot flushes. JAMA 245: 1741 -4, 1981.

80. Campbell S, Whitehead M. Estrogen therapy and the menopause syndrome. Clin Obstet Gynecol4:31-47, 1977.

81. Stteingold KA, Laufer L, Chetkowski R J et al. Treatment of hot flashes with transdermal estradiol administration . J Clin Endocrinol Metab 61 :627-632, 1985.

82. Sonnedecker EUW, Polakow ES. Effects of conjugated equine estrogens with and without the addition of cyclical medrogesterone on hot flushes, liver function, blood pressure, and endocrinological indices. S Afr Med 77:281-285, 1990.

83. Marslaw U, Christiansen C. Ddesogestral in hormone replacement therapy: Long-term effect on bone, calcium, and lipid metabolism, climacteric symptoms, and bleeding . Eur J Clin Invest 21:601-607, 1991.

84. Schiffff I, Tulchinsky D, Cramer D. Oral medroxyprogesterone in the treatment of postmenoipausal symptoms. JAMA244:1443, 1980.

85. Erlik Y, Meldrum DR, Lagasse LD et al. Effect of megestrol acetate on flushing and bone metabolism in postmenopausal women. Maturitas 3:167-172, 1981.

86. Bolli P, Simpson FO. Clonidine and menopausal flushing: A double blind trial. N Z Med J82: 196-200, 1982.

87. Hammond MG, Hatley L, Talbot LM. A double blind study to evaluate the effect of methyldopa on menopausal hot flushes. J Clin Endocrin Metab 58:1158-1160, 1984.

88. Sentenac J, and Timiras PS. The Menopause: Clinical Aspects and Current Trends in therapy, in Hormones and aging (Timiras PS, Quay WD& Vernadakis A Ed.), pp. 135-152, CRC Press, New York, 1995.

89. Brincat M, Moniz CJ, Studd JWW, et al. Long-term effects of the menopause and sex hormone on skin thickness. Br J Obstet Gynecol 92:256-9, 1985.

90. Brincat M, Kabalan S, Studd JW, et al. A study of the decrease of skin collagen content, skin thickness, and bone mass in the postmenopausal women. Obstet Gynecol 70:840-5, 1987.

91. Brincat M, Yuen AW, Studd JW, et al. Response of skin thickness and metacarpal index to estradiol therapy in postmenopausal women. Obstet Gynecol 70:538-41, 1987.

92. Losif CS, Batra S, Sek A et al. Estrogen receptors in the human female lower urinary tract. AmJObstetGynecol 141:817-82, 1981.

93. Ingelman-sundberg A, Rosen J, Gustafsson SA, et al. Cytosol estrogen receptors in the urogenital

tissues in stress-incontinent women. Acta Obstet Gynecol Scand 60:586, 1981.

94. Zuckerman S. Morphological and functional homologies of the male and female reproductive system. Br Med J 2:264, 1936.

95. Raz S, Ziegler M, Caine M. The vascular component in the production in intrauethral pressure. J Urol 108:93-96, 1972.

96. Walters S, Wolf H, Barlebo H et al. Urinary incontinence in postmenopausal women treated with estrogens . Urol Int 33:135-143, 1978.

97. Scotti RJ, Ostergard DR. The urethral syndrome. Clin Obsteet Gynecol 27:515-529, 1984.

98. OulanderJG, Bruskewitz R. Disorders of micturition in the aging patient. Adv Intern Med 34:165-190, 1989.

99. Ulmsten U, Henriksson L, Losif S. The unstable female urethra. Am J Obstet Gynecol 144:93-97, 1982.

100. Bhatia NN, Bergman A, Kararam MM. Effects of estrogen on urethral function in women with urinary incontinence . Am J Obstet Gynecol 160: 176-81, 1989.

101. Wilson PD, Faragher B, Butler B et al. Treatment with oral piperazine oestrone sulphate for genuine stress urinary incontinence in postmenopausal women. Br J Obstet Gynaecol 94:568, 1987.

102. Oriloa HA, Mibach HI. Vulvar transdermal water loss (TEWL) decay curves. Effect of occlusion, delipidation, and age. Acta Derm Venereol (Stokh) 69:461-5, 1989.

103. Pansini F, Albertazzi P, Bonaccorsi G, Zanotti L et al. Trazodone: a non-hormonal alternative for neurovegetative climacteric symptoms. Cllin Exp Obstet Gynecol 22(4):341-4,1995.

104. Freedman RR, Renner JH. Natural alternative therapies: do they have a place in treatment? Menopause Management. March:24-27, 1994.

105. Myers JK, Lindenthal JJ, Peper MP. Life events, social integration, and psychiatric symptomatology. J Health Soc Behav 16:421-7, 1975.

106. Sherwin BB. Hormones, Mood, and Cognitive Functioning in Postmenopausal Women. Obstetrics & Gynecology 87(2 Suppl): 20S-26S, 1996.

107. Luine VN, McEwen BS. Effect of estradiol on turnover of type A monoamino oxidase in brain. J Neurochem 28: 1221 -7, 1977.

108. Aylward M. Plasma tryptophan levels and mental depression in postmenpausal subjects. Effects of oral piperazine-oestrone sulphate. IRCS Med SCI 1 :30-4, 1973.

109. Sherwin BB, Suranyi-Cadotte BE. UP-regulatory effect of estrogen on platelet 3Himipramine binding site in surgically menopausal women. Biol Psychiatry 28:339-48, 1990.

110. Montgomery JC, Bricart M, Tapp A, et al. Effect of estrogen and testosterone on psychological disorders in the climacteric. Lancet i:297-9, 1987.

111. Sherwin RB, Gelfand MM. Sex steroids and affect in the surgical menopause: A doubleblind, crossover study. Psychoneuroendocrinology 10:325-35, 1985.

112. Hammond CB. The climacteric IN: Scott JR, DiSaia, Hammond CB, Spellacy WN, eds. Danforth's obstetrics and gynecology. 7th ed. Philadelphia: Lippincott:777, 1994.

113. Goldstein MK and Teng NN. Gynecologic factors in sexual dysfunction of the older woman. Clin Geriat Med 7(1):41-61,1991.

114. Hunter MS. Emotional well-being, sexual behavior and hormone replacement therapy. Maturitas 12(3):299-314, 1990.

115. Ansbacher R. Nonestrogenic Therapy For The Menopause. Comprehensive therapy 21(5):242-244, 1995.

116. Coope J. Hormonal and non-hormonal interventions for menopausal symptoms. Maturitas 23(2):159-68, 1996.

117. Vaillant L, Callens A. Hormone replacement treatment and skin aging. Therapie 51(1):767-70, 1996.

118. Pierard GE, Letawe C, Dowlati A, Pierard-Franchimont C. Effect of hormone replacement therapy for menopause on the mechanical properties of skin. J Am Geriatr Soc 43(6):6625, 1995.

119. Bachmann GA. Influence of menopause on sexuality. Int J Fertil Menopausal Stud 40 Suppl 1: 16-22, 1995.

120. DitkoffEC, Crary WG, Cristo M et al. Estrogen improves psychological function in asymtomatic postmenopausal women. Obstet Gynecol 78:991-995,1991.

121. Canto DE, Cetina TE. Hormone replacement therapy in the climacteric. Rev Invest Clin 47(1):49-61, 1995.

122. Ross PD. Osteoporosis. ARCHInternalMed 156(13):1399-1411.

123. Kanis JA. Osteoporosis and osteopenia. J Bone Min Res. 5:209-211, 1990.

124. Brazel U. Osteoporosis: taking a fresh look. Hospital Practice, May 15:59-68, 1996.

125. Kanis JA, Melton LJ III, et al. The diagnosis of osteoporosis. J Bone Miner. Res 9: 1137-1141, 1994.

126. Kane RL, Ouslander JG, Abrass IB. Essentials of Clinical Geriatrics, 3rd Ed. Pp. 234-241, McGraw-

THE MENOPAUSE

Hill, Inc., 1994.

127. Johnston CC Jr., Slemenda CW. Pathogenesis of osteoporosis. Bone 17(2 Suppl): l9S-22S, 1995.
128. Greenspan SL, Maitland-Ramsey L, Myers E. Classification of osteoporosis in the elderly is dependent on site-specific analysis. Calcif Tissue Int 58(6):409-14, 1996.
129. Lindsay R. The menopause and osteoporosis. Obstet Gynecol 87(2 suppl.): 16S-19S, 1996.
130. Krane SM, Holick MF. Metabolic Bone Disease, in Harrison's Principles Of Internal Medicine, 13th Ed. (Isselbacher KJ, et al. Ed.), pp. 2172-2177. McGraw-Hill, Inc., St. Louis 1994.
131. Riggs B, Melton L. Involutional osteoporosis. N Eng J Med 314: 1676, 1986.
132. Gallagher JC: Estrogen: prevention and treatment of osteoporosis, in Osteoporosis (Marcus R, Feldman D, KelseyJ, ED.), pp.1191-1208. Academic Press, 1995.
133. Lane JM, Riley EH et al. Osteoporosis: Diagnosis and Treatment. The Journal of Bone and Joint Surgery 78-A(4):618-632, 1996.
134. Girasole G, Jilka RL, Passeri G, et al. 17 beta-estradiol inhibits interleukin-6 production by bone marrow-derived stromal cells and osteoblasts in vitro: a potential mechanism for the anti-osteoporotic effect on estrogens. J Clin. Invest. 89:883-891, 1992.
135. Jilka RL, Hangon G, Girasole G, et al. Increased osteoclast development after estrogen loss: mediation by interleukin-6. Science 257:88-91, 1992.
136. Oursler MJ, Osdoby P, Pyfferoen J, Riggs BL, and Spelsberg TC. Avian osteocalsts ass estrogen target cells. Proc. Nat. Acad. Sci. 88:6613-6617, 1991.
137. Hui SL, Slemenda CC, Johnston and Applendorm CR. Effects of the menopause on vertebral bone density, Bone Miner 2: 141-146, 1987.
138. Ribot C, Tremonlliers JM, Louvet JP, and Guiraud R. Influence of the menopause and aging on spinal density in French women. Bone Miner 2: 141-1`46, 1987.
139. Hedlund LR and Gallagher JC. The effect of age and menopause on bone mineral density of the proximal femur. J Bone Miner Res 4:639-641, 1989.
140. Nordin BEC, Need BE, Chatterton BE, Horwitz M and Morris HA. The relative contribution of age and years since menopause to postmenopausal bone loss. J> Clin Endocrinol Metab 70:83-88, 1989.
141. Gallagher JC, Goldgar D, MOY A. Total bone calcium in normal women: effect of age and menopause status. J Bone Miner Res 2: 491-6, 1987.
142. Lindsay R, Hart DM, Aitken JM, McDonald EB, Anderson JB, Clarke AC. Long-term prevention of postmenopausal osteoporosis by estrogen: evidence for an increased bone mass after delayed onset of estrogen treatment . Lancet 1: 1038-41, 1976.
143. Grenant HK, Cann CE, Ettingert B, Gordan GS. Quantitative computed tomography of vertebral spongiosa: a sensitive method for detecting early bone loss after oophorectomy. Ann Inter Med 97:699-705, 1982.
144. Nordin BEC, Need AG, Bridges A, Horwitz M. Relative contribution of years since menopause, age, and weight to vertebral density in postmenopausal women. HJ Clin Endocrinol Metab 74:20-3, 1992.
145. Quigley ME, Martin PL, Burnier Am, Brooks P. Estrogen therapy arrests bone loss in elderly women . Am J Obstet Gynecol 156: 1516-23, 1987.
146. Elders PJ, Netelenbos JC, Lips P, et al. Accelerated vertebral bone loss in relation to the menopause: a cross-sectional study on lumbar bone density in 286 women of 46 to 55 years of age. Bone Miner 5:11-19, 1988.
147. Elders PJ, Netelenbos JC, Lips P, et al. Perimenopausal bone mass and risk factors. Bone Miner 7:289-99, 1989.
148. Ribot C, Tremollieres F, Pouilles JM, et al. Influence of the menopause and aging on bone mineral density in French women. Bone Miner 5:89-97, 1988.
149. Hedlund LR, Gallagher JC. The effect of age and menopause on bone mineral density of the proximal femur. J Bone Miner Res 4:639-42, 1989.
150. Stevenson JC, Lees B, Devenport M, et al. Determinants of bone density in normal women: risk factors for osteoporosis? BMJ 298:924-8, 1989.
151. Sowers MR, Clark MK, Hollis B, et al. Radial bone mineral density in pre- and perimenopausal women: a prospective density of rates and risk factors for loss. J Bone Miner Res7:647-57, 1992.
152. Gnudi S, Mongiorgi R, Figus e et al. Evaluation of the relative rates of bone mineral content loss in postmenopause due to both estrogen deficiency and aging . Boll Soc Ital Biol Sper 66:1153-9, 1990.
153. Nilas L, Christiansen C. Bone mass and its relationship to age and the menopause. J Clin Endocrinol Metab 65 :697-702, 1987.
154. Recker RR, Lappe JM, Davies KM, et al. Changes in bone mass immediately before menopause . J Bone Miner Res 857-62, 1992.
155. Falch JA, Gautvik KM. A longitudinal study of pre- and postmenopausal changes in calcium

metabolism. Bone 9: 15-19, 1988.

156. Johnston CC Jr, Hui SL, Witt RM, et al. Early menopausal changes in bone mass and sex steroids. J Clin Endocrinol Metab 61 :905-11, 1985.

157. Mazzuoli G, Minisola S, Valtraeten A, et al. Changes in mineral content and biochemical bone markers at the menopause . Isr J Med Sci 21 :875-7, 1985.

158. Slemenda C, Hui SL, Longcope C, et al. Sex steroids and bone mass: a study of changes at time of menopause. J Clin Invest 80:1261-9, 1987.

159. Kelly PJ, Pocock NA, Sambrook PN, et al. Age at menopause-related changes in indices of bone turnover . Clin Endocrin Metab 69: 1160-5, 1989.

160. Pansini F, Bonaccorsi G, Calisesi M, et al. Evaluation of bone metabolic markers as indicators of osteopenia in climacteric women. Gynecol Obstet Invest 33:231-5, 1992.

161. Ribot C, Tremollieres F, Pouilles JM, et al. Obesity and postmenopausal bone loss: the influence of obesity on vertebral density and bone turnover in postmenopausal women. Bone 8:327-31, 1987.

162. Mole PA, Walkinshaw MH, Robins SP, et al. Can urinary pyridium crosslinks and urinary estrogens predict bone mass and rate of bone loss after the menopause? Eur J Clin Invest 22:767-71, 1992.

163. Nordin BEC, Plley KJ. Metabolic consequences of the menopause: a cross-sectional, longitudinal, and intervention study on 557normal postmenopausal women. Calcif Tissue Int 41(suppl):S1-59, 1987.

164. Reid IR, Ames R, Evans MC, et al. Determinants of total body and regional bone mineral density on normal postmenopausal women- a key role for fat mass. J Clin Endocrnol Metab 75:45-51, 1992.

165. Riggs BL, Melton III. The prevention And Treatment Of Osteoporosis. N Eng J Med 327(9):620627, 1992.

166. Aramowicz M (Ed.) New Drugs For Osteoporosis. The Medical Letter 38(965): 1-4, 1996

167. Khosla S, Riggs BL. Treatment options for osteoporosis. Mayo Clin Proc 70(10):978-82, 1995.

168. Beatriz JE, Perry III M. Age-related Osteoporosis. Clinics In Geriatric Medicine 10(4):575-587, 1994.

169. Weiss NS, Ure CL, Ballard JH, Williams AR. Decreased risk of fractures of the hip and lower forearm with postmenopausal use of estrogen. N Eng. J Med. 303: 1195-8, 1980.

170. Ettinger B, Genant HK, Cann CE. Long-term estrogen replacement therapy prevents bone loss and fractures. Ann Intern Med 102:310-24, 1985.

171. Lindsay R, Tohme JF. Estrogen treatment of patients with established postmenoapusal osteoporosis. Obstet Gynecol 76:290-5, 1990.

172. Lufkin EG, Wahner HW, O'Fallon WM, et al. Treatment of postmenopausal osteoporosis with transdernmalestrogen. AnnInternMed 117:1-9, 1992.

173. Field CS, Ory SJ, Wahner HW, Hermann RR, Judd HL, Riggs BL. Preventive effects of transderrnnal 17 beta-estradiol on osteoporotic changes after surgical menopause: a twoyear placebo-controlled trial. Am J Obsteet Gynecol 168(1 pt 1): 114-21, 1993.

174. Lufkin EG, Riggs BL. Three-year follow-up on effects of transdermal estrogen [letter]. Ann Intern Med 125(1):77, 1996.

175. Williams JK, Adams MR, Klopfenstein HAS. Estrogen modulates responses of atheosclerotic coronary arteries, Circulation 81:1680-7, 1990.

176. Felson DT, Zhang Y, Hanna MT, Kiel DP, et al. The effects of postmenopausal estrogen therapy on bone density in elderly women. N Eng J Med 329(16): 1141-1146, 1993.

178. Colditz GA, Egan KM, and Stampfer MJ. Hormone replacement therapy and risk of breast cancer: Results of epidemiologic studies. Am J Obstet Gynec. 168: 1473-1480, 1993.

179. Lindsay R, Hart DM, And Clark DM. The minimum effective dose of estrogen for prevention of postmenpausal bone loss. Obstet Gynecol 63:759-763, 1984.

180. Oursler MJ, Kassem M, Turner R, Riggs BL, Spelsberg TC. Regulation of bone cell function by gonadal steroids, in Osteoporosis (Marcus R, Feldman D, Kelsey J, Ed.), pp. 237-260. Academic Press, 1995.

181. Cauley JA, Seeley DG, Ensrud K, Ettinger B, et al. Estrogen replacement therapy and fractures in older women. Study of Osteoporotic Fracture Research Group. Ann Intern Med 122(1):9-16, 1995. Dawson-Hughes B. The Role of Calcium in the Treatment of Osteoporosis, in Osteoporosis (Marcus R, Feldman D, Kelsey J, Ed), pp. 1159-1168. Academic Press, 1995.

183. Dawson-Hughes B, Dallal GE, Krall EA, et al. A placebo-controlled trial of calcium supplementation in postmenopausal women. N Eng J Med 323 :878-883,1990.

184. Elders PJ, Netelenbos JC, Lips P, et al. Calcium supplementation reduces vertebral bone loss in perimenopausal women: A controlled trial in 248 women between 46 and 55 years of age. J Clin Endocrinol Metab 73:533-540, 1991.

185. Aloia JF, Vaswani JK, Yeh PL, et al. Calcium supplementation with or without hormone

replacement therapy to prevent posstmenopausal bone loss. Ann Intern Med 120:97-103, 1994.

186. Recker RR, Kimmel DB, Hinders S, and Daviies M. Antifracture efficacy of calcium in elderly women. J Bone Miner Res 9(sl): 135, 1994 [Abstract].

187. Optimal Calcium Intake, NIH Consensus Development Panel on optimal calcium intake. JAMA272:1942-1948, 1994.

188. National Research Council Subcommittee on the Tenth Edition of the RDAs, 10~ rev. ed., Food and Nutrition Board, Commission of life Sciences, National Research Council. National Academy Press, Washington DC, 1989.

189. Feldman D, Malloy PJ, and Gross Coleman. Vitamin D: Metabolism and Action, in Osteoporosis (MarcusR, Feldman D, Kelssey J, Ed.),pp. 205-235. Academic Press, 1995.

190. Chapuy MC, Arlot ME, Duboeuf F, et al. Vitamin D3 and calcium to prevent hip fractures in the elderly women. N Eng J Med 327(23): 1637-42,1992.

191. Chapuy MC, Chapuy P, Thomas JL, et al. Biochemical effects of calcium and vitamin D supplementation in elderly, institutionalized, vitamin D-deficient patients. Rev Rheum Eng Ed 63(2): 135-40, 1996.

192. Aloia JF, Vasawani A, Yeh JK, et al. Calcitriol in the treatment of postmenopausal osteoporosis. Am J Med 84:01-408, 1988.

193. Gallagher JC, Riggs BL. Action of 1,25-dihydroxyvitamin D3 on calcium balance and bone turnover and its effect on vertebral fracture rate. Metabolism 39(Suppl 1):30-34, 1990.

194. Tilyard M. Low-dose calcitriol versus calcium in established postmenopausal osteoporosis. Metabolism 39(4 Suppl 1):50-2, 1990.

195. Tilyard MW, Spears GFS, Thomson J, Dovey S. Treatment of postmenopausal osteoporosis with calcitriol or calcium. N Eng J Med 326:357-62, 1992.

196. Bishop CW, Valliere C, Knutson JC, et al. Oral toxicity of 1 alpha-hydroxyvitamin D2(1 alpha OHD2) in rats. J Bone Miner Res 5: Suppl 2: S196. Abstract, 1990.

197. Meczel J, Foldes J, Steinberg R, et al. Aflacalcidol (alpha D3) and calcium in osteoporosis. Clin Orthop 300:241-7, 1994.

198. Papapoulos SE. Bisphosphonates in Osteoporosis (Marcus R, Feldman D, Kelsey J, Ed.), pp. 1209-1234. Academic Press, 1995.

199. Libernan UA, Weiss S, Broli J, et al. Effects of oral alendronate on bone mineral density and the incidence of fractures in postmenopauasal osteoporosis. N Eng J Med 333: 14371443, 1995.

200. Body JJ. Calcitonin for prevention and treatment of postmenopausal osteoporosis. Clin Rheumatol 14 Suppl 3:18-21, 1995.

201. Lyritis GP, Tsakalakos N, Magiasia B, Karachalios T, et al. Analgesic effect of salmon calcitonin in osteoporotic vertebral fractures: a double-blind placebo-controlled clinical study. Calcif Tissue Int 49:369-72, 1991.

202. Kleerekoper M, and Avioli LV. Evaluation and treatment of postmenopausal osteoporosis. In Primer on the metabolic bone Disease and Disorder of Mineral Metabolism, edited by Favus MJ MJ. Ed.2, pp.223-229, New York, Raven Press, 1993.

203. Reginster JY, Dnis D, Droisy R, et al. Long-term (3years) prevention of trabecular postmenopausal bone loss with low-dose intermittent nasal salmon calcitonin. J Bone and MinRes9:69-72, 1994.

204. Ellerington MC, Hillard TC, Whitcrof SI, et al. Intranasal salmon calcitonin for the prevention and treatment of postmenopausal osteoporosis. Calcif Tissue Int 59(1):6-11, 1996.

205. Boivin G, Dupuis J, and Meunier PJ. Fluoride and osteoporosis. In Osteoporosis: Nutritional Aspects. World Review of Nutrition and Diet, edited by A.P. Simopoulos and C. Gailli. Vol. 73, pp. 80-103. Basel, Switzerland, Karger, 1993.

206. Farley SM, wergedal JB, Farley, Javier GN, et al. Spinal fractures during fluoride therapy for osteoporosis: relationship to spinal bone density. Osteoporosis Internat 2:213-218, 1992.

207. Pak CYC, Sakhaee K, Piziak V, et al. Slow-release sodium fluoride in the management of posmenopausal osteoporosis. Ann Intern Med 120(8):625-623, 1994.

208. CYC, Sakhaee K, Adams-Huet B, et al. Treatment of postmenopausal osteoporosis with slow-release sodium fluoride. Ann Intern Med 123(6):401-408.

209. Riggs BL, Hodgson LJ, III. The prevention and treatment of osteoporosis. New England J Med 327:620-627, 1992.

210. Riggs BL, O'Fallon WM, Lane A, et al. Clinical trial of fluoride therapy in postmenopausal osteoporotic women: extended observations and additional analysis. J Bone Min Res 96:265-275, 1994.

211. Sullivan JM, and Fowlkes LP. The Clinical Aspects of Estrogen and the Cardiovascular system. Obstet Gynecol 87:36S-43 S, 1996.

212. Kuller LH, Meilahn EN, Gutai J, et al. Lipoproteins, oestrogens, and the menopause: biological and

clinical consequences of ovarian failure: evolution and management. Norwell, MA: Serono Symposia USA: 179-97, 1990.

213. Lerner DJ, Kannel B. Patterns of coronary heart disease morbidity and mortality in the sexes: A 26-year follow up of the Framingham population. Am Heart J 111:383 -90, 1986

214. Wild RA. Estrogen: Effects on the Cardiovascular Tree. Obstet & Gynecology. 87(2 suppl):27S-35S, 1996.

215. Sarrel PM. Ovarian hormones and the circulation. Maturitas 12:287-98, 1990.

216. Miller VT, Muesing RA, Laosa JC, et al. Effects of conjugated equine estrogen with and without three different progestogens and lipoproteins, high density lipoprotien subtractions, and apolipoproteins, high density lipoprtein subtractions, and apoprotein A-I. Obstet Gynecol 77:235-40, 1991.

217. Whal PW, Walden CE, Knopp H, Wallace R, Rifkind B. Effect of estrogen/progestin potency on lipid/lipoprotein cholesterol. N Eng J Med 308:862, 1983.

218. Adams MR, Kaplan JR, Manuck SB, et al. Inhibition of coronary artery atheroscleosis by 17-beta estradiol in ovriectomized monkeys. Lack of an effect of added progesterone. Arteriosclerosis 10:1051-7,1990.

219. Keany JF Jr, Shwaery GT, Xu A, et al. 17 beta-Estradiol preserves endothelial vasodilator function and limits low-density lipoprotein oxidation in hypercholesterolemic swine. Circulation 89:2251-9, 1994.

220. Negre-Salvayre A, Pieraggi MT, Mabile L, Salvayre R. Protective effect of 17 betaestradiol against the cytotoxicity of minimally oxidized LDL to cultured bovine aortic endothelial cells. Atheosclerosis 99:207-17, 1993.

221. Sullivan JM, Zwaag RV, Lemp GF, et al. Postmenopausal estrogen use and coronary atherosclerosis. Ann Intern Med 108:358-63, 1988.

222. Losordo DW, Kearney M, Kim EA, Jekanowski J, Isner JM. Variable expression of the estrogen receptor in normal and atherosclerotic coronary arteries of premenopausal women. Circulation 89: 1501-10, 1994.

223. Steinbrecher UP. Role of lipoprotein peroxidation in the pathogenesis of atherosclerosis. Clin Cardiol 14:865-7, 1991.

224. Sarrel PM, Lufkin EG, Oursler MJ, Keefe D. Estrogen actions in arteries, bone, and brain. Sci Am Sci Med 1:44-53, 1994.

225. Schouw YT, Graaf YV, et al. Age at menopause as a risk factor for cardiovascular mortality. Lancet 347.March 16; 347(9003):714-8, 1996.

226. Sullivan JM, Vander Zwag R, Lemp GF, et al. Postmenopausal estrogen use and coronary atherosclerosis. Am Heart J 115:954-63, 1988.

227. Gruchow HW, Anderson AJ, Barboriak JJ, et al. Postmenopausal use of estrogen and occlusion ofcoronaryarteries. Am Heart J 115:954-63, 1988.

228. McFarland KF, Boniface ME, Hornung CA, et al. Effects of estrogen replacement therapy on serum lipid values and angographically defined coronary artery disease in postmenopausal women. Am J Cardiol 69: 176-8, 1992.

229. Hong Mk, Romm PA, Reagan K, et al. Effects of estrogen replacement therapy on serum lipid values and angiogrphically defined coronary artery disease in postmenoppausal women. Am J Cardiol 69: 176-8, 1992.

230. Sullivan JM, Vander Zwaag R, Hughes JP, et al. Estrogen replacement and coronary artery disease-effect on survival in postmenopausal women. Arch Intern Med 150:255762, 1990.

231. Bush TL, Barrett-Conner E, Cowan LD, et al. Cardiovascular mortality and noncontraceptive use of estrogen in women: Results form the Lipid Research Clinics Program Follow-Up Study. Circulation 75: 1102-9, 1987.

232. Adams MR, Kaplan JR, Manuk SB, et al. Inhibition of coronary artery atherosclerosis by 17B estradiol in ovariectomized monkeys: Lack of an effect of added progesterone. Arteriosclerosis 10:1051-7, 1990.

233. Falkenborn M, Persson I, Adami H-O, et al. The risk of acute myocardial infarction after estrogen and estrogen-progestogen replacement. Br J Obstet Gynaecol 99:821-8, 1992.

234. Reginster JY, Christiansen C, Dequinze B, et al. Effect oftransdermal 17 beta-estradiol and oral conjugated equine estrogens on biochemical parameters of bone resorption in natural menopause. Calcif Tissue Int 53(1): 13-6, 1993.

235. Haines CJ, Chug TK, Masarei JR, et al. The effect of percutaneous estrogen replacement therapy on Lp(a) and other lipoproteins. Maturitas 22(3):219-25, 1995.

236. Walsh BW, Li H, Sacks FM. Effects of postmenopausal hormone replacement with oral and transdermal estrogens on high density lipoprotein metabolism. J Lipid Res 35(11):2083-93, 1994.

237. Henderson BE. The cancer question: an overview of recent epidemiological and retrospective data. Am J Obstet Gynecol 161:1859-64, 1989.
238. Whitehead MI, Townsend PT, Pryse-Davies J, et al. Effects of estrogens and progestins on the biochemistry and morphology of the postmenopausal endometrium. N Eng J Med 305: 1599-605, 1981.
239. Voigt LF, Weiss NSc Chu J, Dalling JR, McKnight B, Van Belle G. Progestagens supplementation of exogenous estrogens and risk of endometrial cancer. Lancet 338:274-7, 1991.
240. Key TJA, Pike MC. The role of estrogens and progestagens in the epidemiology and prevention of breast cancer. Eur J Cancer Clin Oncol 24:29-43,1988.
241. Steinberg KK, Thacker SB, Smith SJ, et al. A meta-analysis of the effect of estrogen replacement therapy on the risk of breast cancer. JAMA 265: 1985-90, 1991.
242. ACOG Technical Bulletin. April, pp. 1-7, 1992.
243. Padwick MI, Pryse-Davies J, Whitehead MI. A simple method for determining the optimal dosage of progestin in postmenopausal women receiving estrogens. N Eng J Med 315:930-934, 1986.
244. Whitehead MI, Hillard TC, Crook D. The role and use of progestogens. Obstet Gynecol 75(suppl):59S-76S, 1990.
245. Gibbons WF, Judd HL, Moyer D et al. Evaluation of sequential versus continuous estrogen/progestin replacement therapy on uterine bleeding patterns and endometrial histology. Presented at the 38 th Annual Meeting of the Society of Gynecologic Investigations, March 20-23,1991,Ab 490.
246. Osmers P, Valksen M, Schauer A. Vaginosonography for early detection of endometrial carcinoma . Lancet 355: 1569-1571, 1990.
247. Granberg S, Wikland M, Karlson B, et al. Endometrial thickness as measured by endovaginal ultrasonography for identifying endometrial abnormality. Am J Obstet Gynecol 164:47-52, 1991.
248. Love RR, Mzess RB, Barden HS, et al. Effects of tamoxifen on bone mineral density in postmenopausal women with breast cancer. N Eng J Med 326(13): 852-6, 1992.
249. Love RR, Barden HS, Mazess RB, et al. Effects of tamoxifen on lumbar spine bone mineral density in postmenopasal women after 5 years . Arch Intern Med 154(22):2585-8, 1994.
250. Fentiman CM, Rodin A, Murby A, and Fogelman I. Bone mineral content of women receiving tamoxifen for mastalgia . Br. J Cancer 60:262-264, 1989.
251. Love RR, Wiebe DA, Feyzi JM, Newconb PA, Chappell RJ. Effects of tamoxifen on cardiovascular risk factors in postmenopausal women after 5 years of treatment. J Natl CancerInst86(20):1534-9, 1994.
252. Love RR, Newconmb PA, Wiebe DA, et al. Effects of tamoxifen therapy on lipid and lipoprotein levels in postmenopausal patients with node-negative breast cancer. J Natl CancerInst82(16):1327-32, 1990.
253. Love RR, Newcomb PA, Wiebe DA, et al. Effects of tamoxifen therapy on cardiovascular risk factors in postmenopausal women. Ann Intern Med 115(11): 8604, 1991.
254. Mamby CC, Love RR, Lee KE. Thyroid function test changes with adjutant tamoxifen therapy in postmenopausal women. Breast Cancer, J Clin Oncol 13(4):854-7, 1995.
255. Maamby CC, Love RR, Feyzi JM. Protein S and protein C level changes with adjuvant tamoxifen therapy I postmenopausal women. Breast Cancer Res Treat 30(30):311-4, 1994.
256. Riggs BL. Tibilone as an alternative to estrogen for the prevention of postmenopausal osteoporosis in selected postmenopausal osteoporosis in selected postmenopausal women [editorial]. J Clin Endocrinol Metab. 81(7):2417-8, 1996.
257. Bjarnason NH, Bjarnson K, Haarbo J, Rosenquist C, and Christiansen C. Tibilone: Prevention of bone loss in Late Postmenopausal Women . J Clin Endocrinol Metab 81(7):2419-2422, 1996.
258. Rymer J, Fogelman, Chapman MG. The incidence of vaginal bleeding with tibilone treatment. Br J Obstet Gynaecol 101(1):53-6, 1994.
259. Rymer J, Chapman MG Fogelman I, and Wilson. A study of the effect of tibilone on the vagina in postmenopausal women. Maturitas 18(2):127-23, 1994.
260. Rymer J, Chapman MG, Fogelman I. Effect of tibilone on postmenopausal bone loss. Osteoporos Int 4(6):314-9, 1994.
261. Ginsburg J, Prelevic G, Butler D, Okolo S. Clinical experience with tibilone (Ivial) over 8 years. Maturitas 21(1):71-6, 1995.
262. Milner MH, Sinnott MM, Coole TM, et al. A 2-year study of lipid and lipoprotein changes in postmenopausal women with tibilone and estrogen-progestin. Obstet Gynecol 87(4):593-9, 1996.
263. Rymer J, Crook D, Sidhu M, et al. Effects of tibilone on serum concentrations of lipoprotein (a) in postmenopausal women. Acta Endocrinol (Copenh) 128(3):259-62, 1993.
264. Haenggi W, Riesen W, Birkhaeuser MH. Postmenopausal hormone replacement therapy with

tibilone decreases serum lipoprotein (a). Eur J Clin Biochem 31(10):645-50, 1993.

265. Rhe Writing Group for the PEPI trial. Effects of estrogen or estrogen/progestin regimens on heart disease risk factors in postmenopausal women. JAMA 273: 199-208, 1995.

266. Farish E, Barnes JF, Rolton HA, et al. Effects of tibilone on lipoprotein (a) and HDL subfraction. Maturitas 20(2-3):215-9, 1994.

267. Black LJ, Sato M, Rowley ET< et al. Raloxifene (LY139481 HCL) prevents bone loss and reduces serum cholesterol without causing uterine hypertrophy in ovariectomized rats. J Clin Invest 93:63-69, 1994.

268. Sato M, McClintock C, Kim J, et al. Dual-Energy X-ray absoptiometry of raloxifene effects on the lumbar vertebrae and femora of ovariectomized rats. Journal of Bone an Mineral Research 9(5):715-24, 1994.

269. Draper MW, Flowers DE, Neidle JA, Huster WJ, and Zerbe RL. Antiestrogenic properties of raloxifene. Pharmacology 50(4):209- 17, 1995.

270. Yang NNS, Hardikar JK, and Sato M. Raloxifene, an anti-estrogen stimulates the effects of estrogen on inhibiting bone resorption through regulating TGFB-3 expression in bone. J Bone Miner Res (Suppl):S118, 1993. Glasebrook Al, Phillips DL, and sluka JP. Multiple binding sites for the antiestrogen raloxifene. J bone minerl Rs (Suppl 1):S268, 1993.

272. Glasebrook AL, Phillips DL, and Sluka JP, et al. Estrogen and Raloxifene stimulate transforming growth factor-B3 gene expression in rat bone: A potential mechanisms for estrogen-or raloxifene-mediated bone maintenance. End 137(5):2975-2084, 1996.

273. Yang NN, Venugopalan M, Hardikar S, and Glaibrook A. Identification of an estrogen response element activated by metabolites of 17B-estradiol and raloxifene. Science 273:1222-12225, 1996.

274. McKinlay SM, Mckinlay JB. The impact of menopause and social factors on health, in Hammond CB, Haseltine FP, Shiffl, editors, Menopause: Evaluation, Treatment, and Health Concerns, Alan R, Liss, New York, 1989, ppl37-161.

INFLUENCE OF AGE ON THE STRUCTURE AND FUNCTION IN RESPIRATORY SYSTEM; SPECIAL REFERENCE TO AGED WOMEN

S. TERAMOTO*, T. MATSUSE*, Y. FUKUCHI**, Y. OUCHI*

* Department of Geriatrics, Faculty of Medicine, University of Tokyo, Tokyo, Japan. ** Department of Respiratory Medicine, Juntendo University, Tokyo, Japan. Address all correspondence to: Shinji Teramoto, M.D. Department of Geriatrics, Faculty of Medicine, University of Tokyo, 7-3-1 Hongo Bunkyo-ku, Tokyo, 113, Japan Phone +81-3-5800-8652, Fax +81-3-5689-2483

Abstract : *The function of respiratory system gradually, but consistently declines with age. The loss of lung elastic recoil is a characteristic feature of functional alteration with aging in respiratory system, which is associated with airspace enlargement with aging. Because the respiratory system is directly open to the environment, it is difficult to differentiate the physiologic aging without noxious insult, i.e. "senile lung", and pathologic aging in association with cumulative environmental effects including cigarette smoke and pollutants, i.e. chronic obstructive pulmonary disease (COPD). It is, therefore, important to understand the normal progression of the changes in respiratory function, and the implications of the loss in pulmonary reserve for the elderly person with lung disease. There are significant gender differences in lung function and respiratory muscle strength. Although some respiratory disorders seen frequently in elderly including COPD and sleep apnea syndrome (SAS) are considered to be diseases predominantly of men, the osteoporosis-related thoracic change is severely investigated in aged female rather than aged male, and affect many pulmonary function primarily in woman. The significant influence of age and gender on respiratory system should be carefully considered in elderly patients with pulmonary diseases.*

Key words : *senile lung, physiologic aging, pathologic aging, women, pulmonary function, gender difference, osteoporosis*

INTRODUCTION

Aging is an inevitable process, and characterized by a progressive decline in the functional capacity of organ systems. One of the most prominent declines in function with aging is the respiratory system [1]. Because the healthy respiratory system of a young adult is immensely overdesigned, the respiratory system in an elderly person is still capable of supporting gas exchange at a level. Even so, it is important to understand the normal progression the changes in respiratory function, and the implications of the loss in pulmonary reserve for the elderly person with lung disease [2]. In this article, we described the significant influence of age on respiratory system in special reference to aged women.

I - PHYSIOLOGIC AGING OF RESPIRATORY SYSTEM

Age-related alteration of lungs and chest wall without noxious insults can be determined as the physiologic aging changes in respiratory system. The most notable functional changes in the respiratory system seen in the elderly are the loss of lung elastic recoil [3,4] and the decreased compliance in the chest wall [5]. The former is associated with the age-related morphologic alteration in lungs, i.e., ductectasia and airspace enlargement, whereas the latter is consistent with the increased anteroposterior diameter of the chest owing to rib and vertebral decalcification. The loss of elastic recoil with aging is clinically assessed by a decline in forced expiratory volume in one second (FEV_1) (Figure 1). FEV_1 peaks at around age 25 and declines progressively at a mean rate of 29 ml per year for men and 24 ml per year for women in our Japanese population(Figure 1). The results are consistent with the previous data in caucasian peoples, those non-smoking females show slightly lesser rates of decline than non-smoking males (FEV_1, 19 to 26 ml/year in females; 23 to 32 ml/year in males) [6,7].

The changes in compliance of the chest wall increases the work of breathing. Thus, the contribution of the abdominal muscles and diaphragm to respiration is greater in older subjects. Further, the stiffer thorax seen in elderly persons also affect the ventilatory pattern during exercise.The greater participation of diaphragmatic motion together with rapid shallow breathing at lower graded exercise in the elderly as compared to that in the young [8]

Figure 1
Age-related changes in forced expiratory volume in one-second (FEV1);
Open circles = male subjects (n=120); Closed circles = female subjects
(n=120).

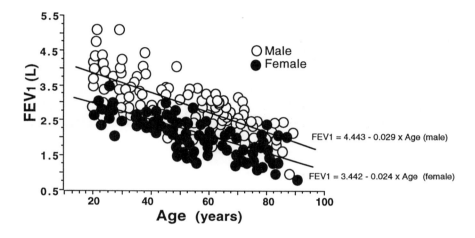

The weakening of respiratory muscles is the other feature of physiologic aging in respiratory system. The strength of diaphragm, which is the most important muscle in the respiratory system, is decreased with aging, and age-related decrease in diaphragm strength may predispose elderly patients to diaphragm fatigue in the presence of conditions that impair inspiratory muscle function or increase ventilatory load [9]. Maximal inspiratory (PImax) and expiratory (PEmax) pressures produced at the mouth are considered to be an acceptable method to evaluate the respiratory muscle strength including diaphragmatic pressure, and decreased with aging [10,11]. Further there is a significant sex difference in static respiratory pressures (Figure 2). The smaller respiratory pressures in aged female than in aged male may be partly explained by the smaller muscle mass in aged women and different constitution of muscles between female and male [12].

Figure 2
Age-related changes in maximal expiratory pressure (PEmax); Open
circles = male subjects (n=120); Closed circles = female subjects (n=120).

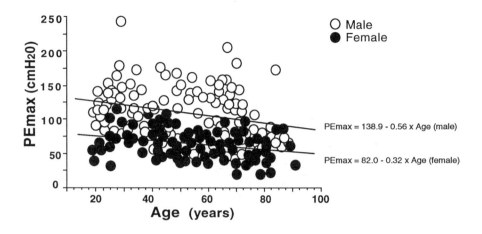

II - SENILE LUNG OR AGING LUNG

Because the airspace enlargement including ductectasia and loss of
elastic recoil of the lung are commonly investigated in aged humans
without noxious insults, Verbeken and coworkers proposed that the
structural and functional characteristics caused by isolated airspace
enlargement seen in elderly as "senile lung", differentiated from
emphysema by the absence of alveolar wall destruction [13,14]. The
ductectasia and airspace enlargement without alveolar wall destruction
was quantitavely assessed by the morphometric indices, e.g. mean linear
intercept and destructive index, while the loss of lung elastic recoil is
assessed by the left-sided shifts of pressure-volume curves of lungs and
by the exponential equivalent K [15].

In an old literature, age-associated alteration in thorax including
hyperkyphosis called as aging lung. Although the changes in thorax
affect the lung function, the hyperkyphosis related thoracic alteration
should be differentiated from "senile lung".

III - POSSIBLE ANIMAL MODEL FOR SENILE LUNG

It is difficult in human lungs to separate the true age effect, i.e., physiologic aging, from the cumulative environmental effects, i.e., the combination of physiologic and pathologic aging, since the human respiratory system is directly open to the environment, continuously exposing the lung to air and pollution. Appropriate animal models are required for the study of the senile lung in relations to physiologic as well as pathologic changes with aging. Recently, senescence-accelerated mouse (SAM) has been proposed as a good model to investigate the differences between senile lung and cigarette smoke-related airspace enlargement [15-19]. The airspace enlargement seen in senescence- prone strain of SAM with aging is not accompanied by the alveolar wall destruction so that SAM is a suitable animal model of senile lung [20]. The airspace enlargement induced by chronic exposure to cigarette smoke is investigated in SAMP strains in association with imbalances of oxidant-antioxidant and elastaseantielastase. The exploration of the differences in the pathogenesis between progressive emphysema and simple airspace enlargement including senile lung may help further our understanding of the significance and pathogenesis of senile lung and senile emphysema.

IV - EFFECT OF OSTEOPOROSIS ON THE FUNCTION OF RESPIRATORY SYSTEM

Osteoporosis is particularly common in elderly females. Osteoporotic fractures increase in number and incidence with age, have a higher incidence in aged women than in men[21,22]. The hyperkyphosis and deformation of the thoracic cage secondary to osteoporosis impair pulmonary function, and in particular the vital capacity in aged woman [23]. The thoracic hyperkyphosis as measured by Cobb's angle is significantly associated with the forced vital capacity (FVC) in woman referred for osteoporosis evaluation. Because the height is considerably affected by the fractures, Leech and coworkers have proposed that arm span should be used for predicting lung function in stead of height [23]. Further, we also found that the thoracic hyperkyphosis as measured by Cobb's angle was significantly associated with the PImax in elderly females (Figure 3). Because the PImax is influenced by the curvature of diaphragm, the hyperkyphosis-related alteration of diaphragmatic shape may reduce the pressure of inspiratory muscles. The understanding of the potential complications of osteoporosis in aged woman may help the argument in favor of active prevention of osteoporosis in adult woman.

Figure 3
The relationship between maximal inspiratory pressure (PImax) and
hyperkyphosis measured as Cobb's angle in female subjects (n=120)

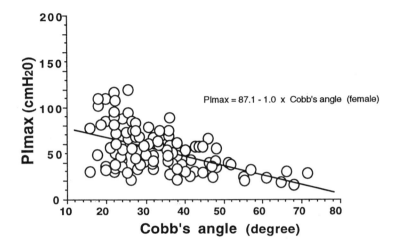

V - EFFECTS OF AGE ON LUNG DEFENCE FUNCTIONS

Aged persons appear to have slowed clearance of particles from the airway probably due to impaired mucociliary function with aging [24]. Significantly elevated numbers of neutrophils and IgG in bronchoalveolar lavage fluid in old normal individuals compared with young normal subjects [25]. In contrast, the antibacterial or phagocytic functions of alveolar macrophages do not appear to be altered in old animals.

Oxidant stress and oxidant injury are implicated in the pathogenesis of age-associated lung disorders inducing pulmonary emphysema. It has been suggested that lung antioxidant capacity decreased in elderly persons [26], and that aged animals may not be maintain pulmonary reducing equivalents as efficiently as adult animals in the face of antioxidant insults [27]. Glutathione (GSH) is the most abundant intracellular antioxidant in mammals, and decreases with aging in lungs and epithelial lining fluid in animals [28,29]. In addition, chronic exposure to cigarette smoke reduces the total GSH and impaired the GSH redox cycle in lungs in aged mice rather than in young mice, suggesting that the effect of cigarette smoke on GSH metabolism was substantially found in aged animals.

The elderly patient with cancer are liable to compromised host due to decrease of immunity with aging [30,31]. Infection is the most serious complications in elderly patients with lung cancer receiving chemotherapy. Although a decrease of oxygen radicals generation by blood following chemotherapy is found both in elderly and adult, the oxygen radical generating activity per leukocyte was not different before and after the therapy in elderly or adult with lung cancer [32].

VI - RESPIRATORY DISEASES

6.1. Chronic obstructive pulmonary disease (COPD)

Pulmonary emphysema increases in frequency with age and is found most frequently in patients in the seventh decade [1, 33]. Although the number of elderly patients diagnosed with chronic obstructive pulmonary disease (COPD) has increased, some of these patients lack the usual history of cigarette use, which suggests the possible role of environmental pollution and passive smoking [34,35].

The COPD is slowly but progressive disease, the main purposes of the treatment for COPD are prevention from the exacerbation of the disease, and production of a significant bronchodilating effect for maintaining lung functions, subsequently achievement a standard level of the quality of life (QOL) [36]. At present, B2-adrenergic agonists are usually the first line bronchodilators for treatment of COPD [37]. Inhaled anticholinergic drugs are also effective for COPD patients, since the pathogenesis of COPD is closely related to the bronchomotor tone, which is based on the sympathetic and parasympathetic balance [38,39]. We have reported that the inhaled anticholinergic drug, oxitropium bromide, produces useful improvements in dyspnea and exercise capacity in both elderly and middle-aged patients with COPD [40.41]. The favorable effects last at least one-year period of treatment with anticholinergic inhalation [42,43]. However, many elderly patients with COPD are often untreated in spite of some reversibility of airways obstruction to the drugs. Because the inhaled anticholinergic drug may well be beneficial in these individuals in terms of reducing symptoms and improving the quality of life, the older patients with chronic airflow limitation should be treated by the inhaled drugs.

6.2. Gender differences in aged patients with lung cancer

Lung cancer is increased progressively among aging samples, and the most common cause of death from cancer in the United States (US) and Japan. Because cancer risk is associated with increasing age, the incidence of lung cancer will likely increase as the population ages [44,45]. In US, lung cancer incidence is gradually leaving off in men but is continuing to rise in women. The odds ratios for major lung cancer types have been reported to be higher for women than for men at very level of exposure to cigarette smoke [46]. The gender difference may not be explained by differences in smoking history and body size, and is likely due to the higher susceptibility to tobacco carcinogens in women.

6.3. Gender differences in aged patients with sleep apnea syndrome

Sleep apnea, primarily obstructive sleep apnea syndrome (OSAS), is known to increase with aging, and predominantly a male disorder.However, OSAS is found in middle-aged female subjects more than one would expect, and under-representation of women among patients with diagnosed sleep apnea has been recognized[47,48,49]. For women, snoring is the most sensitive and strongest predictor of sleep apnea [50].

OSAS is frequently found in patients with hypothyroidism. Because hypothyroidism increase with advancing age,the nocturnal disturbed breathing in aged patients with hypothyroidism should be paid attention by geriatricians. However, it has been suggested that the obstructive sleep apnea in hypothyroidism is related to obesity rather than to hypothyroidism per se [51,52]. Although it has been reported that male gender is a factor for increased incidence of OSAS in hypothyroidism [51], male gender may not be a critical factor in aged hypothyroidism in our experience [53].

6.4. Hyperventilation syndrome in aged women

Hyperventilation is an abnormality of respiratory control and is defined as breathing in excess of metabolic requirements, i.e.CO_2 production[54]. Woman are believed to be more vulnerable to symptomatic hyperventilation. In young women, the effect of progesterone that reduce $PaCO_2$ by up to 8 mmHg in the second half of the menstrual cycle, is implicated in the cause of premenstrually hyperventilation [55]. However, hyperventilation in elderly persons is rarely recognized. We have experienced that a 92-year-old woman showing the excitation, howling, and the numb of hands [56]. Arterial blood gas analysis revealed a marked alkalemia and hypocapnia.

Paper bag re-breathing is effective for relieving the symptom. Because there was no lesion in the lungs or the brain that would account for hyperventilation and convulsions, the attack was considered to be a manifestation of hyperventilation syndrome.The case suggests that hyperventilation syndrome can be found in older persons, and should be considered in the differential diagnosis of disturbance of consciousness even in elderly patients.

Acknowledgements : This study was aided by grants from the smoking research foundation of Japan and Sumitomo marine welfare foundation (Japan).

REFERENCES

1. Thurlbeck WM . Chronic airflow obstruction. In: Pathology of the lung. Edited by Thurlbeck WM and Churg AM. New York: Thieme Medical Publishers, Inc.; p780-825, 1995
2. Gail DB, Lenfant C. The ageing respiratory system. In: . Edited by and. New York: Thieme Medical Publishers, Inc.; p337-348, 1995
3. Turner JM, Mead J, Wohl ME. Elasticity of human lungs in relation to age. J Appl Physiol 25: 664-671, 1968.
4. Knudson RJ, Clark DF, Kennedy TC, Knudson DF Effect of aging alone on mechanical properties of the normal adult human lung. J Appl Physiol 43:1054-1062, 1977.
5. Mittman C, Edelman NH, Norris AH, Schock NW. Relationship between chest wall and pulmonary compliance and age. J Appl Physiol 20:1211-1216,1965.
6. Ware JH, longitudinal and cross-sectional estimates of pulmonary function decline in never-smoking adults. Am J Epidemiol 132:685,1990
7. Crapo RO,: Reference spirometric values using techniques and equipment that meet ATS recommendations. Am Rev Respir Dis 123:659,1981
8. Teramoto S, Fukuchi Y, Nagase T, Matsuse T, Orimo H. A comparison of ventilation components between young and elderly men during exercise. J Gerontol (Biol Sci) 50:B34-B39,1995
9. Tolep K, Higgins N, Muza S, Criner G, Kelsen S. Comparison of diaphragm strength between healthy adult elderly and young men. Am J Respir Crit Care Med 152:677-682,1995
10. Enright PL, Kronmal RA, Manolio TA, Schenker MB, Hyatt RE. Respiratory muscle strength in the elderly: correlates and reference values. Am J Respir Crit Care Med 1994; 149:430-438, 1994.
11. Chen H-I, Kuo C-S. Relationship between respiratory muscle function and age, sex, and other factors. J Appl Physiol 66:943-948,1989.
12. Suzuki M, Teramoto S, Ogawa K, et al. Age-related changes in static maximal inspiratory and expiratory pressures Jpn J Thorac Dis 1997(in press)
13. Verbeken EK, Cauberghs M, Mertens I, Clement J, Lauweryns JM, Van de Woestijne KP . The senile lung: comparison with normal and emphysematous lungs:1.structural aspects. Chest 101:793-799,1992.
14. Verbeken EK, Cauberghs M, Mertens I, Clement J, Lauweryns JM., Van de Woestijne KP . The senile lung: comparison with normal and emphysematous lungs: 2.functional aspects. Chest 101:800-809,1992.
15. Teramoto S, Fukuchi Y, Uejima Y, Teramoto K, Oka T, Orimo H: A novel model of senile lung: senescence-accelerated mouse (SAM). Am J Respir Crit Care Med 150:234-244,1994.
16. Teramoto S, Fukuchi Y, Uejima Y, Teramoto K, Orimo H: Biochemical characteristics of senescenceaccelerated mouse (SAM). Eur Respir J 8:450-456,1995.
17. Uejima Y, Fukuchi Y, Nagase T, Mastuse T, Yamaoka M, Tabata R, Orimo H: Influences of inhaled tobacco smoke on senescence accelerated mouse (SAM). Eur Respir J 3:1029-1036,1990.
18. Uejima Y, Fukuchi Y, Nagase T, Tabata R, Orimo H: A new murine model of aging lung: the senescence accelerated mouse (SAM)-P. Mech Ageing Dev 61:223-236,1991.
19. Teramoto S, Uejima Y, Oka T, Teramoto K, Mastuse T, Ouchi Y, Fukuchi Y. Effects of chronic

cigarette smoke inhalation on the development of senile lung in senescence-accelerated mouse. Res Exp Med: 197:1-11, 1997.

20. Teramoto S, Fukuchi Y. The model of senile lung characterized by hyperinflation without alveolar wall destruction: senescence-accelerated mouse (SAM) [letter] . Am J Respir Crit Care Med 156:-,1997 (in press)

21. Cummings SR, Kelsey JL, Nevitt MC, O'Dowd KJ. Epidemiology of osteoporosis and osteoporotic fractures. Epidemiol Rev 7:178-208,1985

22. Riggs BL, Melton LI 3d. The prevention and treatment of osteoporosis. N Engl J Med 327;620-627,1992

23. Leech JA, Ghezzo H, Stevens D, Becklake MR. Respiratory pressures and function in young adults. Am Rev Respir Dis 1983;128:17-23.

24. Krumpke PE, Knudson RJ, Parsons G, Reiser K. The aging respiratory system. Clinics in Geriatric Medicine 1:143-175,1985

25. Thompson AB, Scholer SG, Daughton DM, Potter JF, Rennard SI. Altered epithelial lining fluid parameters in old normal individuals. J Grontol (Med. Sci.) 47:M171-M176,1992.

26. Kondo T, Tagami S, Yoshioka A, Nishimura M, Kawakami Y. Current smoking of elderly men reduces antioxidants in alveolar macrophages. Am J Respir Crit Care Med 149:178-182,1994.

27. Montgomery MR, Raska-Emery P, Balis JU. Age-related difference in pulmonary response to ozone. Biochem Biophys Acta 890:271-274,1987

28. Teramoto S, Fukuchi Y, Uejima Y, Teramoto K, Ito H, Orimo H. Age-related changes in antioxidant screen of distal lung in mice. Lung 172:223-230,1994.

29. Teramoto S, Uejima Y, Teramoto K, Ouchi Y, Fukuchi Y,. Effect of age on alteration of glutathione metabolism following chronic cigarette smoke inhalation in mice. Lung 174: 119-126, 1996.

30. Schwab R, Walters C, Weksler M. Host defense mechanisms against aging. Semin Oncol 10:20-27,1988.

31. Emmerling P, Hof H, Finger H. Age-related defense against infection with intracellularp athogens. Gerontology 25:327-335,1979.

32. Teramoto S, Fukuchi Y, Chu C-Y, Orimo H. Influences of cisplatin combination chemotherapy on oxygen radical generation by blood in elderly and adult patients with lung cancer. Chemotherapy 41:222-228,1995.

33. Teramoto S, Fukuchi Y. Bullous emphysema. Curr Opin Pulmo Med 2: 90-96, 1996.

34. Chretien J. Pollution (atmospheric, domestic, and occupational) as a risk factor for chronic airways disease. Chest 96 (suppl): S316-S317,1989.

35. Kalandidi A, Trichopoulos D, Hatzakis A, et al. Passive smoking and chronic obstructive lung disease. Lancet ii: 1325-1326,1987.

36. Mahler DA . Chronic obstructive pulmonary disease. In: Mahler DA, editor. Pulmonary disease in the elderly patient. New York: Marcel-Dekker,Inc.,1993,pp 159-188.

37. Kesten S, Chapman KR. Physician perceptions and management of COPD. Chest 104:254-258,1993.

38. Gross NJ. Ipratropium bromide. N Engl J Med 319: 421-425,1988.

39. Gross NJ, Skorodin MS. Role of the parasympathetic system in airway obstruction due to emphysema. N Engl J Med 311: 421-425,1984.

40. Teramoto S, Fukuchi Y, Orimo H. Effects of anticholinergic drug on dyspnea and gas exchange during exercise in chronic obstructive pulmonary disease (COPD). Chest 103:1774-1782,1993

41. Teramoto S, Fukuchi Y. Improvements in exercise capacity and dyspnea by inhaled anticholinergic drug in elderly patients with chronic obstructive pulmonary disease (COPD). Age Ageing 24: 278 - 282,1995

42. Teramoto S, Matsuse T, Sudo E, Ohga E, Katayama H, Suzuki M, Ouchi Y, Fukuchi Y. Long-term effects of inhaled anticholinergic drug on lung function, dyspnea, and exercise capacity in patients with chronic obstructive pulmonary disease. Intern Med 35: 772-778, 1996.

43. Teramoto S, Matsuse T, Ouchi Y, Fukuchi Y. Influence of one-year treatment period on responses to anticholinergic inhalation in patients with chronic obstructive pulmonary disease. Curr Ther Res :-58:78-87, 1997.

44. Yancik R, Ries LG: Cancer in the aged. Cancer 68:2502-2510,1991.

45. Holms R, Hearne E: Cancer stage-to age relationship: implications for cancer screening in the elderly. J Am Gerit Soc 29:1009-1014,1981.

46. Zang EA, Wynder EL. Differences in lung cancer risk between men and women: examination of the evidence. J Natl Cancer Inst 88:183-192,1996

47. Young T, Palta M, Dempsey J, Skatrud J, Webber S, Badr S. The occurrence of sleep-disordered breathing among middle-aged adults. N Engl J Med 328:1230-351,1993.

48. Redline S, Kump K, Tishler PV, Browner I, Ferrette V. Gender differences in sleep disordered breathing in a community- based sample. Am J Respir Crit Care Med 149: 722-726,1994.

49. Guilleminault C, Stoohs R, Young-do K, chervin R, Black J, Clerk A. Upper airway sleep disordered

breathing in women. Ann Intern Med 122: 493-501, 1995.

50. Young T, Hutton R, Finn L, Badr S, Palta M. The gender bias in sleep apnea diagnosis: are women missed because they have different symptoms? Arch Intern Med 156: 2445-2451,1996.

51. Pelttari L, Rauhala E, Polo O, Hyyppfi T, Kronholm E, Viikari J, Kantola I. Upper airway obstruction in hypothyroidism. J Intern Med 236:177-181,1994.

52. Lin C-C, Tsan K-W, Chen P-J. The relationship between sleep apnea syndrome and hypothyroidism. Chest 102:1663-1667,1992.

53. Teramoto S, Nagase T, Fukuchi Y. Nocturnal upper airway obstruction in hypothyroidism [letter]. J Intern Med 238: 473474,1995.

54. Gardner WN. The pathophysiology of hyperventilation disorders. Chest 109:516-534,1996

55. Damas-Mora J, Davies L, taylor W, et al. Menstrual respiratory chnages and symptoms. Br J Psychiatry 136:492-497,1980

56. Teramoto S, Sugai M, Saito E, Matsuse T,Eto M,Toba K, Ouchi Y. Hyperventilation syndrome in a very old woman. Jpn J Geriat 34: 226-229, 1997.

THE PROS AND CONS OF HORMONE REPLACEMENT THERAPY IN THE FEMALE: A PRACTICAL GUIDE FOR EVALUATING CLINICAL NEEDS

C. A. CEFALU *, M. L. MARZIANO**

* Director of Geriatrics and Associate Professor, Department of Family Medicine, Georgetown University School of Medicine, 3800 Reservoir Road NW, Washington, DC 20007. ** Instructor of Family Medicine and Geriatric Medicine Fellow, Department of Family Medicine, Georgetown University School of Medicine, 3800 Reservoir Road, Washington, DC 20007

Abstract : *Hormone replacement therapy is a complex issue for the primary care physician. Estrogens have been shown to be beneficial in preventing osteoporosis and coronary artery disease. Estrogens and progesterones have been shown to have beneficial and deleterious effects on the female. This article summarizes the positive and negative effects of hormone replacement therapy (HRT). A decision to use HRT should be based on four major factors: 1) the patient's age; 2) presence or absence of an intact uterus and ovaries; 3) the presence or absence of osteoporosis risk factors; 4) the presence or absence or cardiovascular risk factors. As important are adequate allotment of time for evaluation and education of the patient for informed decision making and appropriate documentation in the medical record.*

Key Words : *Estrogen, Progesterone, Female, Osteoporosis, Atherosclerosis*

INTRODUCTION

The clinical decision of whether or not to use hormone replacement therapy (HRT) for women is a complex issue for the practicing primary care physician. This is complicated by the recent, constantly changing, and controversial literature on the subject, often conflicting views of various specialists in the field, and the tremendous amount of publicity bombarding women in periodicals, newspapers, television, and radio.

The busy physician often finds himself in a difficult and frustrating situation trying to answer this question for the women who just happens to ask the question in the course of a routine office visit. There is obviously no straightforward right or wrong answer, while the appropriate answer for a particular woman is dependent on a host of general factors relating to age of the patient, length of time without estrogen replacement, family history, historical events, physical findings, laboratory and possible radiological evidence.

In order to make such a decision, a thorough knowledge of benefits and adverse effects of estrogen and progesterone and relative or absolute contraindications to their use are essential.

I - CASE PRESENTATION

A 51 year old Caucasian female asks whether she should be placed on hormone replacement therapy. Her last menstrual cycle was 3 months ago. She complains of daily hot flashes and vaginal dryness. She is concerned about estrogen because her aunt developed breast cancer at the age of 68 years. Her father developed heart disease at around the age of 55. The patient has hypertension. She still has her uterus. She is a smoker and drinks 1 glass of wine per day. Her breast examination reveals no evidence of masses or adenopathy. Her pelvic examination reveals a uterus that is normal in size and no adnexal masses palpable.

1.1. Positive and Negative Effects of Estrogen and Progesterone

The use of estrogens in females has been shown to prevent osteoporosis at all cortical and trabecular bone sites [1]. The use of supplemental calcium is also recommended [2]. It is thought that progesterone may actually have a beneficial effect on osteoporosis as well [3,4]. Estrogen has been shown to be a powerful agent useful for the reduction of total cholesterol, while lowering the (low density) LDL cholesterol, and raising the (high density) HDL cholesterol level [5,6].

However, long-term unopposed estrogen use carries a risk of development of uterine adenocarcinoma [7]. In one study, investigators analyzed all cases of adenocarcinoma in consecutive women taking long-term unopposed estrogens with intact uteri. The adenocarcinomas that developed in such women were well differentiated and slow growing and were not significantly related to increased mortality [8]. To nullify this increased risk of uterine cancer, studies show that adding progesterone either sequentially or in combination reduces significantly the chances of development of uterine cancer, but also reduces substantially the positive effects of the estrogen on the cholesterol profile, depending on the progesterone used [3,9]. The data is conflicting as to whether adding progestin reduces the positive effects of estrogen on the cholesterol profile. The Postmenopausal Estrogen/Progestin Interventions (PEPI) Trial showed that women treated with estrogen with micronized progesterone or estrogen with medroxyprogesterone had a higher HDL level then placebo [10]. Recently, investigators have shown that the addition of progestin does not decrease the protective effects of estrogen therapy [11].

For postmenopausal women with coronary artery disease and angina, estrogen therapy given sublingual estradiol 17^B has been shown to decrease the frequency of chest pain and ST segment depression on electrocardiogram [12]. Other positive cardiovascular effects of estrogen include a reduced risk for myocardial infarction, [13] less intimal thickening of the carotid arteries as determined by carotid ultrasound, [14] and reduction of stroke risk in postmenopausal women [15]. Other positive effects of estrogen therapy on postmenopausal women include improved quality of life, [16] reduction of the frequency of urinary tract infections in these women with atrophic vaginitis, [17] and reduces the risk of osteoarthritis of the hip in elderly Caucasian females [18].

Controversy exists as to whether estrogen replacement therapy increases the risk of breast cancer. In June 1995, the Nurses' Health Study, a prospective cohort, reported an increased risk of invasive breast cancer in postmenopausal women who were taking estrogen alone or estrogen and progesterone. Women who had a significant risk were women over the age of 55 years and who used hormone replacement therapy for 5 years or more [19]. At approximately the same time, another population-based case-control study did not show an "increased risk of breast cancer in middle-aged women" who used estrogen with progesterone [20].

A promising benefit of estrogen replacement is the potential for reduced incidence of Alzheimer's Disease. Paganini-Hill and Henderson using a case-control design nested in a population-based prospective cohort study showed that the risk of Alzheimer's Disease was less in women who used estrogen [21]. In addition, Robinson et al showed that estrogen improved recall of proper names [22]. A recent cross-sectional study also showed enhanced cognitive functioning and decreased rate of ischemic brain damage in postmenopausal women who used estrogen replacement [23].

1.2. Contraindications

Absolute contraindications to the use of estrogen include a family history of "suspected breast cancer", active venous thrombosis, and undiagnosed vaginal bleeding [24,25]. It is controversial as to whether a history of breast cancer or endometrial cancer is an absolute contraindication to estrogen replacement therapy [25]. Estrogens should be used with caution in patients with congestive heart failure, hypertension, migraine headache, previous myocardial infarction, angina, stroke, or chronic renal failure due to their tendency to cause fluid retention especially in big doses [24]. Side effects of estrogen include development of gall stones, abnormal glucose tolerance test, headache, nausea, breast swelling and tenderness, elevated triglyceride level, fluid retention, and edema [24] (Table I).

Table 1
Positive and Negative Effects of Estrogen and Progesterone

ESTROGEN

+++++++++++++	----------------
1. Prevent Osteoporosis and Hip Fracture	1. Breast Tenderness Or Swelling
2. Decreased Cardiovascular Morbidity and Mortality	2. Elevated Blood Pressure
3. Decreased Total Cholesterol, and LDL Cholesterol, Increased HDL Cholesterol	3. Uterine Adenocarcinoma
4. Increased Quality of Life	4. Migraine Headache
5. Improved Memory Recall in Older Women	5. Edema

6. Reduced Frequency of Urinary Tract Infection in Older Women With Atrophic Vaginitis

6. Elevated Glucose Tolerance

7. Elevated Triglyceride Level
8. Contraindicated In "Suspected" Breast Cancer or Undiagnosed Vaginal Bleeding

PROGESTERONE

++++++++++++++++

----

1. Nullifies Risk Of Uterine Adenocarcinoma In Women With Intact Uteri

1. Nullifies Partially The Positive Effects Of Estrogen On The Lipid Profile

1.3. Current Guidelines for Therapy

Guidelines for use of hormone replacement therapy in women vary depending on the presence or absence of a uterus and the preference of the patient and prescribing physician. Patients taking unopposed estrogens with an intact uterus should have a baseline endometrial biopsy [26]. If uterine bleeding occurs and no recent evaluation has been done, endometrial evaluation should be performed. If bleeding does not occur, screening endometrial evaluation should be done probably as often as every year even though the optimal interval for screening has not been established [26]. Women may choose to take a cyclic estrogen plus progestin regimen or both continuously. For these two options, baseline or routine endometrial evaluation is not required because the risk of endometrial cancer is not increased with the addition of the progesterone component [26]. The most practical and hassle-free option for older women involves taking a combination estrogen and progesterone regimen. In such cases, 30-50% of women will develop erratic endometrial bleeding during the first 3-6 months of therapy. These women should report any bleeding and an endometrial evaluation performed if bleeding is prolonged (more than 10 days) or heavy (heavier than the woman's normal menses). For all women using hormone replacement therapy, a yearly clinical breast examination and mammogram should be performed [26]. Older females taking estrogen should be advised that regular periods are to be expected while using hormone replacement therapy. Many older women, for this reason, often decide not to take them [22,26].

1.4. Factors To Consider When Recommending HRT

Recommendations regarding the use of HRT then depend on four main factors. The first includes the presence or absence of an intact uterus and ovaries. The presence of an intact uterus necessitates more caution and monitoring in the use of estrogens with the subsequent need for progesterone as discussed previously. However, a female with an intact uterus and ovaries may be at less risk for the development of osteoporosis depending on age and the presence of symptoms of hormone deficiency such as hot flashes, sweating, insomnia, anxiety and depressive symptoms, weight loss, and anorexia.

The second factor involves the age of the patient (pre-, peri-menopausal, or geriatric age group). The current thinking regarding the development of osteoporosis relates to the amount of time in years that the patient has been without the benefit of estrogens, either through the use of supplemental estrogens for the hysterectomized and oophorectomized patient, or naturally for the women with an intact uterus and ovaries. Often the question arises as to how long an elderly postmenopausal woman should take estrogens in order to continue having an effect on prevention of osteoporosis. Though specifics are undetermined, the longer the time from the menopause to the introduction of hormone replacement therapy, the lesser the window of opportunity and thus the lesser effect on preventing osteoporosis [27]. A woman who has had a hysterectomy and oophorectomy at or around middle age may be at increased risk for premature primary osteoporosis as opposed to an older female in which in the risk may be the same or greater but the "window of opportunity" is reduced [27]. A recent study of 69 long-term users of estrogen (greater then 7 years) showed that long-term protective effect was most apparent in those less than 75 years of age, not significant in those over 75 years of age and less evident in smokers [28].

The third factor involves the presence or absence of osteoporosis risk factors [29]. Since the diagnosis of osteoporosis is a diagnosis of exclusion, medical causes of secondary osteoporosis should be ruled out, especially when it presents prematurely [30]. (Table II) Major risk factors are listed in Table III [27]. However, a recent study contradicts current thinking regarding chronic alcohol use as a risk factor for osteoporosis [31]. The fourth factor involves the presence or absence of a family history or history of cardiovascular risk factors, the lipid profile of the patient, and quality of life issues [9]. (Table III)

Table II

Causes and Laboratory Workup for Secondary Osteoporosis

Secondary Causes	Laboratory Workup
1. Hyperparathyroidism	1. Serum & Ionized Calcium
2. Thyrotoxicosis	2. Parathormone Level
3. Excess Exogenous Thyroid Administration	3. Phosphorus Level
4. Diabetes Mellitus	4. Protein Electrophoresis
5. Endogenous or Exogenous Glucocorticoid Excess Administration	5. Cortisol Level
6. Hyperprolactinemia	6. Complete Blood Count
7. Hypogonadism	7. Vitamin D Level
8. Multiple Myeloma	8. Urinary Hydroxyproline Level
9. Leukemia or Lymphoma	
10. Immobilization	
11. Medication glucocorticoid heparin thyroid medications anticonvulsants antacid use (phosphate binding) phenothiazines	

Table III

Risk Factor Assessment for Hormone Replacement Therapy

Osteoporosis Risk Factors	Cardiovascular Risk Factors
1. Family History	1. Family History
2. Sedentary Activity	2. Sedentary Activity
3. Early Menopause	3. Previous Stroke
4. Tall Statue	4. Previous Myocardial Infarction
5. White or Oriental Race	5. History of Congestive Heart Failure
6. Low Body Weight	6. Diabetes Mellitus
7. History of Smoking	7. Peripheral Vascular Disease
8. Regular Ethanol Use	8. Obesity
9. Decreased Calcium and Vitamin D Intake	9. Hypertension
10. Excessive Protein and Phosphorus Intake	

A laboratory work-up may be necessary to rule out secondary causes of osteoporosis [9] (Table II). Routine radiographs often do not show evidence of thinning of bone or osteoporosis until late in the disease. However, in questionable cases, a bone densitometry may be beneficial in screening high risk women, [9] but is of limited or no value in following the short term progression of the disease.

1.5. Treatment

The recommended calcium dose for the post-menopausal woman who is not on hormone replacement therapy is 1500 mg per day and for the woman taking replacement a minimum of 1000 mg per day is recommended [25]. A minimum of "0.625 mg of oral conjugated equine estrogen, 1.0 mg of oral estradiol, or 50-100 ug of transdermal estradiol per day" are necessary to prevent osteoporosis and provide cardiovascular benefits [25]. Smaller doses of estrogen could also be beneficial if combined with extra calcium [32]. For cyclic/combined therapy, the conjugated estrogen or oral estradiol should be given on days 1 through 25 with medroxyprogesterone given 10 to 14 days per month.25 A dose of 2.5 to 5 mg of medroxyprogesterone is usually recommended for cyclic/combined therapy [25]. In addition, a multivitamin with 400 IU of Vitamin D is a practical part of the prophylaxis and therapy for postmenopausal osteoporosis [9]. Commercial sequential and combination hormone replacement therapy preparations are currently available in a convenient instructional package form that makes their use patient friendly.

II - EXPLANATION FOR CASE PRESENTATION

The woman in question is beginning to enter menopause since she has experienced amenorrhea for 3 months. As her physician, you should counsel her that even though her aunt had breast cancer, she would have a higher risk if she had a first degree relative, such as a sister, mother, or daughter with breast cancer. A family history of breast cancer is not an absolute contraindication for hormone replacement therapy. She has 3 risk factors for coronary disease: family history, hypertension, and smoking. She should be educated regarding the cardioprotective effect of estrogen replacement. Also, she needs to be instructed that starting estrogen immediately will reduce bone loss and protect against bone loss. Since she still has a uterus, this patient should be advised that she should take progesterone to protect against endometrial cancer. If she chooses cyclic progesterone, she should be informed that she will have a menstrual cycle. This patient should also be counseled to quit smoking since it is also a risk factor for osteoporosis. Her diet should be evaluated to ensure adequate calcium intake. A yearly mammogram is also recommended.

CONCLUSIONS

Finally, the physician should allow enough time in an office visit for proper evaluation and investigation of the needs for estrogen, an explanation of benefits and risks to the patient, and adequate time for the patient to make an informed decision about treatment. The physician has a responsibility to be fully informed about the risks and benefits of hormone replacement therapy and necessary work-up. He or she must practice good patient communication skills and have provided appropriate documentation of the findings and the patient's decision.

REFERENCES

1. Fogelman L. Viewpoint: Oestrogen, The Prevention Of Bone Loss And Osteoporosis. British Journal Of Rheumatology. 30:276-281. (August), 1991.
2. Reid IR et al. Effect Of Calcium Supplementation On Bone Loss In Postmenopausal Women. N Engl J Med. 18, 328:460-464, Feb. 18, 1993.
3. ERT: Helping Women Decide. An Editorial-Journal Watch. 10, 5:40.
4. Prince RL. Prevention of Post-menopausal Osteoporosis-A Comparative Study Of Exercise, Calcium Supplementation, and Hormone-Replacement Therapy. N Engl J Med. 325:1189-95, October 24, 1991.
5. Stampfer MJ et al. Postmenopausal Estrogen Therapy And Cardiovascular Disease-Ten Year Follow-up From The Nurses's Health Study. N Engl J Med. 325:756-762, Sept 12, 1991.
6. Goldman L & Tosteson ANA: Uncertainty About Postmenopausal Estrogen-Time For Action, Not Debate. N Engl J Med. 325:800-802, Sept. 12, 1991.
7. Voight LF et al. Progesterone Supplementation Of Exogenous Estrogens And Risk Of Endometrial Cancer. Lancet. 338:274-277, Aug, 3, 1991.
8. Disaia PJ, Creasman WT. Andenocarcinoma of the Uterus. Clinical Gynecologic Oncology. St. Louis, Mosby, 1981, p. 128.
9. Hazzard WR, Andres R, Bierman EL & Blass JP. Principles Of GERIATRIC MEDICINE AND GERONTOLOGY, 2nd ed. McGraw-Hill Information Services Company, New York, New York. 1990. p. 782,785,786, 58, 819, 822.
10. The Writing Group for the PEPI Trial. Effects of Estrogen or Estrogen/Progestin Regimens on Heart Disease Risk Factors in Postmenopausal Women: The Postmenopausal Estrogen/Progestin Interventions (PEPI) Trial. JAMA, 273:199-208.
11. Grodstein F et al. Postmenopausal Estrogen and Progestin Use and the Risk of Cardiovascular Disease. N Engl J Med. 1996;335:453-61.
12. Rosano, GMC; et al. Beneficial effect of Oestrogen on Exercise-induced Myocardial Ischaemia In Women With Coronary Artery Disease. Lancet. 342:133-136, July 17, 1993.
13. Psaty BM et al. The Risk of Myocardial Infarction Associated with the Combined Use of Estrogens and Progestins in Postmenopausal Women. Arch Intern Med. 154:1333-1339, June 27, 1994.
14. Manolio TA et al. Associations of Postmenopausal Estrogen Use With Cardiovascular Disease and Its Risk Factors in Older Women. Circulation. 88:2163-2171, November 1993.
15. Finucane FF et al. Decreased Risk of Stroke Among Postmenopausal Hormone Users: Results From A National Cohort. Arch Intern Med. 153:73-79, January 11, 1993.

16. Daly E; et al. Measuring The Impact of Menopausal Symptoms On Quality of Life. BMJ. 307:836-840, October 2, 1993.
17. Raz R; Stamm WE. A Controlled Trial of Intravaginal Estriol in Postmenopausal Women With Recurrent Urinary Tract Infections. N Engl J Med. 329:753-756, September 9, 1993.
18. Nevitt MC et al. Association of Estrogen Replacement Therapy With the Risk of Osteoarthritis of the Hip in Elderly White Women. Arch Intern Med. 156:2073-2080. October 14, 1996.
19. Colditz GA et al. The Use of Estrogens and Progestins and the Risk of Breast Cancer in Postmenopausal Women. N Engl J Med. 1995;332:1589-93.
20. Stanford JL et al. Combined Estrogen and Progestin Hormone Replacement Therapy in Relation to Risk of Breast Cancer in Middle-aged Women. JAMA. 1995;274:137-142.
21. Paganini-Hill A & Henderson VW. Estrogen Deficiency and Risk of Alzheimer's Disease in Women. AM J Epidemiol. 1994;140:256-61.
22. Robinson D. et al. Estrogen Replacement Therapy and Memory in Older Women. J Am Geriatr Soc. 42:919-922, September 1994.
23. Schmidt R et al. Estrogen Replacement Therapy and Memory in Older Women. A Neuropsychological and Brain MRI Study. JAGS. 1996;44:1307-13.
24. Physicians Desk Reference, 47th Edition. Medical Economics Data, 1993. p. 2624.
25. Evans MP, Fleming KC, & Evans FM. Hormone Replacement Therapy: Management of Common Problems. Mayo Clin Proc. 1995;70:800-805.
26. American College of Physicians. Guidelines for Counseling Postmenopausal Women about Preventive Hormone Therapy. Annals of Internal Medicine 117:1038-1041; December 15, 1992.
27. Beck JC. GERIATRIC REVIEW SYLLABUS-A Core Curriculum In Geriatric Medicine. American Geriatrics Society, New York, New York, 1989-1990 ed., p. 108-110.
28. Felson DT et al. The Effect of Postmenopausal Estrogen Therapy on Bone Density In Elderly Women. N Engl J Med. 329:1141-1146, October 14, 1993.
29. Bourguet CC, Hamrick GA & Gilchrist VJ: The Prevalence Of Osteoporosis Risk Factors And Physician Intervention. The Journal Of Family Practice. 32:265-271, March 1991.
30. Luftin EG & Zilkoski M. Diagnosis and Management of Osteoporosis. Am Fam Physician Monograph No. 1, 1996.
31. Holbrook TL & Barrett-Conner E. A Prospective Study Of Alcohol Consumption And Bone Mineral Density. British Medical Journal. 306:1506-1509, June 5, 1993.
32. Bellantoni M. Osteoporosis Prevention and Treatment. Am Fam Physician 1996;54:986-992.

ANALYTIC QUANTIFICATION OF SKIN CHANGES DURING CLIMACTERIC AGING AND HORMONE REPLACEMENT THERAPY

G. E. PIÉRARD *, C. LETAWE *, C. PIÉRARD-FRANCHIMONT *, U. GASPARD**

* Belgian SSTC Research Unit 5596, Department of Dermatopathology, and ** Center of Menopause, University Medical Center of Liège, Belgium. Address : G. Piérard, MD, PhD. Department of Dermatopathology, CHU Sart Tilman, B-4000 Liège, Belgium

Abstract : Skin is increasingly recognized as a hormone-dependent organ. Like other systems in the body, some cutaneous functions deteriorate during the perimenopause. With advancing development of noninvasive biometrological techniques in dermatology, it is possible to precisely characterize some menopause-associated functional decrements. The same techniques bring information to monitor the corrective effect of hormone-replacement therapy. Recent studies show that climacteric aging of the skin is not an inevitable and unavoidable process as previously thought.

Key words : Dermis, Epidermis, Hormone replacement therapy, Hydroxyacid, Menopause, Retinoids, Skin, Stratum corneum.

INTRODUCTION

Cutaneous aging is a complex process which manifests itself as a progressive reduction in maximal function and reserve capacity of the epidermis, dermis and hypodermis [1, 2]. Two major types of cutaneous aging are usually distinguished, namely the chronologic or intrinsic aging which is opposed to photoaging that occurs in habitually sun-exposed skin. There are many striking differences between their clinical expression . In our opinion, such simple classification does not precisely describe the wide diversity of factors influencing cutaneous aging [3]. Seven distinct types of factors should be considered (Table I). In such classification, the cutaneous climacteric aging enters the spectrum of endocrine aging.

Table I
The 7 types of cutaneous aging (from ref 3).

Type	Determinant Factor
Chronologic aging	passage of time
Genetic aging	genetics (premature aging, phototype, ...)
Photoaging	ultraviolet and infrared irradiations
Behavioral aging	diet, tobacco, alcoholic abuse, drug addiction, ...
Catabolic aging	chronic intercurrent debilitating disease (infections, cancers, ...)
Endocrine aging	dysfunction or aging of hormonal systems (ovaries, testes, thyroid, ...)
Gravitational aging	gravitation force

While aging has always been associated with failing health, it is the unprecedented size of the elderly population, a tribute to medical advances, that now compels research to understand the physiological changes related to aging. Recently, hormonal involvement in aging processes of the skin has attracted increased interest. Skin is a hormone-dependent organ, rich in estrogen receptors and associated proteins [4, 5]. The effect of menopause on skin biology and the influence of hormone replacement therapy (HRT) are among the challenges shared by dermatologists and gynecologists. During the climacteric period, the function of the ovaries is reduced to fail at the menopause. Until recently, the effect of such hormonal changes on skin remained largely unsubstantiated despite the importance of the dermatological aspects of aging in that population [3, 6-10].

HRT is aimed at alleviating the effects of estrogen deficiency on target tissues. It has long been known to effectively counteract menopausal symptoms such as flushing, irritability and vaginal dryness, and has long term benefits in the prevention of osteoporosis and cardiovascular disorders. In contrast to these acknowledged effects, the menopause and its specific HRT still leave a great many challenges unresolved for the dermatologist. In particular, they address the issues of HRT effects on the physiological functions of the epidermis and dermis. In that field, dissension and controversy are rife. Glaring discrepancies are present in the current literature.

The influence of menopause on skin and its correction by HRT and specific topical treatments are difficult to objectivate by clinical inspection alone. Several relevant aspects may, however, be rated semiquantitatively. The visual and tactile analysis of skin is a valuable tool in clinical dermatology. However, it lacks sensitivity and reproducibility when comparative evaluations are made over a prolonged period of time. In addition, the external appearance is sometimes misleading compared to the actual changes induced by treatment [11]. Noninvasive objective methods of biometrology are well suited for improving the reliability and preciseness of assessments.

I - TOPICAL TREATMENTS OF CUTANEOUS AGING

During the past decade, several topical formulations designed for correcting signs of photoaging have been launched on the market. The active ingredients, which are unrelated to sex hormones, may also show some effect on climacteric aging. These are the all - trans - retinoic acid (tretinoin) and its prodrugs retinol and retinaldehyde, and the 13 - cis - retinoic acid (isotretinoin) [12-15]. The a-hydroxyacids and a ß-lipohydroxyacid are also available in such indication [15-18].

Topical estrogen therapy has been used experimentally in order to alleviate cutaneous signs thought to relate to the menopause [11, 19, 20]. Discrepant data have been reported. None of these studies have brought unequivocal conclusions. Further controlled trials are therefore warranted before considering estrogen topical treatment as a safe and promising approach to contest cutaneous climacteric aging.

II - MENOPAUSE, HRT AND THE EPIDERMIS

The climacteric changes occurring in the epidermis have been rarely addressed in the literature [7, 9, 10, 21-23]. Hence, convincing beneficial effects of HRT on the epidermis have been lacking for a long time [9, 23]. Recent investigations shed some light on this biological aspect.

The principal purpose of epidermal differentiation is to generate the stratum corneum which is a barrier preventing water to evaporate from the body and exogenous substances to follow the reverse route. It is widely acknowledged that the water-holding capacity of the stratum corneum is correlated to the quality of the barrier function of the epidermis.

In absence of treatment during the perimenopause, there is evidence that the structure of the stratum corneum is somewhat modified, leading to subtle alterations in the skin barrier function [21], and even to climacteric xerosis known to the laity as "dry skin" [7]. As a result, menopausal skin seems to be more sensitive than skin of youngers to some environmental threats [21, 22]. This is particularly evident on skin exposed to sun [7, 21] and to cold weather [22]. By contrast, postmenopausal women apparently react less frequently and more slowly to some chemical irritant challenges than premenopausal women [24].

Noninvasive biometrological methods are available for assessing both the water-holding capacity and the barrier function of the horny layer. The water content of the superficial layers of the epidermis can be monitored in vivo by measuring the electrical capacitance of the stratum corneum. The water flux across the stratum corneum can be also measured by the transepidermal water loss (TEWL). The plastic occlusion stress test (POST) is a more sensitive method used to discriminate subtle functional changes in the water-holding capacity of the skin [25, 26]. The test consists of positioning an occlusive device on the skin surface and sealing it firmly in order to induce an increase in the water content trapped in the stratum corneum. A 24 h - occlusion is convenient to reach saturation in water inside the stratum corneum. When occlusion is removed, values of electrical skin capacitance are increased and the skin-surface water loss (SSWL) is higher than the physiological variable TEWL (Fig. 1). When the excess in water has evaporated, SSWL equals TEWL, and electrical skin capacitance decreases to reach an equilibrium. The rate of desorption of water during POST gives information on the water-holding capacity of the stratum corneum and on the integrity of the cutaneous barrier function.

Previous studies failed to reveal any significant improvement in electrical skin capacitance and TEWL values of the skin after HRT [9, 23, 27]. However, other studies have suggested that HRT was responsible for a trend toward a decrease in "dryness" and responsiveness of skin toward environmental threat [7, 22]. More recently the sensitive POST method showed that transdermal estrogen HRT (Systen TTS®, Janssen - Cilag) was responsible for an improvement in the water-holding capacity of the stratum corneum which might be correlated with a better barrier function of the epidermis [27]. Such finding is presently confirmed on a larger number of subjects receiving oral HRT with conjugated estrogens (Premarin ®, Ayerst) (Figs. 2 and 3).

Fig. 1

Example of the decay in skin surface water loss (SSWL, g/m2/h) after releasing occlusion in the POST test. The evaporation of the free water in the stratum corneum takes place during the first 10 min. Later, the bound-water compartment is interested by evaporation. The lowest values of SSWL correspond to the physiological transepidermal water loss (TEWL).

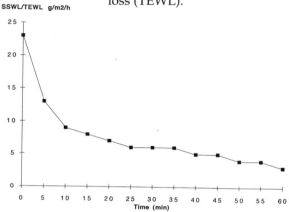

Fig. 2

Effect of HRT on the variation (%) in skin surface water loss (SSWL, g/m2/h) compared to the 60 - min value in the POST test. Average SSWL values in HRT - treated menopausal women (n = 37) show a steeper bound - water decay than in untreated women (n = 37). This indicates a positive effect of HRT on the stratum corneum barrier function.

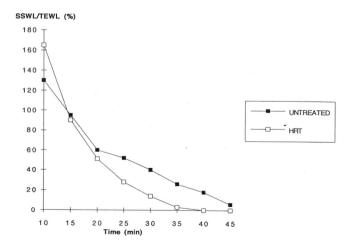

Fig. 3

Effect of HRT on electrical capacitance of skin using POST test. Mean values are higher in HRT - treated women (n = 37) than in untreated women (n = 37), yielding an overall significant increase (+ 7.1 %, $p <$ 0.05) in stratum corneum hydratation.

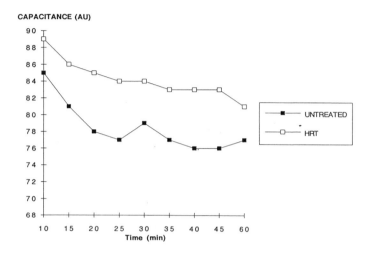

III - MENOPAUSE, HRT AND THE DERMIS

Studies using quantitative laboratory methods have shown a menopause-related reduction in the collagen content of the dermis, and a trend in improvement in this aspect by adequate HRT [6, 28-33]. Nowadays, noninvasive evaluations are made possible using ultrasound measurements of the dermal thickness and computerized analysis of the cutaneous mechanical properties.

Age is an important factor responsible for the biomechanical qualities of skin [34-37]. This aspect is illustrated in Figs 3 and 4. It has also been shown that gender and cyclic variations in female sex hormones may influence these properties [37, 38]. Recent studies attempted at measuring the impact of menopausal hormone deficiency and hormone replenishment in such aspect of cutaneous aging [10, 39, 40]. Increased slackness of skin was the key point which was demonstrated during menopause [39, 40]. This slackness was likely related to the decline in both skin collagen content and skin thickness which occurs following menopause [6, 29, 32]. Another factor responsible for skin slackness could be the elastic fibers which might be altered with estrogen deprivation [7]. Some studies have shown that HRT limits the extent of skin collagen loss in the initial postmenopausal years [30-32, 41, 42] and increases the proportion of type III collagen [33]. However, the possibility of elastic tissue repair during HRT is a matter of controversy [7, 19]. Data collected in our laboratory do not show such improvement. The biomechanical study [39] indicated that HRT using conjugated estrogens (Premarin®, Ayerst) in sequence with medrogestone (Colpro®, Ayerst) slows the progress of deterioration in skin extensibility, while it appears to have less effect upon other age-related viscoelastic changes.

There is evidence that skin collagen content and bone mass are influenced by estrogen deficiency, both of them declining in the years following menopause . A correlation between skin atrophy and osteoporosis is suggested by a few works [43-47], and there is some evidence that biometrological evaluations of skin properties may predict the effect of HRT on osteoporosis prevention [47].

Fig. 4

Biomechanical properties of skin recorded using a Cutometer SM 474®. Typical curve of elevation of skin (E, mm) during a 5-s traction - 5-s relaxation cycle (T, s) under a negative pressure of 500 mbar transmitted through a 4-mm probe. The main variables are the maximum deformation (MD) and the residual deformation (RD). The time - dependant recoil of the skin after deformation is evaluated by the biologic elasticity (BE = 102 (MD - RD) MD-1). Skin laxity related to climacteric aging is characterized by both increased MD and decreased BE.

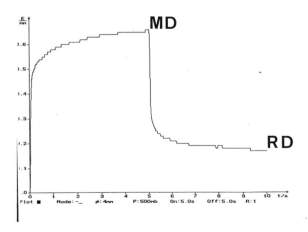

Fig. 5

Trends in biomechanical properties of skin observed in the comparison between HRT - treated and untreated menopausal women. A series of 100 short (0.1 s) successive cycles is applied at the same test site. In these caricatural examples an untreated menopausal woman (a) shows skin laxity (high MD values and small BE) compared to a HRT - treated woman (b). Statistical analysis on large series of subjects confirms the reality of such trend.

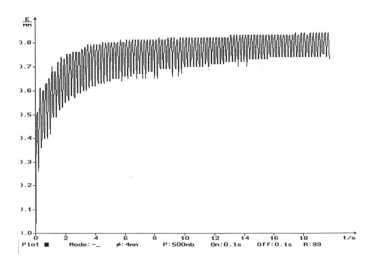

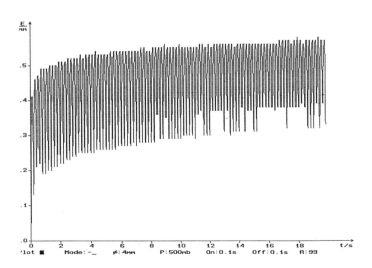

CONCLUSION

There is mounting evidence that menopause affects some functions of the skin. HRT appears to limit some of the climacteric aspects of cutaneous aging. It seems likely that changes that occur in skin with advancing age, particularly during the perimenopause, may be of some prognostic value in monitoring the senescent process not only for that organ, but perhaps for the entire individual as well. With the increasing development of noninvasive bioengineering techniques, the correlation with other consequences of estrogen depletion and replenishment could be pursued as an area for future research.

REFERENCES

1. Lapière Ch M, Piérard GE. The mechanical forces, a neglected factor in the age-related change of the skin. Giorn It Chir Dermatol Oncol 1987; 2: 201-210.
2. Piérard GE, Lapière Ch M. The microanotomical basis of facial frown lines. Arch Dermatol 1989; 125: 1090-1092.
3. Piérard GE. The quandary of climacteric skin ageing. Dermatology 1996; 193: 273-274.
4. Hasselquist MB, Goldberg N, Schroeter A, Spelsberg TC. Isolation and characterization of the estrogen receptor in human skin. Clin Endocrinol Metab 1980; 50: 76-82.
5. Schmidt JB, Lindmaier A, Spona J. Hormone receptors in pubic skin of premenopausal and postmenopausal females. Gynecol Obstet Invest 1990; 30: 97-100.
6. Brincat M, Moniz CF, Studd JWW, Darby AJ, Magos A, Cooper D. Sex hormones and skin collagen content in postmenopausal women. Br Med J 1983; 287: 1337-1338.
7. Bolognia JL, Braverman IM, Rousseau ME, Sarel PM. Skin changes in menopause. Maturitas 1989; 11: 295-304.
8. de Lignières B. Hormones ovariennes et vieillissement cutané. Rev Fr Gynecol Obstet 1991; 86: 451-454.
9. Piérard GE. Ménopause et vieillissement cutané. Rev Med Liège 1994; 49: 199-203.
10. Callens A, Vaillant L, Lecomte P, Berson M, Gall Y, Lorette G. Does hormonal skin aging exist ? A study of the influence of different hormone therapy regimens on the skin of post-menopausal women using non-invasive measurement techniques. Dermatology 1996; 193: 289-294.
11. Creidi P, Faivre B, Agache P, Richard R, Haudiquet V, Sauvanet JP. Effect of a conjugated oestrogen (Premarin®) cream on ageing facial skin. A comparative study with a placebo cream. Maturitas 1994; 19: 211-223.
12. Grove GL, Grove MJ, Leyden JJ, Lufrano L, Schwab B, Perry BH, Thorne EG. Skin replica analysis of photodamaged skin after therapy with tretinoin emollient cream. J Am Acad Dermatol 1991; 25: 231-237.
13. Sendagorta E, Lesiewicz J, Amstrong RB. Topical isotretinoin for photodamaged skin. J Am Acad Dermatol 1992; 27: 515-518.
14. Shukuwa T, Kligman AM, Stoudemayer T. The effect of short - term (one - month) topical tretinoin on photodamaged forearm skin. J Dermatol Treat 1993; 4 : 139-143.
15. Piérard GE, Henry F, Piérard-Franchimont C. Comparative effect of short-term topical tretinoin and glycolic acid on mechanical properties of photodamaged facial skin in HRT - treated menopausal women. Maturitas 1996; 23: 273-277.
16. Lévêque JL, Corcuff P, Gonnord G, Montastier C, Renault B, Bazin R, Piérard GE, Poelman MC. Mechanism of action of a lipophilic derivative of salicylic acid on normal skin. Skin Res Technol 1995; 1: 115-122.
17. Ditre CM, Griffin TD, Murphy GF, Sueki H, Telegan B, Johnson WD, Yu RJ, Van Scott EJ. Effects of a-hydroxy acids on photoaged skin: a pilot clinical, histologic, and ultrastructural study. J Am Acad Dermatol 1996; 34: 187-195.
18. Piérard GE, Nikkels-Tassoudji N, Piérard-Franchimont C, Lévêque JL. Dermo-epidermal stimulation elicited by a b-lipohydroxyacid. A comparison with salicylic acid and all-trans retinoic acid. Dermatology 1997; 194: 398-401.

19. Punnonen R, Vaajalahti P, Tiesala K. Local oestradiol treatment improves the structure of elastic fibers in the skin of postmenopausal women. Ann Chir Gynaecol 1987; 76, S202: 39-41.
20. Schmidt JB, Binder M, Macheiner W, Kainz Ch, Gitsch G, Bigelmayer Ch. Treatment of skin ageing symptoms in perimenopausal females with estrogen compounds. A pilot study. Maturitas 1994; 20: 25-30.
21. Piérard GE, Nikkels-Tassoudji N, Piérard-Franchimont C. Recreational sunbeds and climacteric xerosis. J Eur Acad Dermatol Venereol 1995; 5: 24-27.
22. Paquet F, Piérard-Franchimont C, Fumal I, Goffin V, Paye M, Piérard GE. Sensitive skin at menopause, dew point and electrometric properties of the stratum corneum. Maturitas (in press).
23. Jemec GBE, Serup J. Short-term effects of topical 17 beta-oestradiol on human post-menopausal skin. Maturitas 1989; 11: 229-234.
24. Elsner P, Wilhelm D, Maibach HI. Sodium laurylsulfate - induced irritant contact dermatitis in vulvar and forearm skin of premenopausal and postmenopausel women. J Am Acad Dermatol 1990; 23: 648-652.
25. Osmark K, Wilson D, Maibach H. In vivo transepidermal water loss and epidermal occlusive hydration in newborn infants: anatomical region variation. Acta Dermatol Venereol 1980; 60: 403-407.
26. Berardesca E, Maibach H. Monitoring the water-holding capacity in visually non-irritated skin by plastic occlusion stress test (POST). Clin Exp Dermatol 1990; 15: 107-110.
27. Piérard-Franchimont C, Letawe C, Goffin V, Piérard GE. Skin water-holding capacity and transdermal estrogen therapy for menopause. A pilot study. Maturitas 1995; 22: 151-154.
28. Brincat M, Moniz CJ, Studd JWW, Darby A, Magos A, Emburey G, Versi E. Long-term effects of the menopause and sex hormones on skin thickness. Br J Obstet Gynaecol 1985; 92: 256-259.
29. Punnonen R, Vilska S, Rauramo L. Skinfold thickness and long-term postmenopausal hormone therapy. Maturitas 1984; 5: 259-262.
30. Brincat M, Moniz CF, Kabalan S, Versi E, O'Dowd T, Magos AL, Montgomery J, Studd JWW. Decline in skin collagen content and metacarpal index after the menopause and its prevention with sex hormone replacement. Br J Obstet Gynecol 1987; 94: 126-129.
31. Brincat M, Versi A, Moniz CF, Magos A, de Trafford J, Studd JWW. Skin collagen changes in postmenopausal women receiving different regimens of estrogen therapy. Obstet Gynecol 1987; 70: 123-127.
32. Castelo-Branco C, Duran M, Gonzalez-Merlo J. Skin collagen changes related to age and hormone replacement therapy. Maturitas 1992; 15: 113-119.
33. Savvas M, Bishop J, Laurent G, Watson N, Studd J. Type III collagen content in the skin of postmenopausal women receiving oestradiol and testosterone implants. Br J Obstet Gynaecol 1993; 100: 154-156.
34. Grahame R. A method for measuring human skin elasticity in vivo with observations on the effects of age, sex and pregnancy. Clin Sci 1970; 39 : 223-238.
35. Lévêque JL, Corcuff P, de Rigal J, Agache P. In vivo studies of the evolution of physical properties of the human skin with age. Int J Dermatol 1984; 23: 322-329.
36. Piérard GE. Mechanical properties of aged skin. Indentation and elevation experiments. In : Skin aging : properties and functional changes as measured by non invasive technologies. Ed. J.L Lévêque, P. Agache. New York M. Dekker 1993; 49-56.
37. Piérard GE, Kort R, Letawe C, Olemans C, Piérard-Franchimont C. Biomechanical assessment of photodamage. Derivation of a cutaneous extrinsic ageing score. Skin Res Technol 1995; 1: 17-20.
38. Berardesca E, Gabba P, Farinelli N, Borroni G, Rabbiosi G. Skin extensibility time in women. Changes in relation to sex hormones. Acta Derm Venereol 1989; 69: 431-433.
39. Piérard GE, Letawe C, Dowlati A, Piérard-Franchimont C. Effect of hormonal replacement therapy for menopause on mechanical properties of skin. J Amer Geriatr Soc 1995; 43: 662-665.
40. Henry F, Piérard-Franchimont C, Cauwenbergh G, Piérard GE. Age-related changes in facial skin contours and rheology. J Am Geriatr Soc 1997; 45: 220-222.
41. Punnonen R, Villska S, Rauramo L. Skinfold thickness and long term post-menopausal hormone therapy. Maturitas 1984; 5: 259-262.
42. Maheux R, Naud F, Rioux M, Grenier R, Lemay A, Guy J, Langevin M. A randomized, double-blind, placebo-controlled study on the effect of conjugated oestrogens on skin thickness. Am J Obstet Gynecol 1994; 170: 642-649.
43. Brincat M, Ten Yuen W, Studd JWW, Montgomery J, Magos AL, Savvas M. Response of skin thickness and metacarpal index to estradiol therapy in postmenopausal women. Obstet gynecol 1987; 70 : 538-541.
44. Nilas L, Christiansen C. Rates of bone loss in normal women: evidence of accelerated trabecular bone loss after the menopause. Eur J Clin Invest 1988; 18: 529-534.
45. Chappard D, Alexandre Ch, Robert JM, Riffat G. Relationships between bone and skin atrophies during aging. Acta Anat 1991; 141: 239-244.
46. Castello-Branco C, Pons F, Gratacos E, Fortuny A, Vanrell JA, Gonzalez-Merlo J. Relationship between skin collagen and bone changes during aging. Maturitas 1994; 18: 199-206.
47. Kluge A. Hautdickenmessung mit Ultraschall-Früherkennung eines Osteo-poroserisikos. Exp Gynaecol 1992; 16: 40-42.

OLDER WOMEN'S EXPECTATIONS REGARDING FUTURE SUPPORTIVE HOUSING AND LONG TERM CARE

J. T. ROBISON

Department of Epidemiology and Public Health, Yale School of Medicine and Braceland Center for Mental Health and Aging Institute of Living, Hartford Hospital. Address correspondence to Julie T. Robison, PhD, Braceland Center for Mental Health and Aging, Institute of Living, 400 Washington St., Hartford CT 06106. Research supported by the National Institute on Aging (#IT50 AG11711-01), Karl Pillemer and Phyllis Moen, Co-Principal Investigators; and (#T32-AG00153), research training grant in the Epidemiology of Aging.

Abstract: This study draws on data from the Cornell Retirement and Well-Being project to examine older women's preferences, plans, and expectations about their future housing and long term care arrangements. Due to a higher prevalence of chronic disease, disability, and widowhood, older women face a greater likelihood than their male counterparts to need adjustments in their housing situations later in life. Yet when asked about their expectations regarding eight specific housing options, including aging in place, living in a retirement community, or purchasing long term care insurance, women are overall less likely than men to expect to change their housing. However, examining interactions between gender and other life circumstances shows that older women's housing expectations are quite heterogeneous.

Key Words: housing, long term care, aged women

INTRODUCTION

As the population of older Americans grows, the demand for various levels of supportive housing also increases. The majority of people over age 65 are healthy and living independently in their own homes. However, people over age 80, who are disproportionately women, represent the fastest growing segment of older people and this group faces an increasing likelihood of chronic disease, frailty, and widowhood [1]. Frequently, the need for more supportive housing accompanies such changes. The wide diversity of individual needs and preferences demands a broad range of available types of housing for older adults, including independent living, retirement communities with various services, and informal home sharing, in addition to assisted living and long term care facilities.

Although older women report similar overall subjective health to that reported by men, older women have more functional limitations and subsequently higher needs for assistance [2]. Because women live longer than men, they are significantly more likely to become widows, to live alone, and to need to make alternative arrangements for their own care, either in the form of extended family networks or in a supportive living environment. Previous research has found that older women are more likely to move than their male counterparts, especially in later age ranges [3]. Older women are commonly at a financial disadvantage relative to older men as well. Changes in marital status, such as divorce or widowhood, frequently result in decreased income for women. In addition, women's life courses are typically marked with periodic entrances and exits from the labor market, rather than a continuous career, which are accompanied by smaller or nonexistent retirement benefits [4, 5]. Thus, those women physically capable of maintaining their own independent household may need financial alternatives, such as a reverse mortgage or home sharing, to enable them to age in place.

A life course perspective underlines the importance of the process of development and change over the life span [6]. One key proposition of the life course perspective is its focus on the importance of context, the circumstances shaping perspectives and choices. Decisions are not made in a vacuum; rather, ongoing roles, involvements, and situational factors influence actions and expectations. Older women's plans and expectations about their later life housing arrangements are undoubtedly influenced by their individual circumstances, such as marital status, age, health and commitments to employment, family, and community.

In spite of the innumerable considerations necessary for planning for suitable housing in later life, many people do not make these arrangements until they find that their current housing can no longer support them [6]. Little is known about expectations regarding shifts in housing in later life and how these plans and expectations vary by gender as well as how life events, opportunities, and situational constraints influence such choices. While we have seen that older women face greater pressures to adjust their housing and prepare for long term care needs than do men, the question remains as to whether women just entering later life have different housing expectations than men and whether these expectations are in line with their likely future needs. This study draws on data from the Cornell Retirement and Well-Being Project to examine older women's post-retirement housing and long term care plans, expectations, and preferences.

I - METHODS

Seven hundred fifty-two randomly selected retirees and active workers, ages 50 to 72, from six large organizations (manufacturing firms, utility industries, hospitals, and universities) in upstate New York, were interviewed in 1995 about their plans and activities for the future. These organizations were chosen to represent large corporations and service organizations from both metropolitan and non-metropolitan areas. The sample includes both men and women as well as workers and retirees from a wide range of occupational levels. In total, 295 not-yet-retired and 458 retired men and women completed the survey with an overall response rate of 67 percent. In order to minimize the effects of missing values, the analyses below include only those respondents for whom we have data on all relevant questions (N= 702).

Respondents' expectations, plans, and dispositions about their current and future housing arrangements were assessed using modified questions based on the 1989 version of the American Association of Retired Persons (AARP) Understanding Senior Housing for the 1990s survey [8]. The dependent variables in the present study, respondents' expectations of ever making each of eight different housing or long-term care arrangements, are arrayed on a scale from 0 to 100. The eight options include: always living in one's current home, modifying one's home for special needs, living in a retirement community, purchasing long-term care insurance, getting a reverse mortgage, living with a family member, sharing a household with unrelated people, or living in a separate housing unit located on a relative's property (ECHO cottage). This method of asking respondents to assess the probability of choosing each of these options on a 100 point scale measures the strength of the respondents' expectations rather than simply asking whether or not they will move at some point in the future. This approach elicits much finer information and more accurately reflects expectations about future behavior [9, 10].

The analyses examine gender in relation to several other housing-related measures as well, including type (single family versus not), tenure (rent, own with mortgage, own outright), living alone, amount of planning for future housing (a lot, some/a little, not at all), whether respondents are counting on their children for help, whether they want to live alone, number of moves since age 30, years in the current home, and whether they have already made a retirement move.

Other socio-demographic characteristics included in these analyses are gender, nonmetropolitan versus metropolitan residence, income (under $3,000 to $100,000), age (50-72), marital status (married versus not married), racial/ethnic background (white versus non-white), and retirement status (retired -- defined as drawing a pension after having left one's "career" job with the contact company -- versus preretired worker). Social integration measures include whether or not respondents are volunteering or caregiving, amount of contact with neighbors and relatives (see them more than once a month), whether they live near grandchildren, and their religious involvement (go to church more than once a month). Health measures include objective physical health (any major illness, injury, or disability in the year preceding the interview), subjective health (zero - very serious health problems - to ten - in the very best health), psychological health (CES-D depression scale [10] and Rosenberg's self-esteem scale [11]), spouse's health during the past year, and respondent's and spouse's health histories (the number of major illnesses, injuries, or disabilities since the respondent was 30 years old).

Differences between older women and men's housing preferences, amount of planning, and expectations about each of the eight housing options described above are first examined bivariately, using t-test and chi-square tests of significance. Next, social and demographic factors including gender (which were chosen based on a previously developed model) are examined in separate multivariable analyses for each housing option with ordinary least squares regression techniques. The results of these analyses are described more fully elsewhere [13]; this paper focuses on the findings for gender. Finally, interactions between gender and several other factors are examined to look at the complexities among women in their projected housing arrangements.

II - RESULTS

The sample is 46 percent female and ranges in age from 50 to 71, with an average age of 61. Three-quarters of respondents are married, 43 percent have a high school education or less while 37 percent have a college degree. Income is distributed fairly evenly, with 32 percent earning less than $30,000, 38 percent earning $30,000 to $59,999 and 30 percent earning $60,000 or more. Retirees comprise 61 percent of the sample. Ninety-five percent of respondents are white.

Table 1 shows women and men's current housing characteristics, preferences, and mean future housing expectations. Even in this relatively early period of old age, women are significantly more likely than men to live alone (30% versus 18%). However, at this stage women have no greater propensity to live in alternative housing types (i.e., non single family), to rent, or to have planned more for their future housing. While women do not report counting on their children for future help significantly more than men do (in fact, roughly 80% of both men and women deny this disposition), women are almost twice as likely as men to say that they want to live alone. This latter difference may reflect an expectation for women to lose their spouses (if they are not already widowed) and a reluctance to move in with another family member. Approximately one-quarter of retirees have already made a move during their retirement, but women do not significantly outnumber men in this group.

Of the eight potential housing and long term care arrangements, three show significant gender differences in terms of respondents' expected probabilities. Again, respondents stated the likelihood that they would choose each option at some time in the future on a scale from 0 (absolutely no chance) to 100 (certain to or already done). Table 1 displays mean responses to these eight scales for women and men. In spite of the probable increased need for women to change their living arrangements in later life, women in late middle age have higher expectations than men to stay in their current homes for the rest of their lives; on average women predict a 60 percent likelihood that they will never move, versus men's predicted 54 percent likelihood. On the other hand, women expect to modify their current homes for special needs at a significantly higher rate than do men (52% versus 46% likelihood). Women also display a trend toward a greater expectation than men have to live with a family member (other than the spouse) at some future time (14% versus 11% likelihood). Note the overall low expectations about this option as well as for shared housing and living in an ECHO cottage for both genders. These latter two choices, as well as moving to a retirement community, purchasing long term care insurance, and obtaining a reverse mortgage show no gender differences.

Table 1

Housing characteristics, preferences, and expectations of women and men.

Housing Measures	Women	Men
Percentages in each category:		
Housing type		
Single family	86	88
Semi-detached, multi-unit, mobile home	14	12
Tenure		
Rents	7	8
Owns, with mortgage	43	48
Owns, outright	50	44
Lives alone		
Yes	30	18**
No	70	82
Planning for future housing		
A lot	32	34
Some/a little	39	39
Not at all	29	27
Counting on children for future help		
Yes	12	10
No	78	82
Don't know	10	8
Want to live alone		
Yes	29	15**
No	63	78
Don't know	9	8
Made a retirement move		
(retirees only, n=427)		
Yes	26	23
No	74	77
Mean Expected Probabilities for Future Housing Arrangements		
(scale = 0 - 100):		
Never move	60	54*
Stay in own home with modifications for special needs	52	46*
Move to a retirement community	23	23
Purchase long term care insurance	32	35
Obtain a reverse mortgage	17	20
Move in with a family member	14	11+
Share home with a non-relative	8	10
Live in an ECHO cottage	8	7

$**p<0.01$ $*p<0.05$ $+p<0.10$

Table 2 shows the multivariable models tested for expectations about each of the eight housing options. Each model includes a selection of background factors, measures of housing history, measures of social integration, and health indicators, following a hypothesized theoretical model of factors influencing housing expectations (discussed in detail elsewhere [13]). Unstandardized coefficients for gender as well as for age, income, marital status, retirement status, volunteering, caregiving, and objective health are displayed in Table 2. These measures were selected based on significant bivariate relationships with particular housing options to examine in more detail as potential moderators of the effects of gender (see below). Other measures included in the analyses, but not shown in Table 2 are: area of residence, race, years in the home, number of moves, tenure, contact with relatives and neighbors, proximity to grandchildren, religious involvement, subjective health, psychological health, spouse's health, and health history (see [13] for complete models).

Similar relationships appear when adjusting for social and demographic factors as seen in the bivariate comparisons of gender and housing choices, with two changes. That is, women are still more likely than men to expect to stay in their current homes for the rest of their lives, but also to expect to modify their homes for special needs. Now, however, there is no gender difference in the expectation to live with a family member (in fact, only marital status influences this option, with married people far less likely to forsee such an arrangement). In addition, women show a significantly lower expectation than men to share their home with a non-family member in exchange for rent and/or household services.

The final set of analyses examines the possibility that other life circumstances may moderate the relationship between gender and several of the housing choices of particular policy relevance. Older women represent an extremely heterogeneous group with wide variation in health, marital and retirement status, income level, age, and obligations to family and communities. Interactions between gender and age, marital status, income, retirement status, volunteering, caregiving, and objective health are tested in separate regression models (each of which holds constant age, income, and race), for four of the housing options: never moving, living in a retirement community, buying long term care insurance, and obtaining a reverse mortgage. The significant findings from these interactions are exhibited in Figure 1.

Table 2

Older Women's Expectations About Future Housing Arrangements, Net of Socio-demographic Factors

Unstandardized Coefficients (Standard errors in parentheses)

Housing Options:	never move	modify home	retirement community	LTC insurance	reverse mortgage	family member	shared housing	ECHO cottage
Constant	46.21*	37.43	32.80+	29.00	60.76**	41.50**	48.75*	60.76**
	(25.55)	(26.28)	(19.87)	(24.71)	(20.22)	(14.96)	(12.52)	(12.81)
Women	5.19+	6.70*	-1.59	-2.76	-1.68	1.80	-2.45*	-.54
	(2.79)	(2.86)	(2.17)	(2.71)	(2.20)	(1.65)	(1.37)	(1.40)
Age	.45	-.19	-.06	-.31	-.25	-.14	-.40*	.19
	(.32)	(.33)	(.25)	(.31)	(.26)	(.19)	(.16)	(.16)
Income	-3.19**	-.58	1.60**	1.89**	.08	-.53	.07	-.46
	(.74)	(.76)	(.57)	(.72)	(.58)	(.44)	(.37)	(.37)
Married	6.05	4.45	-8.17**	-6.59+	.63	-5.77**	-5.70**	-1.26
	(3.69)	(3.77)	(2.86)	(3.55)	(2.92)	(2.15)	(1.82)	(1.84)
Retired	5.97	3.89	3.41	-3.67	-1.77	-2.16	-2.54	-1.81
	(3.86)	(4.00)	(3.02)	(3.73)	(3.06)	(2.27)	(1.91)	(1.94)
Volunteering	5.21+	-2.04	3.84+	7.05*	2.42	.54	1.90	.43
	(2.85)	(2.93)	(2.22)	(2.74)	(2.25)	(1.68)	(1.41)	(1.43)
Caregiving	-3.18	-.36	7.61**	7.00*	.11	1.23	-.85	-1.67
	(3.30)	(3.40)	(2.57)	(3.18)	(2.57)	(1.94)	(1.62)	(1.65)
Objective health: ill in past year	-.73	.61	1.45	2.63	-3.08	-2.79	-1.49	-.92
	(3.36)	(3.43)	(2.59)	(3.26)	(2.63)	(1.96)	(1.65)	(1.68)
F	6.08**	2.39**	2.09**	2.73**	1.45*	1.75*	2.52**	1.06
R2	.21	.10	.08	.11	.06	.07	.10	.04
N	586	565	584	559	568	571	579	580

** p<.01   * .01<p<.05   + .05<p<.10

184

Figure 1
Moderating Effects of Marital Status, Age, Retirement Status, Health, and Volunteering on Gender for Expectations about Future Housing Arrangments."

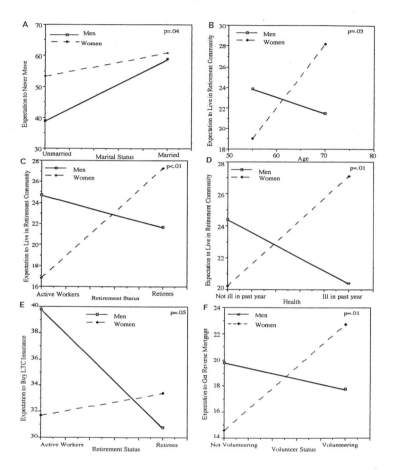

Figure 1a shows that unmarried women have a much higher expectation to stay in their current home than unmarried men, while married men and women have similar expectations. Age, retirement status and health all moderate women's expectations about living in a retirement community (Figure 1b-d). Women in their early 70s predict a much higher likelihood of choosing this option than women in their late

50s. Similarly, retired women and those in worse health also forsee a greater chance of moving to a retirement community than those not yet retired and those in good health. Intriguingly, men show the exact opposite reaction in each of these cases. Retired women show a stronger preference for purchasing long term care insurance than working women, while men who are still working have much higher expectations to make this investment than retired men (Figure 1e). Finally, volunteer status appears to influence women's expectation to get a reverse mortgage, with current volunteers predicting a higher likelihood than non-volunteers (Figure 1f). Life circumstances clearly influence older women's expectations about their future housing.

CONCLUSION

Although older women on the whole will face greater pressures than will men on their ability to age-in-place and continue to live independently in the community, women in this study report lower expectations than men of ever moving from their current homes. Responses to the question of how likely they are to move in the future may strongly reflect their desires, in spite of the reality that their needs for supportive housing will probably exceed men's needs. Gender does not differentiate among those 102 respondents who have actually moved, equal proportions of men and women among this "young-old" group have in fact already made a retirement move (roughly one-quarter of retirees). Women in this sample are more likely to live alone, and to prefer to do so, than men. Perhaps because of the greater propensity for women (versus men) to become widowed, older women expect to live alone at some time and feel they will be able to do so independently throughout old age.

Women's strong expectation, or desire, to remain in their current homes is also reflected in their higher predictions of modifying their homes to adjust for special needs. It may be that women feel stronger ties to their communities and they hope to adjust to any future disabilities through home remodeling rather than moving. It is interesting to note, however, that women predict no higher likelihood of obtaining a reverse mortgage or buying long term care insurance (which could be used to finance home health care), and a lower likelihood of sharing their homes with a non-relative, all of which would also enable one to age in place.

Significant interactions between gender and other important characteristics point to the complexity and diversity within the larger group of older women in determining who expects to move at all, move to a retirement community, purchase long term care insurance, or obtain a reverse mortgage. For example, women consider moving to a retirement community or purchasing long term care to be more likely when they are in their late 60s and 70s, retired, or in poor health. Breaking down the marital status variable into three levels (never married, formerly married, and currently married) shows some interesting variations. For example, women who have never married have even stronger expectations of aging in place, of modifying their homes, and of sharing their homes than those in the other two categories. On the other hand, women who were formerly married are much more likely to expect to live with a family member or to live in an ECHO cottage on a family member's property than those who never married (and presumably do not have children) or those currently married (who do not yet feel such a need).

Thus, a general conclusion may be drawn that women in their late 50s, 60s, and early 70s overall do not anticipate making any major changes in their housing arrangements which would involve moving from their current homes, nor do they predict using financial strategies like long term care insurance or reverse mortgages. They do, however, see modifying their homes to accomodate potential disability as a likely scenario. Applying a life course perspective and examining variation within this group of older women highlights the important differences in housing expectations related to marital status, age, health, and outside committments.

REFERENCES

1. Kinsella, K. Aging and the family: Present and future demographic issues. In: R. Blieszner and V. Bedford (Eds.), Handbook of Aging and the Family. Westport, CT: Greenwood Press, 1995.
2. Spitze,G, Logan, J. Gender differences in family support: Is there a payoff? Gerontologist 1989; 29:108-113.
3. Watkins, J. Gender and race differentials in elderly migration. Research on Aging 1989; 11:33-52.
4. Moen, P. A life course approach to postretirement roles and well-being. In: L. Bond, S. Cutler, and A. Grams (Eds.), Promoting Successful and Productive Aging. Thousand Oaks, CA: Sage, 1995.
5. Moen, P. Gender, age, and the life course. In: RH Binstock, and LK George (Eds.), Handbook of Aging and the Social Sciences, fourth edition. San Diego: Academic Press, 1995.
6. Elder, GH Jr. The life course paradigm: Historical and developmental perspectives. In: P. Moen, GH Elder, Jr, and K. Luscher (Eds.), Examining Lives in Context: Perspectives on the Ecology of Human Development. Washington, DC: American Psychological Association, 1995.
7. Golant, SM. Housing America's Elderly: Many Possibilities/Few Choices. Newbury Park: Sage, 1992.
8. American Association of Retired Persons. Understanding Senior Housing for the 1990s. Washington, DC: AARP, 1992.
9. Juster, FT. Anticipations and Purchases: An Analysis of Consumer Behavior. Princeton, NJ: Princeton University Press, 1964.
10. Juster, FT. Consumer Buying Intentions and Purchase Probability: An Experiment in Survey Design. New York: National Bureau of Economic Research, 1966.
11. Radloff, LS. The CES-D scale: A self-report depression scale for research in the general population. Applied Psychological Measurement 1977; 1:385-401.
12. Rosenberg, M. Conceiving the Self (reprint edition). Melbourne, FL: Academic Press, 1986.
13. Robison, JT, Moen P. (submitted). Housing expectations of older workers and retirees.

OSTEOPOROSIS:EPIDEMIOLOGY AND RISK ASSESSMENT

P. D. ROSS

Hawaii Osteoporosis Center, Honolulu. Reprint requests and correspondence to: Dr. Philip D. Ross, Hawaii Osteoporosis Center, 401 Kamakee Street, Honolulu, Hawaii 96814 USA. Tel: 808-592-2636 Fax: 808-592-2638

INTRODUCTION

Until fairly recently, osteoporosis was considered an unavoidable, and untreatable, consequence of aging. The disease affects most women, and many men, resulting in fragile bones which are easily broken from minor trauma, such as a fall from standing height. In severe cases, vertebral fractures can occur spontaneously, causing height loss and spinal deformity. Spine and nonspine fractures, especially those of the hip, can lead to declines in physical function and quality of life which persist long beyond the fracture healing period. Fortunately, it is possible to identify people at risk before fractures occur, using noninvasive measurements of bone density and other risk factors. Furthermore, effective treatments are available for reducing the risk of fractures.

I - EPIDEMIOLOGY

The incidence of fractures increases dramatically with age beginning soon after menopause for women, and somewhat later for men. The spine is the most common site of osteoporotic fractures [1]. The incidence of vertebral fractures is close to zero before age 50, but increases approximately exponentially to more than 3% per year (>3 out of 100 women each year) after age 85 [1-6]. It appears that more than half of all women will experience at least one vertebral fracture during their lives, and about half of the women with fractures develop multiple fractures [5,7,8]. However, only one-third of all vertebral fracture cases are diagnosed clinically, partly because only half of all cases report pain associated with the fracture [3,7,9,10].

Most nonspine fractures among the elderly are the result of minor or moderate (nonviolent) trauma, such as a fall from standing height, or less [11,12]. Like vertebral fractures, the incidence of hip fractures increases exponentially from almost zero at age 50 to approximately 3% per year after age 85 [13-16]. Fracture incidence increases exponentially with age at many skeletal sites [17]. However, the incidence of wrist fractures increases soon after menopause, but plateaus at 0.7% per year after age 60 [1,13,16,18]. Almost all types of fractures among the elderly are associated with low bone density [19,20].

Left untreated, more than half of all women, and about one-third of men in the US will eventually develop osteoporotic fractures, and many of these people will develop multiple fractures [21]. The high proportion with fractures is related to the rapid increase in fracture incidence at older ages, combined with the large number of potential fracture sites in the skeleton and the fact that many women and men are now living to advanced ages.

Hip fractures increase the risk of death during the subsequent 12 months by two to five times [14,22-25]. The average lifetime risk of dying from hip fracture is almost 3% for US Caucasian women, but the risk for individuals with low BMD or other risk factors can be much higher. Some data also suggests a progressive increase in mortality among women with vertebral fractures (but not wrist fractures), compared to those without fractures [24]. However, many fracture cases had pre-existing comorbid conditions, and the extent to which increased mortality is truly attributable to fractures and their complications remains uncertain. People with low BMD also appear to have an increased risk of death which is related to stroke rather than fractures [26,27].

Although most people with osteoporosis do not die as a direct result of the disease, osteoporotic fractures cause pain, disfigurement, and disability, which often lead to loss of independence and declines in quality of life during their remaining years. Postmenopausal women currently live to age 82 on average, and many women and men now survive into their nineties. Thus, the high incidence of fractures beginning in the sixties and seventies can affect the quality of life for many years.

The expense of treatment, hospitalization, and nursing homes puts an enormous economic burden on patients and society. The health care costs due to osteoporosis have been estimated to be $6 to $10 billion each year in the US [28]. Almost all hip fracture cases are hospitalized, and approximately half are discharged to nursing homes or other institutions [23,25,29]. Hip fractures account for half of all hospitalizations due to osteoporosis, but only 10% of the 2.3 million outpatient services each year [30]. Nursing homes account for approximately half of the health care costs for hip fracture cases [23,30].

Most fractures cause pain and physical impairment which can last weeks or months, and often result in long-term or permanent declines in physical function among the elderly. Among hip fracture cases who survive the first year, approximately half are unable to walk, almost 90% are unable to climb stairs without assistance, and 10% eventually become functionally dependent [31-34]. In one study, only 9% of hip fracture cases could walk outdoors by themselves 6 years later, compared to more than half of people without fractures [35]. Furthermore, 31% of the hip fracture patients (but only 1.5% of controls without fractures) were bedridden after 6 years. Other nonspine and spine fractures also contribute to long-term declines in physical function [36-38]. Years later, women with osteoporotic fractures are two to six times more likely than those without fractures to report difficulties with activities of daily living. These declines increase the risk of falls, and fears of falling often lead to further reductions in physical activity and independence. Declines in physical function and changes in appearance (such as kyphosis) also contribute to social isolation and loss of self-esteem, impairing quality of life [39,40]. Pressure sores, urinary tract infections, and pneumonia are other common morbid consequences of physical inactivity among the elderly [29,41].

II - RISK ASSESSMENT

Osteoporosis has been described as a "disease characterized by low bone mass and microarchitectural deterioration of bone tissue, leading to enhanced bone fragility and a consequent increase in fracture risk" [42]. Bone densitometry (absorptiometry) is a quick, safe, noninvasive procedure for measuring bone mineral density (BMD), which correlates strongly with bone strength in vitro, and is an effective predictor of fracture risk in population studies [29,43,44-51]. Furthermore, treatments for osteoporosis are designed to reduce fracture risk by maintaining or increasing BMD. Measurements of BMD can also be used to monitor disease progression or the effectiveness of intervention. Most importantly, BMD measurements can identify those at increased risk before fractures occur. Another major risk factor is a history of previous nonviolent fracture [2,45-47]. Low BMD and existing fractures are complementary risk factors: people with both risk factors have greater risk than people with only one risk factor, who in turn are at higher risk than those with no risk factors. For convenience, three stages of osteoporosis severity have been defined by the World Health Organization [52]:

1) Low bone mass, or osteopenia: BMD values between 1.0 and 2.5 standard deviations (SD) below the mean for young (ages 30-40) healthy adults
2) Osteoporosis: BMD values more than 2.5 SD below the mean for young adults
3) Severe (or established) osteoporosis: low BMD (more than 2.5 SD below the mean) plus history of nonviolent fracture.

However, it is important to recognize that there is a continuum in risk. Consequently, there are much larger differences in risk between people than is implied by these three categories. People with a history of multiple fractures are at much greater risk of future fractures than those with only one fracture in the past [2,45,46,53-55]. Therefore, standard spine radiographs should be considered for identifying undiagnosed vertebral fractures among elderly women or other people at high risk (because only one-third are routinely diagnosed clinically). Differences in fracture risk of at least 10 to 20 times exist between people over the full range of BMD. As a result, BMD is probably the best predictor of fracture risk, and also provides information beyond that obtained from fracture history. Therefore, BMD should be measured even if fractures have already occurred. Furthermore, very low BMD indicates a need to obtain spine radiographs to determine if vertebral fractures have already occurred, especially if there is a history of acute back pain. The relationship between BMD and fracture incidence is similar in magnitude, or greater than, the ability of blood pressure to predict stroke, or serum cholesterol to predict heart attacks [2,19,20,43,45,46]. The risk of fractures increases progressively by 1.5 to 2 times for each standard deviation decrease in BMD. Measurements can be made at any skeletal site, although hip BMD is somewhat better for predicting hip fractures.

In addition to BMD, other bone characteristics influence bone strength. These include bone geometry, such as hip axis length (which can be measured easily during acquisition of hip BMD), and trabecular architecture (such as the number and type of trabecular connections). Quantitative ultrasound (QUS) measurements have not yet been approved by the FDA, but may provide a measure of architecture in addition to other characteristics of bone strength. Studies of QUS suggest that it predicts fractures as well as BMD [6,56].

Much of the variability in BMD is determined by genetic factors, but the remaining variability is of sufficient magnitude to explain large differences in fracture risk between people [57-59]. The increase in size and mass of the skeleton from infancy through adolescence (and probably during fetal development) is strongly influenced by diet and physical activity [29,60-63]. Bone density continues to increase for some years after full height is attained, after which it remains relatively stable during mid-life [64]. Some evidence suggests that bone loss begins prior to menopause, at least at some skeletal sites [65]. Bone loss after menopause causes fracture risk to double every 10 years, on average [66]. Subsequently, women lose about half of their bone mass, and men lose about one-third [29]. Using the definition given earlier (more than 2.5 SD below the young adult mean with or without fractures), almost one-third of women between ages 60-70 have osteoporosis, and the proportion increases to 70% after age 80 [52,67,68]. An enormous number of men and women with osteopenia or osteoporosis are at increased risk, and at least 50% of those with osteoporosis have already experienced fractures.

Some individuals experience more, and some less than, the average amount of bone loss. Changes in BMD can be monitored by repeating measurements, which have very good reproducibility -- precision errors are typically 1% to 2% [65,69-72]. Measurements can be repeated at 1 to 2 year intervals when rapid bone loss is suspected - such as untreated patients soon after menopause. For other patients, 5 year intervals are appropriate unless BMD is already low (high risk), in which case shorter intervals are justified [21,73].

Bone remodeling occurs throughout life; bone resorption causes microscopic pits which are then refilled with new bone tissue. If formation does not keep up with resorption, or if the resorption pits coalesce, a progressive decrease in bone mass and loss of bone structure occurs. Estrogen deficiency and other factors cause an increase in the rate of bone turnover (frequency of remodeling), accelerating the rate of bone loss. One option for evaluating bone turnover is to measure serum or urinary biochemical markers of bone formation or resorption. Formation markers include osteocalcin and skeletal alkaline phosphatase; resorption markers include bone collagen breakdown products such as urinary pyridinoline, deoxypyridinoline, or cross-linked N- or C-telopeptides. Increased markers are correlated with faster rates of bone loss, and increased risk of fractures [74-76]. Furthermore, changes in markers signify treatment effectiveness; markers are elevated after menopause, and decrease dramatically by as much as 70% during treatments which inhibit bone resorption or turnover [74,77].

In addition to BMD and fracture history, a large number of other risk factors have been identified. With some exceptions, most risk factors cannot be used to identify which patients are at greatest risk and who should be treated [23,78,79]. Rather, risk assessment is usually based on BMD and fracture history, as described above.

Some risk factors are associated with rate of bone loss (Table 1). Factors associated with accelerated bone loss include menopause or other causes of estrogen deficiency, corticosteroid use, physical inactivity, dietary (calcium and vitamin D) deficiencies, ethanol abuse, excess caffeine intake, and smoking [80-88]. Postmenopausal women lose BMD most rapidly during the first 5-10 years after menopause (about 2% to 4% per year), and later at about 1% to 2% per year -- twice as fast as men of similar age [69,71,89-93]. Immobility is a particularly potent risk factor; bed rest, paralysis, and post-fracture studies have demonstrated decreases in BMD of as much as 40% in less than a year. Certain health conditions such as gastrectomy, hypogonadism (both male and female), hypercortisolism, hyperthyroidism, hyperparathyroidism, hepatic disease, and disturbances of calcium metabolism, such as Paget's disease, osteomalacia, certain neoplastic diseases, and renal disease can also contribute to bone loss, or otherwise disrupt bone metabolism leading to increased fracture risk [21,80]. Heparin, anticonvulsants, excess thyroid hormone, aluminum-containing antacids, and excess dietary sodium or protein may also increase bone loss [21,79,94].

Factors associated with slower rates of bone loss include estrogen replacement therapy, adequate calcium and vitamin D intake, physical activity, and thiazide diuretic use [80,95,96]. Both estrogens and thiazides have been shown to preserve bone density and long term use (more than 6 years) reduces fracture incidence by about half [96-99]. Treatment with bisphosphonates, which inhibit bone resorption, results in an increase in BMD, and dramatically reduces fracture incidence by at least 50% within two years [100-102]. Alendronate has already been approved by the FDA for treating osteoporosis, and other promising drugs are under investigation.

Some risk factors predict the risk of fractures through mechanisms other than bone loss. For example, the incidence of hip fractures among Blacks and Asians is about half that of Caucasians, but the lower risk among Asians is not related to BMD, which is similar to Caucasians, or lower [15,103-106]. One obvious contributor to fracture risk is risk factors for falls, such as slow walking speed, weak muscle strength, use of psychoactive drugs or sedatives, cognitive impairment, and poor balance [55,107]. Approximately one out of every four postmenopausal Caucasian women fall each year [108,109]. Men fall about half as often as women, and Blacks and Asians fall about half as often as Caucasians [110-112]. The reasons for these racial differences are under investigation, as are interventions to reduce falls [113,114]. A family history of fractures also appears to increase the risk independent of BMD. Women whose mother or sister have a history of hip or wrist fracture are at increased risk of fractures themselves; the overall risk is even greater if their BMD is low [47].

Table 1
Factors contributing to bone loss.

Age	+
Hypogonadism (including postmenopausal women without estrogen)	++
Female gender	+
Immobility/inactivity	++
Increased biochemical markers of bone turnover	++
Alcohol abuse	+
Cigarette smoking	+
Caffeine excess	+
Calcium deficiency	+
Vitamin D deficiency	+
Poor physical function (muscle weakness, etc)	+
Chronic health problems	+
Increased life expectancy (duration of bone loss)	+
Genetics (family history)	?
Thyroid hormone excess	+
Anticonvulsants	?
Corticosteroid use	++

+Associated with bone loss
++Strongly associated with accelerated bone loss
? = Association possible, but not confirmed

SUMMARY

More than half of all women and about one-third of men will develop fractures related to osteoporosis. The consequences of fractures are often severe, and can lead to persistent declines in quality of life and increased mortality rates. Bone density should always be measured to quantitate the degree of fracture risk and provide a baseline value for future comparisons, regardless of whether other risk factors are present, because there are no symptoms other than fractures associated with disease progression, and because effective treatments for low bone density are available. Early detection and intervention is likely to be most effective because irreversible loss of bone structure has taken place by the time fractures begin to occur. Although the use of bone densitometry is on the rise, relatively few people are currently receiving treatment to prevent or reverse bone loss.

REFERENCES

1. Melton LJ III, Cummings SR. Heterogeneity of age-related fractures: implications for epidemiology. Bone Miner 1987;2:321-331.
2. Black DM, Nevitt MC, Palermo L, et al. Prediction of new vertebral deformities. [abstract] J Bone Miner Res 1994;9:S135.
3. Cooper C, Atkinson EJ, O'Fallon WM, Melton LJ III. Incidence of clinically diagnosed vertebral fractures: A population-based study in Rochester, Minnesota, 1985-1989. J Bone Miner Res 1992;7:221-227.
4. Ross PD, Wasnich RD, Vogel JM. Detection of pre-fracture spinal osteoporosis using bone mineral absorptiometry. J Bone Min Res 1988;3:1-11.
5. Ross PD, Fujiwara S, Huang C, Davis JW, Epstein RS, Wasnich RD, Kodama K, Melton LJ III. Japanese women in Hiroshima have greater vertebral fracture prevalence than Caucasians or Japanese-Americans in the US. Int J Epidemiol 24(6):1171-1177, 1995.
6. Ross PD, Huang C, Davis JW, et al. Predicting vertebral deformity using bone densitometry at various skeletal sites and calcaneus ultrasound. Bone 1995;16:325-332.
7. Cooper C. Epidemiology of vertebral fractures in western populations. In: Cooper C and Reeve J, eds. Spine. State of the Art Reviews: Vertebral Osteoporosis. Philadelphia, PA: Hanley and Belfus; 1994;8:1-21.
8   Kiel DP, Hannan MT, Genant HK, Felson DT. Prevalence and incidence of vertebral fractures in the elderly: initial results from the Framingham Study. [abstract] J Bone Miner Res 1994;9(Suppl 1):S129.
9. Melton LJ III, Kan SH, Frye MA, Wahner HW, O'Fallon, WM, Riggs BL. Epidemiology of vertebral fractures in women. Am J Epidemiol 1989;129:1000-1011.
10. Ross PD, Davis JW, Epstein RS, Wasnich RD. Pain and disability associated with new vertebral fractures and other spinal conditions. J Clin Epidemiol 1994;47:231-239.
11. Melton LJ III, Ilstrup DM, Riggs BL, Beckenbaugh RD. Fifty-year trend in hip fracture incidence. Clin Orthop 1982;162:144-149.
12. Owen RA, Melton LJ III, Johnson KA, Ilstrup DM, Riggs BL. Incidence of Colles' fracture in a North American community. Am J Public Health 1982;72:605-607.
13. Melton LJ III, Riggs BL. Risk factors for injury after a fall. Clin Geriatr Med 1985;1(3):525-539.
14. Gallagher JC, Melton LJ III, Riggs BL, Bergstrath E. Epidemiology of fractures of the proximal femur in Rochester, Minnesota. Clin Orthopaed Relat Res 1980;150:163-171.
15. Farmer ME, White LR, Brody JA, Bailey KR. Race and sex differences in hip fracture incidence. Am J Pub Health 1984;74:1374-1380.
16. Melton LJ III. Epidemiology of age-related fractures. In: Avioli , ed. The Osteoporotic Syndrome. Detection, Prevention, and Treatment. 3rd ed. New York, NY: Wiley-Liss; 1993a:17-38.
17. Kanis JA, Pitt FA. Epidemiology of Osteoporosis. Bone 1992;13:S7-S15.
18. Sølgaard S, Petersen VS. Epidemiology of distal radius fractures. Acta Orthop Scand 1985;56:391-393.
19. Seeley DG, Browner WS, Nevitt MC, Genant HK, Scott JC, Cummings SR. Which fractures are associated with low appendicular bone mass in elderly women? Ann Intern Med 1991;115:837-842.
20. Seeley DG, Browner WS, Nevitt MC, Genant HK, Cummings SR. Almost all fractures are osteoporotic. [abstract] J Bone Miner Res 1995;10(Suppl 1):S468.
21. Ross PD. Osteoporosis: Frequency, consequences, and risk factors. Arch Intern Med 156(13):1399-1411, 1996.

22. Fisher ES, Baron JA, Malenka DJ, et al. Hip fracture incidence and mortality in New England. Epidemiology 1991;2:116-122.

23. US Congress, Office of Technology Assessment, Hip fracture outcomes in people age fifty and over -- Background paper, OTA-BP-H-120 Washington, DC:US Government Printing Office; July, 1994.

24. Cooper C, Atkinson EJ, Jacobsen SJ, O'Fallon WM, Melton LJ III. Population-based study of survival after osteoporotic fractures. Am J Epidemiol 1993;137:1001-1005.

25. Magaziner J, Simonsick EM, Kashner TM, Hebel JR, Kenzora JE. Survival experience of aged hip fracture patients. Am J Public Health 1989;79:274-278.

26. Browner WS, Seeley DG, Vogt TM, Cummings SR. Non-trauma mortality in elderly women with low bone mineral density. Lancet 1991;338:355-358.

27. Browner WS, Pressman AR, Nevitt MC, Cauley JA, Cummings SR. Association between low bone density and stroke in elderly women. The Study of Osteoporotic Fractures. Stroke 1993;24:940-946.

28. Peck WA, Riggs BL, Bell NH, et al. Research directions in osteoporosis. Am J Med 1988;84:275-282.

29. Melton LJ III. Hip fractures: A worldwide problem today and tomorrow. Bone 1993;14(Suppl):S1-S8.

30. Phillips S, Fox N, Jacobs J, Wright WE. The direct medical costs of osteoporosis for American women aged 45 and older, 1986. Bone 1988;9:271-279.

31. Chrischilles EA, Shireman T, Wallace R. Costs and health effects of osteoporotic fractures. Bone 1994;15:377-386.

32. Marotolli RA, Berkman LF, Cooney LM. Decline in physical function following hip fracture. J Am Geriatr Soc 1992;40:861-866.

33. Cummings SR, Phillips SL, Wheat ME, et al. Recovery of function after hip fracture. J Am Geriatr Soc 1988;36:801-806.

34. Magaziner J, Simonsick EM, Kashner TM, Hebel JR, Kenzora JE. Predictors of functional recovery one year following hospital discharge for hip fracture: a prospective study. J Gerontol Med Sci 1990;45:M101-M107.

35. Jalovaara P, Virkkunen H. Quality of life after hemiarthroplasty for femoral neck fracture. Acta Orthop Scand 1991; 62: 208-217.

36. Greendale GA, Barrett-Connor E, Ingles S, Haile R. Late physical activity and functional effects of osteoporotic fracture in women: The Rancho Bernardo Study. J Amer Geriatr Soc 1995;43:955-961.

37. Huang C, Ross PD, Wasnich RD. Vertebral fractures and other predictors of back pain among older women. J Bone Miner Res 11(7):1025-1031, 1996.

38. Huang C, Ross PD, Wasnich RD. Vertebral fracture and other predictors of physical impairment and health care utilization. Arch Intern Med 156:2469-2475, 1996.

39. Gold DT, Lyles KW, Shipp KM, Drezner MK. Unexpected consequences of osteoporosis: An evolving basis for treatment decisions. In Osteoporosis, R Marcus, D Feldman, J Kelsey, eds. Academic Press, San Diego, 1996.

40. Gold DT, Drezner MK. Quality of life. In Osteoporosis: Etiology, Diagnosis, and Management, Second Edition. BL Riggs and LJ Melton III, eds. Lippincott-Raven Publishers, Philadelphia 1995.

41. Versluysen M. How elderly patients with femoral fracture develop pressure sores in hospital. Br Med J 1986;292:1311-3.

42. Consensus Development Conference: Prophylaxis and treatment of osteoporosis. Am J Med 1991;90:107-110.

43. Marshall D, Johnell O, Wedel H. Meta-analysis of how well measures of bone density predict occurrence of osteoporotic fractures. Br Med J 312:1254-1259, 1996.

44. Cheng S, Suominen H, Era P, Heikkinen E. Bone density of the calcaneus and fractures in 75- and 80-year-old men and women. Osteoporosis Int 4:48-54, 1994.

45. Ross PD, Davis JW, Epstein RS, Wasnich RD. Pre-existing fractures and bone mass predict vertebral fracture in women. Ann Intern Med 1991;114:919-923.

46. Ross PD, Genant HK, Davis JW, Miller P, Wasnich RD. Predicting vertebral fracture incidence from prevalent fractures and bone density among non-black, osteoporotic women. Osteo Int 1993;3:120-127.

47. Cummings SR, Nevitt MC, Browner WS, et al. Risk factors for hip fracture in White women. N Eng J Med 1995;332:767-773.

48. Cummings SR, Black D. Bone mass measurements and risk of fractures in Caucasian women: A review of findings from prospective studies. Am J Med 1995;98(Suppl 2A):24S-28S.

49. Wasnich RD, Ross PD, Heilbrun LK, Vogel JM. Prediction of postmenopausal fracture risk with bone mineral measurements. Am J Obstet & Gynecol 1985;153:745-751.

50. Gärdsell P, Johnell O, Nilsson BE. Predicting fractures in women by using forearm bone densitometry. Calcif Tissue Int 1989;44:235-242.

51. Black DM, Cummings SR, Genant HK, Nevitt MC, Palermo L, Browner W. Axial and appendicular bone density predict fractures in older women. J Bone Miner Res 1992;7:633-638.

52. Kanis JA, Melton LJ III, Christiansen C, Johnston CC, Khaltev N. The diagnosis of osteoporosis. J Bone Miner Res 1994;9:1137-1141.

53. Kotowicz MA, Melton LJ III, Cooper C, Atkinson EJ, O'Fallon WM, Riggs BL. Risk of hip fracture in women with vertebral fracture. J Bone Miner Res 1994;9:599-605.

54. Lauritzen JB, Schwarz P, McNair P, Lund B, Transbol I. Radial and humeral fractures as predictors of subsequent hip, radial or humeral fractures in women, and their seasonal variation. Osteo Int 1993;3:133-137.

55. Gärdsell P, Johnell O, Nilsson BE, Nilsson JA. The predictive value of fracture, disease, and falling tendency for fragility fractures in women. Calcif Tissue Int 1989;45:327-330.

56. Bauer DC, Gluer CC, Genant HK, Stone K. Quantitative ultrasound and vertebral fracture in postmenopausal women. J Bone Miner Res 1995;10(3):353-358.

57. Kelly PJ, Eisman JA, Sambrook, PN. Interaction of genetic and environmental influences on peak bone density. Osteo Int 1990;1:56-60.

58. Krall EA, Dawson-Hughes B. Heritable and Life-style determinants of bone mineral density. J Bone Min Res 1993;8:1-9.

59. McKay HA, Bailey DA, Wilkison AA, Houston CS. Familial comparison of bone mineral density at the proximal femur and lumbar spine. Bone Miner 1994;24:95-107.

60. Cooper C, Cawley M, Bhalla A, et al. Childhood growth, physical activity, and peak bone mass in women. J Bone Miner Res 1995;10(6):940-7.

61. Slemenda CW, Miller JZ, Hui SL, Reister TK, Johnston, CC Jr. Role of physical activity in the development of skeletal mass in children. J Bone Miner Res 1991;6:1227-1233.

62. Kröger H, Kotaniemi A, Kröger L, Alhava E. Development of bone mass and bone density of the spine and femoral neck -- a prospective study of 65 children and adolescents. Bone Miner 1993;23:171-182.

63. Turner JG, Gilchrist NL, Ayling EM, et al. Factors affecting bone mineral density in high school girls. New Zealand Med J 1992;105:95-96.

64. Teegarden D, Proux WR, Martin BR, et al. Peak bone mass in young women. J Bone Miner Res 1995;10:711-716.

65. Slemenda C, Longcope C, Peacock M, Hui S, Johnston C. Sex steroids, bone mass, and cone loss. A prospective study of pre-, peri-, and postmenopausal women. J Clin Invest 97:14-21, 1996.

66. Davis JW, Ross PD, Wasnich RD, MacLean CJ, Vogel JM. The long-term precision of bone loss rate measurements among postmenopausal women. Calcif Tissue Inter 1991;48:311-318.

67. Looker AC, Johnston CC Jr, Wahner HW, et al. Prevalence of low bone femoral bone density in older women from NHANES III. J Bone Miner Res 1995;10:796-802.

68. Melton LJ III. How many women have osteoporosis now? J Bone Miner Res 1995;10:175-177.

69. Davis JW, Ross PD, Wasnich RD, MacLean CJ, Vogel JM: Comparison of cross-sectional and longitudinal measurements of age-related changes in bone mass. J Bone Miner Res 1989;4:351-357.

70. Hui S, Slemenda C, Johnston C Jr. The contribution of bone loss to postmenopausal osteoporosis. Osteo Int 1990;1:30-34.

71. Harris S, Dawson-Hughes B. Rates of change in bone mineral density of the spine, heel, femoral neck and radius in healthy postmenopausal women. Bone Miner 1992;17:87-95.

72. Ross PD, He Y-F, Davis JW, Epstein RS, Wasnich RD. Normal ranges for bone loss rates. Bone Miner 1994;26:169-180.

73. He Y-F, Ross PD, Davis JW, Epstein RS, Vogel JM, Wasnich RD. When should bone density measurements be repeated? Calcif Tissue Int 1994;55:243-248.

74. Garnero P, Shih WJ, Gineyts E, Karpf DB, Delmas PD. Comparison of new biochemical markers of bone turnover in late postmenopausal osteoporotic women in response to alendronate treatment. J Clin Endocrinol Metab 1994;79:1693-1700.

75. Akesson K, Ljunghall S, Jonsson B, Sernbo I, Johnell O, Gardsell P, Obrant KJ. Assessment of biochemical markers of bone metabolism in relation to the occurrence of fracture: A retrospective and prospective population-based study of women. J Bone Miner Res 1995;10(11):1823-1829.

76 Garnero P, Hausherr E, Chapuy M-C, Marcelli C, Grandjean H, et al. Markers of bone resorption predict hip fracture in elderly women: The EPIDOS prospective study. J Bone Miner Res 11(10):1531-1538, 1996.

77. Gertz BJ, Shao P, Hanson DA, et al. Monitoring bone resorption in early postmenopausal women by an immunoassay for cross-linked collagen peptides in urine. J Bone Miner Res 1994;9:135-142.

78. Ribot C, Tremollieres F, Pouilles J-M. Can we detect women with low bone mass using clinical risk factors? Am J Med 1995;98(Suppl 2A):52S-55S.

79. Ross PD. Risk factors for fracture. In: Cooper C and Reeve J, eds. Spine. State of the Art Reviews: Vertebral Osteoporosis. Philadelphia, PA: Hanley and Belfus. 1994;8:91-110.

80. Bauer DC, Browner WS, Cauley JA, et al. Factors associated with appendicular bone mass in older women. Ann Intern Med 1993;118:657-665.
81. Sowers MR, Clark MK, Hollis B, Wallace RB, Jannausch M. Radial bone mineral density in pre- and postmenopausal women: A prospective study of rates and risk factors for loss. J Bone Miner Res 1992;7:647-657.
82. Dawson-Hughes B, Dallal GE; Krall EA, Harris S, Sokoll LJ, Falconer G: Effect of vitamin D supplementation on wintertime and overall bone loss in healthy postmenopausal women. Ann Intern Med 1991;115: 505-512.
83. Ulivieri FM, Bossi E, Azzoni R, et al. Quantification by dual photon absorptiometry of local bone loss after fracture. Clin Orthop 1990;250:291-295.
84. Minaire P. Immobilization osteoporosis: A review. Clin Rheumatol 1989;852:95-103.
85. Kannus P, Leppala J, Lehto M, Sievanen H, Heinonen A, Jarvinen M. A rotator cuff injury produces permanent osteoporosis in the affected extremity, but not in those with whom the shoulder function has returned to normal. J Bone Miner Res 1995;10:1263-1271.
86. Reid IR. Steroid osteoporosis. In: Cooper C and Reeve J, eds. Spine. State of the Art Reviews: Vertebral Osteoporosis. Philadelphia, PA: Hanley and Belfus; 1994;8:111-131.
87. Saito JK, Davis JW, Wasnich RD, Ross PD. Users of low-dose glucocorticoids have increased bone loss rates: a longitudinal study. Calcif Tissue Int 1995;57:115-119.
88. Laan RFJM, van Riel PLCM, van de Putte LBA, van Erning LJTO, van't Hof MA, Lemmens JAM. Low-dose prednisone induces rapid reversible axial bone loss in patients with rheumatoid arthritis: A randomized, controlled study. Ann Intern Med 1993;119:963-968.
89. Hagino H, Yamamoto K, Teshima R, Kishimoto H, Kagawa T: Radial bone mineral changes in pre- and postmenopausal healthy Japanese women: cross-sectional and longitudinal studies. J Bone Miner Res 1992;7:147-152.
90. Hansen MA, Overgaard K, Christiansen C. Spontaneous postmenopausal bone loss in different skeletal areas - followed up for 15 years. J Bone Miner Res 1995;10:205-210.
91. Davis JW, Ross PD, Vogel JM, Wasnich RD: Age-related changes in bone mass among Japanese-American men. Bone Miner 1991;15:227-236.
92. Orwoll ES, Oviatt SK, McClung MR, Deftos LJ, Sexton G. The rate of bone mineral loss in normal men and the effects of calcium and cholecalciferol supplementation. Ann Int Med 1990;112:29-34.
93. Ensrud KE, Palermo L, Black D, et al. Hip bone loss increases with advancing age: Longitudinal results from the Study of Osteoporotic Fractures. [abstract] J Bone Miner Res 1994;9(Suppl 1):S153.
94. Need AG, Morris HA, Cleghorn DB, De Nichilo D, Horowitz M, Nordin BEC. Effect of salt restriction on urine hydroxyproline excretion in postmenopausal women. Arch Intern Med 1991;151:757-759.
95. Wasnich RD, Ross PD, Heilbrun LK, Vogel JM, Yano K, Benfante R. Differential effects of thiazide and estrogen upon bone mineral content and fracture prevalence. Obstet Gynecol 1986;67:457-463.
96. Cauley JA, Cummings SR, Seeley DG, et al. Effects of thiazide diuretic therapy on bone mass, fractures, and falls. Ann Intern Med 1993;118:666-673.
97. Jones G, Nguyen T, Sambrook PN, Eisman JA. Thiazide diuretics and fractures: Can meta-analysis help? J Bone Miner Res 1995;10:106-111.
98. Ettinger B, Genant HK, Cann CE. Long-term estrogen replacement therapy prevents bone loss and fractures. Ann Intern Med 1985;102:319-324.
99. Weiss NS, Ure CL, Ballard JH, Williams AR, Daling JR. Decreased risk of fractures of the hip and lower forearm with postmenopausal use of estrogen. N Engl J Med 1980;1195-1198.
100. Liberman UA, Weiss SR, Broll J, et al. Effect of oral alendronate on bone mineral density and the incidence of fractures in postmenopausal osteoporosis. New Engl J Med 333:1437-43, 1995.
101. Black DM, Cummings SR, Karpf DB, et al. Randomized trial of alendronate on risk of fracture in women with existing vertebral fractures. Lancet 348:1535-41, 1996.
102. Watts NB, Harris ST, Genant HK, Wasnich RD, Miller PD, Jackson RD, Licata AA, Ross PD, Woodson GC, Yanover M, Mysiw WJ, Kohse L, Rao MB, Steiger P, Richmond B, Chesnut CH. Intermittent cyclical Etidronate treatment of postmenopausal osteoporosis. N Engl J Med 323:73-79, 1990.
103. Baron JA, Barrett J, Malenka D, et al. Racial differences in fracture risk. Epidemiology 1994;5:42-47.
104. Ross PD, Norimatsu H, Davis JW, et al. A comparison of hip fracture incidence among native Japanese, Japanese-Americans, and American Caucasians. Am J Epidemiol 1991;133:801-809.
105. Hagino H, Yamamoto K, Teshima R, et al. The incidence of fractures of the proximal femur and the distal radius in Tottori Prefecture, Japan. Arch Orthop Trauma Surg 1989;109:43-44.
106. Silverman SL, Madison RE. Decreased incidence of hip fracture in Hispanics, Asians, and Blacks: California hospital discharge data. Am J Pub Health 1988;78(1):1482-1483.

107. Grisso JA, Chiu GY, Maislin G, Steinmann WC, Portale J: Risk factors for hip fractures in men: a preliminary study. J Bone Miner Res 1991;6:865-868.
108. O'Loughlin JL, Robitaille Y, Boivin JF, Suissa S. Incidence of and risk factors for falls and injurious falls among the community-swelling elderly. Am J Epidemiol 1993;137:342-354.
109. Luukinen H, Koski K, Hiltunen L, Kivela SL. Incidence rate of falls in an aged population in northern Finland. J Clin Epidemiol 1994;47:843-850.
110. Nevitt MC, Cummings SR, Kidd S, Black D. Risk factors for recurrent nonsyncopal falls. A prospective study. JAMA 1989;261:2663-2668.
111. Tinetti ME, Speechley M, Ginter SF. Risk factors for falls among elderly persons living in the community. N Engl J Med 1988;319:1701-1707.
112. Yasumura S, Haga H, Nagai H, Suzuki T, Amano H, Shibata H. Rate of falls and the correlates among elderly people living in an urban community in Japan. Age Ageing 1994;23:323-327.
113. Tinetti ME, Baker DI, McAvay G, et al. A multifactorial intervention to reduce the risk of falling among elderly people living in the community. N Engl J Med 1994;331:821-827.
114. Myers AH, Young Y, Langlois JA. Prevention of falls in the elderly. Bone 1995;18(1):87S-101S.

SEX DIFFERENCE IN IMPROVEMENT OF ADL AFTER BEHAVIORAL THERAPY FOR FUNCTIONAL URINARY INCONTINENCE IN ELDERLY INPATIENTS

K. TOBA *, K. NAGANO *, N. SUDOH *, M. ETO *, K. KOZAKI *, M. YOSHIZUMI *, M. HASHIMOTO *, J. AKO *, N. SUGIMOTO *, K. YUMITA **, M. HARA **, Y. FUKUSHIMA **, Y. OUCHI *

* Department of Geriatrics, Faculty of Medicine, the University of Tokyo. ** Saitama Kaisei Hospital. Address correspondence to Kenji Toba MD. Department of Geriatrics, Faculty of Medicine, the University of Tokyo, 7-3-1 Hongo, Bunkyo-ku, Tokyo 113 Japan, Tel & Fax +81-3-3812-6739

Summary : *This study was performed to evaluate the influence of gender on the outcome of behavioral intervention for functional urinary incontinence in elderly inpatients (n=22, men 7, women 15) with physical/cognitive impairment. The behavioral therapy for urinary incontinence consisted of timed-toileting and prompt voiding. After the therapy, 80% of the patients did not require a pad. Furthermore, 40% of the patients became able to use the bathroom by themselves. Basic ADLs were also markedly improved after the behavioral therapy. However, except for getting on/off the toilet and dressing, the magnitude of the improvement was significantly greater in women (p<0.05). These results suggest that gender is important in the evaluation of long-term care in elderly subjects.*

Key words: *Urinary incontinence, Behavioral therapy, ADL, Sex difference*

It has been shown that behavioral therapy is effective for urinary incontinence in patients with physical and cognitive impairment [1-6]. However, sometimes therapy has to be discontinued, not only because of unanticipated complications of the patients but also of their reluctance to continue therapy and depressive mood. In these setting, it has not been studied whether gender is involved.

Therefore, in the present study, we compared the outcome and the improvement of activities of daily living (ADLs) by behavioral therapy for functional urinary incontinence between male and female elderly physically impaired inpatients.

I - PATIENTS AND METHODS

Twenty-two patients (7 men; 73.7 ± 3.1 and 15 women; 80.8 ± 1.4, mean±S.E.M. years old) were studied. Patients with recent cerebrovascular accident were excluded from the study. With respect to ADLs, we selected patients who could sit at the end of the bed with or without assistance.

First, the daily pattern of urination was recorded in all patients. Then we designed an individual behavioral therapy schedule considering each urination profile including daily voiding time, assisting device and ADLs.

Four graded urination-related activity levels were classified as follows; Level 0: totally dependent (pad), Level 1: partially dependent (using external device or portable toilet). Level 2: independent using external device or portable toilet. Level 3: independent (using bathroom). These scores were recorded daily. When the final score was greater than that before therapy, the outcome was judged as a therapeutic success. Similarly, a decreased or unchanged score was judged as a therapeutic failure.

Eleven items of basic ADLs were also classified into 4 grades (Independent=3, partly dependent=2, greatly dependent=1, totally dependent or impossible=0). The graded score was recorded before as well as 1 and 3 months after the start of the behavioral therapy. Medical problems and accidents including urinary incontinence, orthostatic hypotension and falls were also recorded.

II - RESULTS

Table 1 summerizes the individual background data of the subjects, the duration of incontinence before the start of behavioral therapy, and the outcome of the behavioral therapy. More than half of the subjects (n=15) suffered from cerebrovascular disease. Hemiparesis (40%) and dementia (48%) were most frequent neurological complications in the subjects. Seventy percent of the subjects had fecal incontinence. The pre-therapy duration of incontinence was not different between male and female subjects (458±228 vs. 209±85 days).

Table 1
Patient background and outcome of behavioral therapy

Age/Sex	Disease	Pre-therapy duration of incontinence (days)	Days of therapy in successful cases
88F	CVD, hip fx	0	failed
86F	DM, disuse atrophy	1	210
81F	SDAT	1	failed
91F	SDAT, OA	2	2
76F	DM, HT, disk hernia	7	3
68F	CVD, DM, HT	16	failed
83F	CHF, Af	21	67
81F	CVD	50	21
82F	CVD	98	37
81F	CVD, hip fx	124	39
78F	DM,HT	150	37
83F	CVD	305	3
75F	Parkinson disease	420	60
81F	CVD, OA, RA	786	30
78F	CVD, SDAT	1163	1
80.8±1.4		209±85	42.5±16.5
78M	CVD, AAA, HT	2	30
65M	CVD, CHF	28	30
80M	CVD,DM,HT	103	24
60M	CVD	133	failed
70M	CVD, hip fx	395	150
81M	CVD, Parkinson disease	940	1
82M	CVD, IIP	1610	30
73.7±3.1		458±228	44.1±21.7

Mean±SEM

CVD; cerebrovascular disease, hip fx, hip fracture, DM; diabetes mellitus, SDAT; senile dementia of Alzheimer type, OA; osteoarthritis deformans, HT; hypertension, CHF; chronic heart failure, Af; atrial fibrillation, RA; rheumatoid arthritis, AAA; abdominal aortic aneurysm, IIP; idiopathic interstitial pneumonia

In total, the successful rate was 82% (18/22). Before behavioral therapy, 16 subjects wore pads, while 82% of them did not require a pad after therapy. Furthermore, 36% (8/22) of them became able to use the bathroom independently (Fig. 1).

Figure 1

Outcome of behavioral therapy

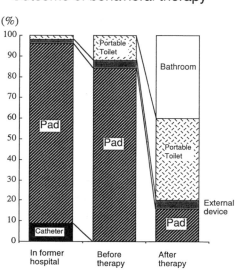

n =22

Outcome of behavioral therapy Behavioral therapy; timed toileting and prompt voiding Former hospital; way of urination in the hospital where subjects were inpatients before admission to our hospital.

The mean duration of incontinence before the behavioral therapy was more than 9 months. However, the duration did not reflect the outcome of behavioral therapy. There was no statistically significant difference in the success rate of behavioral therapy between male and female subjects (6/7 vs. 12/15). Similarly, the mean therapeutic period in the successful cases was almost the same in men and women (Table 1).

The sum of the graded scores of 11 basic ADL items was improved 1 month after the start of behavioral therapy both in men and women. However, at 3 months after the start of therapy, further improvement was observed only in women, and the ADL level was significantly higher in women than men ($p < 0.05$, Fig.2).

Figure 2

Changes in sum of 11 basic ADL scores in men and women before, 1 month and 3 months after the start of behavioral therapy. Values are mean±SEM. See details of 11 of basic ADL items in Figure 3.

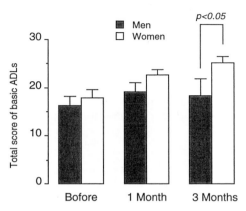

Figure 3

Changes in 11 ADL scores in men and women before (finely shaded), 1 month (roughly shaded) and 3 months (in thick line) after the start of behavioral therapy.

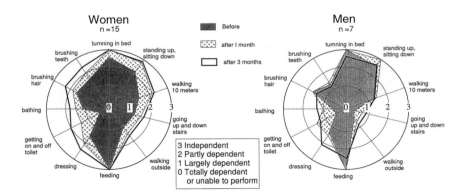

When each of the basic ADL items before behavioral therapy was compared between men and women, male subjects had higher average scores for turning in bed, standing up/sitting down and brushing hair, while women had higher scores for going up/down stairs, walking outside, bathing and brushing their teeth. Three months after the start of behavioral therapy, women showed getting increased average score of basic ADLs. In contrast, in men, except for getting on and off the toilet and dressing, each mean score of basic ADLs was decreased or unchanged.

The most frequent causes of interruption (n=3) or stopping (n=4) of behavioral therapy were acute febrile illness (n=3) and fall (n=2). Only one case was unsuccessful due to severe dementia.

III - DISCUSSION

We previously reported that functional type urinary incontinence is the most frequent type of urinary incontinence in elderly inpatients in Japan [7]. For a long time, little attention has been paid about behavioral intervention in such patients.

In the present study, behavioral therapy for urinary incontinence was successful in more than 80% of very frail elderly subjects. This figure is quite high, compared to that reported in the previous studies [2-6]. One reason may come from the selection of patients, because we set the condition for entry to this study that the subjects should be able to sit at the end of the bed with or without assistance.

On the other hand, behavioral therapy is quite unpopular in Japan [1,7], and for almost all subjects, it was the first time to receive behavioral therapy. This resulted in a long period of incontinence before the start of behavioral therapy in some patients. However, in the present study, the delay of behavioral therapy for urinary incontinence for many days was not a risk factor in treatment failure. This result greatly encourages us to conduct a future trial in elderly people cared in geriatric wards in Japan.

In the present study, effect of the behavioral therapy on basic ADLs was quite different between men and women, except for getting on and off toilet and dressing. It is not clear why in men, the behavioral therapy had no ripple effect on other basic ADLs. It is not likely that the difference was due to the age of the subjects, because the mean age of the female subjects was 7 years older than that of male subjects. In a previous study, there was no obvious difference in the frequency of depression between elderly men and women [8]. And the life-time risk for depression is not higher in men [9]. The background data showed the mean age and the pre-therapy duration of incontinence were not different between men and women. Therefore, we speculate that elderly women were more active and had better communication than elderly men in the hospital, which may have contributed to the difference. In the present study, we tried to record the geriatric depression scale and the morale score of the subjects. However, almost all subjects could not comprehend the questionnaire. An index or scale to judge the vitality of elderly patients with cognitive impairment need to be developed in future.

REFERENCES

1. Natsume O. Yamada K. Samma S. Ozono S. Hirao Y. Okajima E. : A questionnaire survey on urinary incontinence in geriatric nursing home patients. Jpn. J. Urol. 84. 694-9, 1993
2. Ouslander JG; Geriatric urinary incontinence. Disease-A-Month. 38:65-149, 1992
3. Ouslander JG. Simmons S. Schnelle J. Uman G. Fingold S. : Effects of prompted voiding on fecal continence among nursing home residents. J. Am. Geriatr. Soc. 44:424-8, 1996
4. Schnelle JF. MacRae PG. Giacobassi K. MacRae HS. Simmons SF. Ouslander JG. : Exercise with physically restrained nursing home residents : maximizing benefits of restraint reduction. J. Am. Geriatr. Soc. 44:507-12, 1996
5. MacRae PG. Asplund LA. Schnelle JF. Ouslander JG. Abrahamse A. Morris C. : A walking program for nursing home residents: effects on walk endurance, physical activity, mobility, and quality of life. J. Am. Geriatr. Soc. 44:175-80, 1996
6. Schnelle JF. Keeler E. Hays RD. Simmons S. Ouslander JG. Siu AL. A cost and value analysis of two interventions with incontinent nursing home residents. J. Am. Geriatr. Soc. 43:1112-7, 1995
7. Toba K. Ouchi Y. Orimo H. Iimura O. Sasaki H. Nakamura Y. Takasaki M. Kuzuya F. Sekimoto H. Yoshioka H. Ogiwara T. Kimura l. Ozawa T. Fujishima M. : Urinary incontinence in elderly inpatients in Japan: a comparison between general and geriatric hospitals. Aging Clin. Exp. Res. 8:47-54, 1996
8. Nagatomo l. Nomaguchi. M. Matsumoto K. : Sex difference in depression and quality of life in elderly people. Jpn. J. Psychiat. Neurol. 48:511-5, 1994
9. Wilhelm K. Parker G. : Sex differences in lifetime depression rates: fact or artifact?. Psychol. Med. 24:97-111, 1994